MICHIGAN'S
CIVIL WAR
CITIZEN-GENERAL

MICHIGAN'S CIVIL WAR CITIZEN-GENERAL

ALPHEUS S. WILLIAMS

JACK DEMPSEY

THE
History
PRESS

Published by The History Press
Charleston, SC
www.historypress.com

First published 2019

Manufactured in the United States

ISBN 9781467138642

Library of Congress Control Number: 2018966325

*To those who serve
our country
without receiving
full honor due*

CONTENTS

Contents

Though eminently an officer of action,
he had the patience and affability of manners
which won the love and veneration of his men.

—*William Tecumseh Sherman, December 22, 1878*

❧

It is the fate of all great and good men
that their worth is not appreciated until after death.

—*William Ward Duffield, January 29, 1879*

PREFACE

In the nearly century and a half since the death of Alpheus Starkey Williams, only a thirty-page biography published 108 years ago has appeared in book form.[1] Sixty years ago, an edited volume of his personal Civil War correspondence, prefaced by a brief life sketch, was first published.[2] By itself, his wartime experience from 1861 to 1865 merits book-length treatment. His record of local and national public service deserves full examination. His personal life is a story unto itself.

This work attempts a textured treatment that places Williams where his life and Civil War record may be fully understood. By no means was he perfect, and the book does not attempt to make him so. It is based on research first deepened in a recent study of the Antietam Campaign, where he played a part underappreciated by history.[3] It uncovers new sources and provides revelations about Williams, such as the real story of his patrimony and the pathos of his family's mortality. He was an affectionate husband and father; his premature losses—including parents, a beloved wife and half of his six children—have not been appreciated. A quiet, abiding faith needs better understanding. He ran for office many times and often lost, including a major party candidacy for governor. His war-long service on numerous Eastern and Western Theater battlegrounds is for the first time examined in detail. Significant is his role on each of the three days at Gettysburg—still overlooked, in part, because of an extraordinary slight. The book is also the first to detail Williams's involvement with the burning issue of the day: American slavery. Though not an abolitionist, he acted as a liberator.

Born into New England prosperity, graduating from Yale, he chose an uncertain path on the Michigan frontier. In early Detroit, the people entrusted increasing responsibilities to his care. Through occupations as attorney, civic official, judge, newspaper publisher and merchant, his constant avocation was as militia man. Although not a West Pointer, he volunteered for the Mexican-American War and rose to the state's highest civilian military position. He was an antislavery Whig who rebuffed membership in the Republican Party. On the eve of the Civil War, he labored to ready Michigan's troops for the coming fury. Not content with training men once war commenced, he secured an appointment to the battlefield as brigadier general soon after the Union's first defeat. As a Democrat, he fought for the nation and, despite lack of recognition from the administration, aided Lincoln's reelection. His Congressional service, previously covered in passing, takes on a different cast for following principle over party in the contested election of 1876. He also worked on behalf of veterans and civil service reform.

The central theme for the Civil War is his failure at promotion. Williams never rose above brigade-level[4] rank despite commanding divisions and corps in the most demanding combat situations, exhibiting leadership that outshone more formally trained and experienced general officers. Unlike several notable peers, he suppressed disenchantment and chose not to resign his commission, preferring to see the country's greatest crisis through to successful resolution. His contributions proved key at Antietam, to the issuance of the Emancipation Proclamation, to turning back the Confederate high tide at Gettysburg, to the success of the fabled March to the Sea and to final triumph near the Virginia/North Carolina border.

For the soldiers under his command, he was an intrepid leader. They awarded him a favored nickname—"Pap," pronounced "Pop"[5]—and looked to this father figure on many a field of battle for order and clear-headed sagacity. Just before the curtain came down on the war, William Tecumseh Sherman dealt him the last in a long line of affronts by the army commanders he faithfully served.

He was a proud patriot and hero who died while in service to his state and his nation.

PRELUDE

Although a lame duck, the outgoing congressman had duties to uphold on a wintry day in 1878.

Duty. It was his habit, so he would be extolled, to perform the most rigid discharge of every duty that devolved on him. For forty years, he had been at his post, whatever its nature, faithfully serving his family, his community and his nation. Today was no different. This Saturday, December 21, he arose, performed his morning ablution and walked to the U.S. Capitol, where Congressional business awaited. Sixty-eight years old, he had survived two wars with hardly a flesh wound or illness.

This day he mounted the west grand staircase on the House side of the Capitol for business of the Committee on the District of Columbia. He was cheerful and hopeful. He conversed with colleagues about committee work in which he felt a lively interest. He looked, once again, to promote the best interest of the District and the country.

The meeting got underway and proceeded apace. Without warning, in a moment he fell gravely ill. Fellow members rushed to his aid, concerned over what might be a crisis similar to what befell John Quincy Adams in these same precincts.

Would he write a memoir? Would he get to shape Civil War memory? Who would tell his story? Who would remember his name?

Maps

Created by Bruce Worden, Ann Arbor.

CHAPTER 1

NEW ENGLAND DAYS

The American nation was so very young in 1810. That annum marked only the thirty-fourth of the declared independence of these united states and the twenty-first of their Constitution. Signers of the Declaration still lived. Together with the original thirteen, four additional states sent representatives to the 11th Congress. Founder James Madison occupied the White House as the fourth president. A boy named Abraham turned one year old in Kentucky, and Robert Edward Lee had his third birthday in Virginia. Showman P.T. Barnum and future First Lady Elizabeth McCardle were born. As was Alpheus Starkey Williams.

Like those of another future American military hero, the ancestors of A.S. Williams made an early home in Connecticut. Maternal grandfather Timothy Starkey, a sailing man with Revolutionary War militia experience, went by "Captain." His daughter Hepzibah was born on April 6, 1784. Named after her mother, who died in 1786, she married Ezra Williams in 1802 and had five children: Frederic William, born in 1804; Charles, 1806; Ezra Starkey, 1808; Alpheus; and Irene, 1819. Named after his mother's brother, Alpheus was born on September 20, the last of the four boys, in Saybrook, known today as Deep River.[6]

First settled in 1635, the town had grown into a significant manufacturing hub by 1810. The chief product was hair combs. Local invention in 1798 of a mechanized process for cutting ivory jump-started the industry. Ezra Williams established an ivory comb factory in 1802; it "did but little business till 1807," when profits began flowing. After combining with another company in 1816, within three years the enterprise employed two dozen men producing "50,000 dozen combs annually." One of Ezra's partners was brother-in-law Alpheus Starkey. Increasing financial strength in the community fostered better schools for its children, following a long tradition of learning. Saybrook had been selected in 1701 for the home of the college that became Yale University. A.S. Williams likely attended a local private academy that offered a broad curriculum. The family house, a stately Colonial, still stands at a major intersection in Deep River.[7]

Death paid frequent visits to the Williams household. Timothy Starkey died when Alpheus was seven, and Ezra Williams died in 1818, age thirty-nine, severing the comb company from his children's potential ownership. Sometime after 1820, mother and four children moved in with the departed father's parents. Paternal grandfather Samuel died in 1822, leaving grandmother Irene to care for her daughter-in-law and grandchildren. She would be a strong influence in Alpheus's youth and outlived Hepzibah, who died on her forty-fifth birthday, April 6, 1829. By age eighteen, A.S. Williams had lost his parents, three grandparents and brother Charles, whom he never knew, dying when not yet seven months old.[8]

Previously dominated by agriculture, 1820's Connecticut had become more industrial. A steady increase in immigrants from Ireland, Scotland, Scandinavia and the German states was beginning to affect traditional demographics of the Dutch and English settlements. The Federalist Party of George Washington, John Adams and Alexander Hamilton held sway. Negative economic impacts from the War of 1812 increased opposition to the conflict; with peace came a rise in manufacturing. In 1818, a new constitution disestablished the Congregational Church.[9]

This Yankee background had formed the youthful years of Alpheus Williams when, at age seventeen, he was listed among seventy-eight freshmen in the "Catalogue of the Officers and Students in Yale College" at New Haven in November 1827. Only thirty miles separated him from Saybrook, but distance lay more in a map of the mind. To enter, he passed examinations in classical literature, Greek and Latin, grammar, reading and arithmetic. He finished his four years during the 1830–31 school year, living at No. 4 Linonian Rooms as a member of that student literary society in a class of eighty-six. Both morning and evening, all students attended prayer in the college chapel; public worship there was mandatory on Sunday, unless given permission to attend another congregation. The course of instruction emphasized the classics, teaching Horace to freshmen, Euclid to sophomores, Tacitus to juniors and rhetoric, philosophy and theology to seniors. The

Williams family home, Deep River, Connecticut, built circa 1802. *Courtesy of Eric Minotti and owner.*

Interior of the Williams family home. *Courtesy of Eric Minotti and owner.*

Photo of A.S. Williams in "gold locket miniature painted while a student in Yale, 1830." *Burton Historical Collection, Detroit Public Library.*

"object of the system of instruction" was "to *commence* a *thorough* course" and "maintain such a proportion between the different branches of literature and science, as to form a proper *symmetry* and *balance* of character." Tuition, board, books and other expenses for the four years totaled approximately $800. Williams made some fast friends at Yale, among them educator Henry Barnard, lawyer Ninian Gray and author Henry Wikoff. Three decades later, one of his classmates would wait more than a week for Williams to make their rendezvous at Richmond. Emerging from university at age twenty-one, appearing rather highbrow, Williams had been given a foundation for "high intellectual attainments."[10]

What would be next on life's agenda? Decades later, some chroniclers asserted that graduation gifted Alpheus a major inheritance, $75,000, from his father's estate. This princely sum would, they wrote, be spent in profligacy.[11] The story is a myth. The probate file for Ezra Williams concludes with this bequest to his youngest son: $6,320.83.[12] A.S. Williams did stand at a pivot point. He had received a first-rate education, but neither it nor his father's will had provided the basis for a livelihood. As the fourth male child, with no apparent aptitude for manufacturing, another career beckoned.

Williams chose the law. He moved to New York City in late 1831 to study with Wyliss Hall, Yale class of 1824.[13] These lessons lasted until the fall of 1833, when he returned to Yale for admission to its law school. A large portion of his reading also involved military subjects. Studies were interrupted by a number of trips, several with Wikoff, who judged his former classmate "amiable, intelligent, and free from all vice." In January 1832, they journeyed to Washington, where Williams found the Capitol and other public sites to be "magnificent." They visited the Senate and witnessed political heroes Henry Clay and Daniel Webster hold forth. After paying respects at Washington's grave, Williams journaled about the example of patriotism, character and humility set by the Father of the Country. He found the visit to Mount Vernon deeply moving:

"I plucked a bough from a cedar limb & left the consecrated spot with emotions indescribable."[14]

After a voyage to Matamoros, Mexico, with brother Frederic, Williams joined Wikoff on a trip through the South commencing at Charleston in April 1833. He found the region less than satisfactory. Just the month before, South Carolina had repealed its Ordinance of Nullification, which declared invalid the federal Tariff Act of 1832 and threatened civil strife. Reacting to a heightening of the state's military readiness, Williams journaled that such "display of arms and troops in opposition to the general government…falls within Treason." He was also repulsed at the sight of a slave auction. Lost in the Carolina backwoods, Wikoff brooded to Williams that he would rather shoot himself than starve; "'it is not unlikely that we shall have to choose before long,' replied my companion calmly." After Williams received his Yale law degree in 1834, they traveled through Pennsylvania and then down the Ohio River to the Mississippi and St. Louis. Their return took them through Kentucky and western Virginia. Williams reached Connecticut in July. He could have been expected to embark on a legal career.[15]

A.S. Williams's Yale College Law diploma, 1834. *Detroit Historical Society.*

Instead, on November 8, 1834, Williams's diary recorded his arrival at the French port of Havre aboard the sailing packet *Sylvie de Grasse* after a three-week voyage from New York. He went to Paris and took rooms at 2 Rue Castiglione, a location in the first arrondissement that was central to many cultural attractions. He began French lessons and visits to the "curiosities" of Paris, including the Louvre, Notre Dame, the Palace of Luxembourg, the Pantheon, the Tuileries garden and too many others to list ("&c. &c.," he noted). At the nearby Place du Carrousel, he enjoyed a review of troops, and at the Place Vendome just up the street he witnessed a regiment drumming out one of its soldiers. He attended and made skeptical notes regarding Roman Catholic liturgies. Two American companions, "E.F & H.W.," went along to such sites as the Pere Lachaise Cemetery, final resting place of many famous Parisians.[16]

"E.F." signified Edwin Forrest, a friend of Wikoff's from Philadelphia. Regarded as "the first great" American actor, Forrest "so rapidly sprang into popular favor" and maintained his standing that none had "so long held his high rank in his profession." An "undeniable genius" as a Shakespearean tragedian, Forrest's European tours widened his fame. For traveling companions on this great European adventure, Williams had two of the most interesting personalities of the day. For their part, Williams "was an agreeable companion and an indefatigable traveler."[17]

By Christmas 1834, A.S. Williams had relocated to the Hotel de Castiglione, several blocks from his first apartment. He took in the opera, undertook dancing lessons, celebrated the holiday with "egg nogg" and in February 1835 began a trip with his companions to Lyons, Turin, Genoa, Pisa, Rome, Naples, Pompeii, Salerno, Venice and Geneva. The journey had its travails: at one border crossing, he forfeited two pistols as contraband. In May, he again left Paris for a trip with Wikoff through England, commencing in London at the Epsom derby, where he almost wagered his watch after losing all of his cash in a confidence game. They went on to Oxford, Manchester, Liverpool, York, Newcastle and then Scotland for stays in Edinburgh and, on the Fourth of July, Glasgow. Ireland—Belfast and Dublin—came next, followed by a channel crossing to Antwerp and on to Liege, Cologne, Frankfurt, Milan, Vicenza, Munich, Vienna, Prague, Berlin, Amsterdam and The Hague. Williams arrived back in Paris on November 25 to spend a final winter. On March 10, 1836, he embarked for home, his European excursions finally concluded.[18]

Another emprise lay ahead.

CHAPTER 2

GO NORTHWEST, YOUNG MAN

Williams spent only a few months in Connecticut before implementing a life-altering decision. In February, he had written to sister Irene, apparently seeking a fresh start: "I have made up my mind to go early in the summer to the West." On August 1, 1836, he departed for Detroit, the main riverfront town of the Territory of Michigan in the "Old Northwest." Its population when he turned six had been 850 people; Connecticut's was then 250,000. Two years before his arrival, Detroit had increased to nearly 5,000 inhabitants and was expanding by 1,000 a year. New structures "were going up all over town." Once "hardly more than a frontier outpost," in 1836 an estimated 200,000 people would "flood" through the port arriving on ninety steamboats and more than that number of sailing ships.[19]

Michigan was booming. The opening of the Erie Canal in 1825 facilitated transportation of passengers and goods from New England; recovery from the depression of 1828–29 increased ready cash for land sales in the sparsely inhabited territory. Consequently, "the year 1836 was one of the most prosperous in the annals of Detroit." Years later, Williams would describe how "speculating fever" drew many like him to Michigan that year. And many like him were "Yankees," becoming Michigan's largest ethnic group and major influence in the course of its growth.[20]

The case of Fletcher Webster, son of Daniel Webster, is on point. Desiring to make a name for himself, the twenty-two-year-old left Massachusetts in 1835 to settle in an Illinois "town of great expectations." He invested in a Macomb, Michigan bank and soon followed his money to Detroit. First residing at a private boardinghouse, Mr. and Mrs. Webster moved next to the Michigan Exchange Hotel, newly opened in 1835. He "hung out his shingle on Jefferson avenue" and began practicing law.[21]

That same year, a young U.S. Army officer came to Detroit as part of a survey crew attempting to fix the Michigan/Ohio border. During that summer, Robert E. Lee wrote to a friend, "Detroit is for us, though our young Gentlemen Say, for they have all been there, that they talk of nothing but Land Speculations—& that their Standing Toast, Sentiment & dream is 'a Corner Lot running back to An Alley.'" The opportunities on this frontier were extolled: "[P]ersons of even ordinary enterprise and limited means, often attain to affluence in the west, while, in the east, enterprise and moderate capital combined are in a course of years but comparatively little productive." Others like Williams accepted such invitations.[22]

Just as during his European travels, Williams had not made this trip completely on his own. Henry C. Kingsley, Yale Law class of 1836, journeyed with him as far as Cleveland. Kingsley went on to Columbus to begin his career and then joined his elder brother, George, back in the lake city—a town about the size of Detroit but in a state with a population of 1.5 million. They had clients in need of "land agency" work in the Michigan Territory, and their fellow Yale alumnus would be on the ground and in a position to be of assistance. Williams also engaged in communications on legal matters with another acquaintance. Edwin Forrest had Michigan land investments that needed his handling as well.[23]

Although alone, Williams enjoyed Thanksgiving in Detroit at the Michigan Exchange, located at Jefferson Avenue and Shelby Street. He needed to become known. The inexperienced practitioner went to court to study seasoned lawyers arguing their cases. He attended church services periodically. An early and cold winter enabled sleigh rides with new friends on the frozen Rouge River, including a New Year's Eve celebration of the coming of 1837. On its first day, after sleeping in "from fatigues of last night," he took stock of his new circumstances: "I have [ex]changed the gay metropolis for a western town—pleasure for law and study." Assuming his health was "spared," he vowed that this year would be marked by "more activity and industry." On January 2, he paid a number of social calls on ladies of the town and on the fourth witnessed arguments in the Supreme Court. He became a director of the Detroit Young Men's Society during 1837. Writing in the journal exclusively in French, he arrived at the first day of 1838 with a pledge similar to an annum earlier: he hoped that this year would "be more faithfully and profitably spent." Usually, his entries were purely factual, with the only emotion expressed at having not succeeded enough.[24]

Circumstances in the new state of Michigan enabled his ambition to advance and diverted attention from the economic slump. On January 4–6, Williams witnessed "great excitement in streets on Canada matters" and noted that Governor Stevens T. Mason had called a meeting of citizens for the seventh. The so-called Patriot War had come to Detroit when American sympathizers attempted to help a Canadian faction break free from the British Crown. They raided arsenals in Detroit and Monroe, seized a schooner at a Detroit wharf and sailed down to Gibraltar in preparation to take Fort Malden across the river in Amherstburg, Ontario. The federal government called on Mason to thwart this threat to peaceful relations, and the governor called out the militia. Hugh Brady, war veteran and commander of the Detroit garrison, mustered as many volunteers as feasible into the service of the United States, including A.S. Williams. The new soldier spent his first night standing guard over the powder magazine. The next morning, his unit sailed for Fort Gratiot at the mouth of Lake Huron to bring arms stored there safely back to Detroit. After temporarily grounding in Lake St. Clair, the contingent reached the installation and loaded the arms on board the *Macomb*, a wooden sidewheel steamship. The militiamen soon reached Detroit, objectives achieved.

Williams's duty did not finish with this mission. He stood sentinel duty at the magazine, marched to the Dearbornville Arsenal and then to Gibraltar, Mount Clemens and Ecorse and, on February 24, to Fighting Island in the Detroit River as part of a force to confront two hundred "Patriots" who continued militating for Canadian annexation. After Crown forces drove the insurgents onto the frozen river, the Brady Guards disarmed and put the guerrillas under arrest. Williams recorded that he did indeed first discharge his weapon during the hostilities. An active militia and the young men's club confirmed his decision to settle in Detroit, for they demonstrated a rising level of society that encouraged such voluntary organizations.[25]

Having shown martial mettle, Williams exhibited a different type of assertiveness in the courting domain. He was an eligible bachelor, "a handsome, well-dressed, cultured young man," five-feet-eight with "grayish blue eyes and dark brown hair and whiskers." His manner was "placid, cordial" and attractive. He began in 1837, while residing and practicing law out of the Michigan Exchange, to keep company with Jane Hereford Larned, a nineteen-year-old widow. Her father was Charles Larned, War

Photo of miniature of Jane Larned "dated 1831." *Burton Historical Collection, Detroit Public Library.*

of 1812 officer, probate judge, prosecutor, attorney general of the Michigan Territory, U.S. attorney and member of the Board of Trustees of the University of Michigan. The relationship blossomed. At 6:00 p.m. on January 16, 1839, in St. Paul's Episcopal Church, the couple were married by Right Reverend Samuel A. McCoskry. Williams's diary carried a new tone, one of profound satisfaction. Under the heading "My Wedding Day," he recorded, "[M]arried & happy at last—and Janie Pierson is, indeed Janie Williams."[26] At last? His age that winter Wednesday was twenty-eight.

McCoskry was one of two Detroit prelates whose lives intersected Williams's in powerful ways. He had attended West Point for two years and then intended on practicing law before settling on the ministry. Both his father and uncle were Revolutionary War veterans. A friend to explorer Douglass Houghton, McCoskry was a leading figure in Detroit who preached at the consecration of the Mariners Church and on Quinquagesima Sundays. The other prelate, George Duffield, began in 1838 at "the First Presbyterian, then styled 'Protestant' Church" until his death in 1868; "scarcely a man in Detroit was so influential." As the "beloved pastor," his house at Woodward and High Street was the site of many weddings. Williams had many connections to the Duffield family, many of whom would become soldiers and statesmen. His membership in "the most influential religious society in Michigan" marked his commitment to things religious.[27]

The marriage inspired subsequent blissful expressions. At the four-month mark, Williams reflected how life was "flowing on like the peaceful current of a gentle river as happy as the day is long." If the future would "but equal the past few months in the allotments of delightful hours I shall be contented." While he wrote, his wife held the candle and ink; then he read to her from the Bible. Jane made occasional entries in his diary, addressing the notes to "my dear husband." They headed to the market in the mornings, regularly attended church on Sundays and coped with her periodic illnesses—a cold, a headache, an unspecified unwellness—motivating him to stay by her side. She was never seriously ill, for in the summer he left for a visit to

Connecticut, attending a class meeting and commencement in New Haven and conducting legal business. The end of September found him back in Detroit. He rented a new office with his law partner, Theodore Romeyn, and oversaw work on a house that was finished in June 1840. He tended the garden and cared for the house like any happy newlywed.[28]

Marriage did not affect his membership in the Brady Guards. He joined them as U.S. representatives in a birthday event for Queen Victoria at Ontario's Fort Malden and participated in maneuvers with visiting military units. A few months after the wedding, he was elected vice-president of the Detroit Boat Club, his first stint as a leader in a Detroit social organization. On March 1, 1839, he took his first civic post with an appointment by the governor to notary public for Wayne County. Cultural education also continued; he read Gibbon's history of the Roman empire and novels such as *Rob Roy*. In March 1840, he was appointed inspector of elections in his city ward, the first public political activity recorded. The new year had even greater significance with the birth of the couple's first child, a girl, in February. But she died shortly after.[29]

It was a busy year. In July, he was elected to a position of business leadership as a director and vice-president of the Bank of St. Clair; he would be president from 1842 to 1845. More lasting was affiliation with the Whig Party. In May, he and thirty fellow members went on a political excursion to Hamtramck. In October, now thirty years old, he attended the Whig convention in Dearbornville. There he was nominated for a probate judgeship, a position held by Jane's father during his distinguished career. Election Day, November 3, brought success: he defeated his opponent by some one hundred votes—although the margin fell to fourteen after votes from Hamtramck were lost.[30]

Williams's victory came during the party's high-water mark. It captured control of Congress and sent military hero William Henry Harrison to the White House. Henry Clay, Daniel Webster and a new generation of leaders had taken their name from the British political organization that "opposed the monarchy." According to Clay, President Andrew Jackson had acted as "a Chief Magistrate who is endeavoring to concentrate in his own person the whole powers of government." Whigs sought a government that would be active on internal improvements and favor tariff policy that protected domestic commerce. They fought for enfranchising African Americans in the 1835 state constitution. One of their chief spokesmen, Ross Wilkins, noted that the Declaration of Independence did not make "distinctions based on the color of a man's skin." They had elected the governor in 1839 and taken control of both houses of the legislature. Williams was in good company: the Whig stable included Zachariah Chandler and Jacob M. Howard, future U.S. senators. In Illinois, another lawyer found a home in the party. Abraham Lincoln would win election to the U.S. House of Representatives during the coming decade.[31]

New Year's Day 1841 had a different character than previous years. Williams filed his oath as probate judge and, three days later, "embarked upon duties of office." On the twelfth came another first: Charles Larned, eight and one-quarter pounds, made himself known to Detroit; mother Jane was recorded as doing well despite the back-to-back deliveries. Avoiding the summer heat and disease of the town, in June mother and child embarked for Mackinac Island and Green Bay aboard the steamer *Columbus*. While his family sailed the Great Lakes, Williams continued political work on behalf of the party, served with the Brady Guards and orated the Declaration of Independence as part of the Fourth of July observance. Returning home from a wedding, the horse-drawn conveyance "was upset" in front of the Capitol, and Williams "got knocked on head." The injury caused him to be "stupid for awhile."[32]

Alpheus and Jane would have four more children, all of them born in Detroit. Irene ("Rene") came next, born on January 3, 1843. It was another auspicious year: in April, Williams was elected alderman of Detroit's Fifth Ward, becoming a member of the common council legislative body. Frederick Larned arrived on November 8, 1844. Mary Howard, known as "Minnie," arrived on August 10, 1846. Julia Allen was born on February 2, 1848, but would live only until December 23, 1853.[33]

Perhaps due to the educational interest of their children and those of neighbors, Jane Williams appears to have served the Detroit public school system as a school inspector. In November 1841, the Detroit Common Council began a process to reform and improve public schools in the city. A February 1842 state law authorized the council to create a board of education that would fashion a public school system with tax support. The board of education "appointed a standing committee of three ladies from each ward to examine the primary schools." Years later, a family friend chronicling this history discovered that "among them I find the names of... Mrs Alpheus Starkey Williams."[34]

Williams merged politics, business and literacy when he acquired the *Daily Advertiser* on November 10, 1843. Its offices were located on the north side of Jefferson Avenue at Woodward over "Kings store." He would publish the newspaper until selling it on January 1, 1848. The *Advertiser* was the descendant of the weekly *Northwestern Journal*, first published in October 1829 in opposition to the Democratic Party, established by the friends of John Quincy Adams. It had become Michigan's leading Whig mouthpiece, and Williams now supplied advocacy for the party platform in his editorials and commentaries. His writing also revealed a mind taken with "martial imagery and military terms."[35]

In 1844, Williams ran unsuccessfully for another term as judge of probate and was defeated in a race for mayor by twelve votes. He then secured an appointment by the council as city recorder—substituting for the mayor in case of illness, absence or death—and served until 1848. He lost a third election for judge in 1848. National politics came to the rescue when he was appointed postmaster of Detroit under the Whig administration of Zachary Taylor in April 1849; he served until April 1853. The office was in the courthouse building he knew well as a lawyer and jurist; his home was on the north side of Croghan (now Monroe Street) "2 below Brush." According to one historian, the appointment was a patronage plum as an antislavery Whig closely affiliated with William Seward, U.S. senator from New York. Lewis Cass returned to the U.S. Senate, however, and may have helped Williams get the job. When his appointment ended, he opened a shop on Jefferson to purvey lighting products. He also had become a Mason in 1846 and served as "Worshipful Master." Detroit had grown to more than twenty-one thousand residents—no metropolis but more populous than ten years earlier.[36]

AND ADVERTISING GAZETTEER.   780

MICHIGAN

OIL COMPANY,

Union Block, 46 Jefferson Ave.,

DETROIT,   *MICHIGAN.*

MANUFACTURERS OF

MASON'S SPERM OIL,

The best Oil extant for Machinery & Burning, and Warranted not to Gum.

MANF'RS OF LARD OIL & STERINE CANDLES

WARRANTED EQUAL TO ANY MADE.

DEALERS EXCLUSIVELY IN

OILS AND CANDLES.

Have constantly on hand a large supply of all kinds of Oils for burning and machinery.

A. S. WILLIAMS, Agent

DETROIT, MARCH 1, 1854.

Michigan Oil Company ad, 1854 Detroit City Directory. *Burton Historical Collection, Detroit Public Library.*

Taylor's election lay in his success during the recent war with Mexico. In May 1846, following the initial battle between Mexican forces and U.S. troops under Taylor, Michigan's governor received a request from the War Department to raise a regiment of volunteer infantry. The 1st Michigan Volunteers was enrolled and mustered in October 1847. The individual companies hailed from all over the state. Colonel Thomas B.W. Stockton of Flint commanded; second in charge was Lieutenant Colonel A.S. Williams, appointed because of his prominence in Detroit militia affairs and civic record. Here appeared the prime opportunity to put his military interest into action while he was still young enough to serve. He could not miss out even though it meant exposing his wife and little children to risk. The vanguard left Detroit in December 1847; Williams and the remainder left on February 9, 1848.

The next day, Williams wrote to "Dearest Jeanie." He was already missing her: "[W]e don't know how much we love any one till we are separated from them." The regiment's route took it to Cincinnati via rail and then on a steamer to New Orleans. By the eleventh, it was anchored off Vera Cruz and several days later on the way to Córdoba to guard a specie train. On March 16, Williams saw a body of horsemen through his spy glass, and they soon came across the site where Georgians had been attacked by guerrillas. The men stopped to bury the dead. Williams had his baptism of fire when hostile shots were fired from the chaparral. That day proved to be the climax of his service. Although in the field for several months, he never saw battle. The regiment's principal duty involved guarding "supply and specie trains between Vera Cruz and inland posts" against guerrilla forces. On July 12, he telegraphed Jane of being homeward bound.

In Mexico, "Williams won no glory, acquired no combat experience, and was involved only in guerrilla warfare; but he did learn the duties of military life and the responsibilities of managing a military unit." The organized war had concluded before his arrival. Contending with irregular forces in the war's aftermath had its own hazards. His service record showed he enrolled on October 18, 1847, mustered in on December 8 and was discharged on July 29, 1848, all at Detroit. His personal data: age thirty-seven; five feet, eight inches tall; gray eyes; brown hair; light complexion; publisher by trade.[37]

Although the homecoming was joyful, grief soon arrived. Four months after his return, forty days short of their tenth wedding anniversary, on December 8, 1848, at age thirty, Jane Larned Williams died. She left a bereaved husband and five children under eight years old. The devoted service of longtime family housekeeper Ann McIntosh would help keep the family together. In November 1847, Alpheus had purchased a large family plot in Detroit's eastside Elmwood Cemetery, coinciding with the regiment's first departure for Mexico. Its utility came all too soon.[38]

The U.S census taker in August 1850 inventoried the Williams family starting with postmaster Alpheus, age thirty-nine, and four children: Larned (age nine), Irene (seven), Frederick (five) and Mary (four). Also in

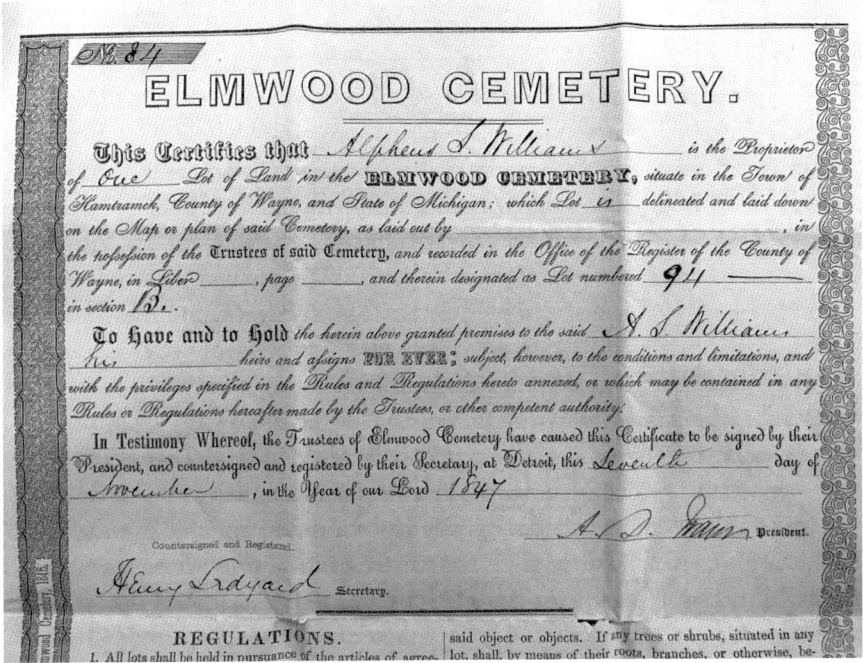

A.S. Williams's deed to Elmwood plot. *Burton Historical Collection, Detroit Public Library.*

the household lived two females—faithful servant Ann McIntosh (thirty-seven) and Catherine Crouch, a twenty-one-year-old German native—and Francisco Miguell, a sixteen-year-old servant born in Mexico. The family of G.S. (listed as an agent) and Mary R. Lansing were also enumerated under the same dwelling-house number.

Five years to the month of her mother's death, right before Christmas 1853, little Julia died. A further bereaved father's concerns now focused on Frederick. Williams's correspondence between 1854 and 1857 spoke frequently of "Freddy" and a chronic leg disorder that periodically caused painful abscesses. At times, Williams had "given up society" to care for his son. His occasional business trips left him wondering about the son's condition while separated. In early 1857, he felt "constant uneasiness about poor Fred." Escorting Minnie to a costume ball at the National Hotel on February 9 may have provided some distraction. In May, he went to Washington on Orphan's Court business, and upon returning in June wrote to Irene to come home. Her brother wanted to see his sister one last time. On August 17, 1857, Fred died.[39]

Politics diverted his attention from such sorrowful matters. The outcome of the Mexican conflict proved troublesome in the North. It cemented inclusion of Texas, a slave state, in the Union and opened the door to others. The "Compromise of 1850" temporarily settled the dispute, admitting California as a free state, banning the slave trade in the District of Columbia and tightening the Fugitive Slave Law that required northerners to aid in the recovery of escaped persons by their master/owners. In 1854, the controversy reignited with passage of the Kansas-Nebraska Act. The bill codified the Democratic doctrine of popular sovereignty espoused by Senators Steven A. Douglas of Illinois and Lewis Cass of Michigan, enabling each territory to decide for itself—rather than Congress—whether to achieve statehood as slave or free. A coalition of antislavery members of various parties gathered in Jackson, Michigan, in July, agreeing to form a new Republican Party dedicated to restricting the expansion of slavery in America. A reconstruction of the major parties was unfolding; traditional Whig issues were overwhelmed as the question of slavery dominated politics after the Kansas-Nebraska Act, and "the center of gravity in the Democratic party shifted southward."[40]

As a Whig, Williams's views on the slave question put him in the middle on the controversy. "Ardently opposed to the institution of slavery," having been raised in New England and seen the reality of the "peculiar institution" during his travels, he nonetheless possessed views on race typical of his time. Abolition could split the country. The practice of slavery injured other races; as "a strong advocate of free labor," Williams saw how a small farm could not compete with a large plantation. The *Advertiser* also criticized the inordinate power by one section over the federal government: "The probable passage of a new so-called 'revenue tariff' is another startling proof of the entire control of southern politicians in Congress." Still, instead of a radical platform, he stood for "gradual emancipation based on constitutional change."[41]

Despite personal antipathy to slavery and local formation of the Republican Party, Williams did not bolt the Whigs. A conference of Whig editors had been held in Jackson in February 1854, and they adopted a policy "looking to the consolidation, in a new party, of all the anti-slavery elements." Separately, future governor Kinsley Bingham, a Democrat, came to Detroit to persuade others to unite under a new banner. He conferred with Jacob Howard, Zachariah Chandler, "General Alpheus S. Williams, E.A. Wales, Henry Barns and others, all Whigs. These interviews were not particularly reassuring. A number of those interviewed were very reluctant to give up the Whig organization, though they all did eventually come in except General Williams and Mr. Wales, who remained irreconcilable to the end." Wales owned the *Advertiser* with Williams as editor; the paper "denounced the results of the Jackson convention and called for a separate Whig convention, which was held October 4, 1854." The effort to preserve a middle ground failed: the "only result" was showing "that to revive the Whig party as a separate organization was hopeless." The *Advertiser* continued to argue, unsuccessfully, for "the formation of a great conservative party" that would "embrace the whole country" rather than opt for sectional appeal.[42]

Williams had notable company in standing by the Whig banner—for a time. No less than Abraham Lincoln initially "remained consciously aloof" from the Republican Party. Like Williams, he sought "to revive flagging support for the Whig Party, avoiding any direct involvement" with the new organization. Lincoln became a Republican only in 1856 "after it became abundantly clear that his beloved Whig Party was no longer functional." Others like Kinsley S. Bingham of Michigan departed their previous affiliation in 1854 and became members, and candidates for office, under the new standard. Bingham had "matured in an evangelical culture of moral imperatives and absolutes." Williams, however, was no evangelical.[43]

Lewis Cass had become Michigan's most famous son by the national election of 1856. The Democratic Party platform embraced the Cass Doctrine on popular sovereignty and Congressional nonintervention on the territorial slavery question. The election resulted in a Democratic victory for James Buchanan, but Republican candidate John C. Frémont carried eleven northern states. Whig candidate Millard Fillmore carried one. In August, Williams had signed an "Appeal of Whigs of Detroit to the Whigs of Michigan" urging colleagues to support Buchanan over Frémont. Republicans trounced Democrats in Michigan statewide races, Frémont beat Buchanan and Bingham was reelected governor. As for Williams, in 1856 his other activities were as member of the Board of Public Instruction and in the militia. Before the decade was out, he would run as a Democrat—and lose—for a seat on the Detroit council.[44]

Now forty-seven, Williams took solace in several public-minded activities during 1858. He served on the committee of arrangements for Detroit's Washington's Birthday celebration. He won a nonpartisan election as school inspector (following in his deceased wife's footsteps) for the Board of Education in the Third Ward. Most notably, he had gained recognition as the preeminent military man in the state due to his various contributions, including helping found the Detroit Light Guard, successor to the Brady Guards. At the August 1858 state militia convention in Detroit, Williams "was called to the chair" to serve as president. The focus of the convocation was to recommend improvements in the Michigan laws concerning the state militia with a view to increasing its size and organization. He also authored a resolution seeking the transfer of Fort Wayne on the Detroit River to the state for use as an armory. The year also included his election to the State Pioneer Society along with Zachariah Chandler (they were members 283 and 284). Once aboard, he joined the committee planning the celebration of the anniversary of the July 24, 1701 settlement of Detroit.

The next year, Republican governor Moses Wisner appointed Williams to the State Military Board, where he would serve into 1861, and at its first meeting he became president. A Lansing militia company formed in 1859 and took its name after Williams. At the board meeting in October 1859, Williams suggested that a compilation of tactics be published drawn from U.S. Army regulations. His compensation for this service: twenty-five dollars in salary and fourteen dollars for expenses.[45]

Williams contended for the office of alderman, Third Ward of Detroit, in the fall of 1859. When the November 8 returns were totaled, the winner was John J. Bagley by a vote of 322 to 256. In February 1860, Williams was appointed a visitor to the board of the Marine Hospital in Detroit. Congress had authorized the hospital's construction in 1854, and it opened in November 1857 on the southwest corner of Jefferson and Mount Elliott Avenues. A monthly tax imposed on seamen funded operations; a record of all sailors was kept at the Detroit Custom House. Williams's commission came from Secretary of the Treasury Howell Cobb. He may have sold his home by now, for a city directory gave his address as "boarding house, 133 Woodbridge St."[46]

In July 1860, the census recorded Alpheus, age forty-eight, without occupation. He owned real estate valued at $24,000, and his personal estate was worth $15,000. Living with him were children Charles (nineteen), Irene (seventeen) and Mary (fourteen). Ann McIntosh and another servant, thirty-year-old Irish immigrant Mary Scott, took care of the family. Also in the house were two Connecticut relatives. Williams lived at 15 Rowland; the street ran from Michigan Avenue north along the west side of Capitol Park and ended at Grand River.[47]

As the calendar turned from 1860, his adopted home had become a city of forty-five thousand inhabitants.[48] A retrospective of Williams's record might have shown someone perhaps expected to lead a rather effete life. Educated, cultured and well traveled, he had by the age of twenty-six seen more of the world than most of his countrymen. His roots in New England went back generations. His second quarter century looked nothing like the first. He moved to the frontier, got down to lawyering, won public offices and the confidence of electors, ran businesses and volunteered for a militia company and rose through its ranks. His politics had proven popular and secured him patronage jobs but then served as an impediment. He stood, on the brink of civil war, as a leader who had proven himself in varied capacities. Service in the conflict with Mexico had not introduced him to mass combat, but it had subjected him to hostile fire. The bloodbath into which America would soon plunge lacked any precedents, least of all for a middle-aged civilian whose martial talents had been tested largely in a reserve organization.

Williams found meaning and comfort in his Christian faith. His "deep religiosity" manifested itself in a lifelong devotion rather than a temporary excitement. To a daughter he wrote, "Remember that religion is not the matter of a single day or of one season of unusual fervor. It is the duty and business of a whole life."[49]

His faith and devotion to duty were about to meet their greatest challenge.

CHAPTER 3

CIVIL WAR

A FIRST RESPONDER

The Detroit theater crowd had settled into their seats to enjoy Friday evening's entertainment. The next day's newspaper told of the unexpected interruption that ensued: "It was a scene of excitement that followed the announcement of hostilities at Charleston." Confederate military forces in that South Carolina city, representing seven seceded states, had fired on Fort Sumter, a U.S. military installation. Civil war had erupted in America. Michigan would be called into action.[50]

According to future Medal of Honor recipient William Withington of Jackson, the state's capacity to respond arose from the volunteer spirit of the militia and its officers. That *esprit* had been cultivated by the state's chief military leader. Withington hailed the August 1860 state encampment in Jackson as critical to Michigan's "awakening," for it "generated the soldierly spirit and pride which from the first infused the Michigan troops, and the leaven of which ran through the war." He identified the officer who brought it "to organization": Alpheus S. Williams.[51]

On April 16, Republican governor Austin Blair arrived in Detroit to map out plans for responding to the president's call for troops to meet the Southern rebellion. He met with his state military officers in the afternoon— A.S. Williams, H.M. Whittlesey, A.W. Williams of Lansing and C.W. Leffingwell—and issued a call for ten companies of volunteers to form the regiment requested by Washington.[52]

Williams served with a coterie of former military men to prepare the Michigan regiment to depart for Washington. Some sources proclaim

Gathering to defend the Union, April 20, 1861, federal building, Griswold south of Michigan's historic capitol. *Archives of Michigan.*

him the first officer to respond after Fort Sumter. Blair quickly approved formation of a Michigan brigade, convinced that a single regiment would prove inadequate to the crisis. Party affiliation did not rule the day: he appointed Williams as its brigadier general on April 18, a salute to long and devoted service in Detroit and state militia affairs. The fifty-year-old volunteer immediately dove in, "working around the clock in an effort to clear away details and wade through the paper work." Drilling commenced, and the troops began to fill up the "Camp of Instruction" that Williams organized at Fort Wayne on the Detroit River.[53]

The nation's regular army in April 1861 comprised sixteen thousand soldiers. Its commander, Winfield Scott, was seventy-four years old. None of its four generals had attended the U.S. Military Academy; three were veterans of the War of 1812. Approximately one thousand West Point graduates were then living, and about 20 percent of the officer corps went over to the Confederacy. The United States needed more good officers.[54]

Given the paucity of leadership resources, the presence of a seasoned militia officer with at least some experience under fire could prove a major

1848 barracks, Historic Fort Wayne, Detroit. *Author's collection.*

asset to the Union cause. It also fulfilled American military tradition. Many officers in the Continental army were self-taught or veterans of conflict, not war college graduates. Among the most famous was Henry Knox, bookseller, avid reader on military subjects, militia member, volunteer at Bunker Hill and eventually major general. Succeeding generations of Americans looked to such a soldier-scholar as a *beau ideal*, especially given concerns over a standing army and suspicion of the behavior of peacetime soldiers. U.S. Chief Justice John Marshall served in the militia, as a lieutenant in the Continental army and in major battles before his distinguished judicial career.

Williams's most recent service as head of the State Military Board familiarized him with army procedures. He was knowledgeable of tactical and staff requirements and had served on courts-martial. His militia experience had taught how to teach discipline. Now his role was to prepare raw recruits for the grim service they would experience. The ninety-day 1st Michigan Volunteer Regiment set off to Washington on May 13, just one month from events in Charleston Harbor. Perhaps one of his proudest moments was in seeing the Detroit Light Guard mustered in as Company A, proof of its readiness. In addition to overseeing training in Detroit, Williams traveled the state to attend to soldier affairs. He went to Grand Rapids to muster in the 3rd Michigan Infantry, joined the contingent on the train ride to Detroit and went on board the steamer *Ocean* across Lake Erie to Cleveland before returning to Michigan.[55]

In May, Lincoln agreed with Blair and requested the states enlist volunteers for three-year terms. Michigan responded with the 2nd and 3rd; its fourth three-year regiment began to form in mid-May. Ordered to rendezvous at Adrian, militia companies arrived to find that the trustees of the local college had made available the use of campus buildings and grounds. The site became known as Camp Williams in honor of the state's leading military officer. When the regiment received its colors on June 21, Williams and other notables, including Senator Chandler and Adjutant General John Robertson, journeyed to Adrian for the ceremony. The brigadier general also saw to training of "the 5th 6th 7th and (in part) 8th Regiments" of infantry. His efforts form part of the "remarkable" performance by Michigan "in accommodating the large number of recruits who responded" in 1861.[56]

No longer youthful, Williams might have sat out the war or continued to serve as the main organizer and training official for Michigan units. He was not content with that role. Although he had not seen combat between armies in Mexico, and despite his age, Williams yearned to participate more actively in the war and put his militia training and experience to defense of the U.S. flag. He decided to seek a commission in the volunteer forces of the United States as a general officer.

In early July, Williams carried to Washington a letter of introduction to the secretary of war from someone of excellent reputation. Ross Wilkins, sixty-two years of age, was a distinguished lawyer and federal judge dating to Michigan's 1837 admission to the Union. Wilkins had gained renown as "a remarkable man" whose "intellectual brilliancy stood alone."[57] Williams could have no better character witness. The document read, in part:

> *This letter is no mere formal introduction. The Bearer thereof is General Alpheus Williams of the First Brigade of Michigan Volunteers, appointed by Governor Blair and truly prophesying the confidence and general respect and affection of our people. He is a military man by education and experience. Courteous and courageous, honorable and high minded, intimately acquainted with the theory and details of military science from a*

captain to colonel, and from company drill, to the government of a Brigade,
to him, more than any one else among us…[58]

On Saturday, July 13, Williams wrote his first Civil War letter, to Minnie, while away from Detroit. His children and other relatives would have to stand in for the spouse with whom he would have dearly loved to share his experiences. He had visited a number of camps and come away "impressed with the immensity of the gathering." He had apparently impressed Secretary of War Simon Cameron and the president, both of whom "very cordially received" him and promised an appointment as soon as Congress made it possible.[59]

The promise was kept. On August 5, the White House transmitted to the Senate a lengthy list of nominations for general officer appointments. Included was this:

I nominate the persons named in the accompanying list for appointment in
the Volunteer force in the service of the United States, as proposed by the
Secretary of War.
    Abraham Lincoln.

…

A.S. Williams, of Michigan, to be brigadier-general, May 17, 1861.

The Senate gave approval later that day, making Williams's one of numerous appointments backdated to May. His name appeared just above Israel B. Richardson of Michigan, a graduate of the U.S. Military Academy and Mexican-American War veteran. Also listed were West Pointers including several under whom he would serve: Ambrose E. Burnside, Ulysses S. Grant, Joseph Hooker, George G. Meade, William T. Sherman, Henry W. Slocum and George H. Thomas. Both Grant and Williams had begun their service in this war as mustering officers in their home states. Both Meade and Grant were known to Williams because of their U.S. military service while stationed in Detroit. With the appointment came annual pay of about $3,600, critical to continuing his children's support.[60]

Several days later, the War Department sorted out assignments. Some, like Grant, went to the Western Department (St. Louis). Others, like Sherman, went to the Department of the Cumberland (Kentucky). The August 24 order directed that "Gen. A.S. Williams is assigned to duty with the Michigan regiments in course of organization in that State."[61] Commission and orders in hand, Williams returned home. While in

Detroit, he was able to secure War Department appointment of the judge's son, William D. Wilkins, to his staff.[62]

The appointment of a non–West Pointer was no singular event, but it was rarer than that of the academy-trained. In the Michigan delegation, Williams was the most prominent citizen-soldier, for he had not attended any military school. Richardson had. Orlando B. Willcox, Christopher C. Augur, George A. Custer, George L. Hartsuff, and Henry J. Hunt all had as well.

On September 17, 1861, Williams's days of training and mustering troops came to an end. He was needed at the front far from Michigan. The War Department order prescribed: "Brig. Gen. A.S. Williams, U.S. Volunteers, after completing the duties on which he is now employed in Michigan, will repair to Washington and report for duty to the commanding general Department of the Potomac. By command of Lieutenant-General Scott." One year later on this date, he would find himself in the greatest test of his life.[63]

In early October, he returned to Washington and awaited assignment. With him went his principal aide-de-camp, Samuel E. Pittman, a lieutenant in the 1st Michigan Infantry. Son Charles ("Larned") came along as a civilian adjutant for the next several months. Williams had a very gracious and kind audience with General-in-Chief Scott and believed that he would command a brigade of Michigan troops. He soon learned that the War Department had a different plan.

Williams had managed to keep his family together through many travails. With the war deepening, he had made the difficult decision to break it up, perhaps forever, in order to lead in combat. He sent Rene to school in Philadelphia, while Minnie remained in the care of family. Separated from his daughters, and soon from his only living son, Williams began the regular practice of detailed and informative correspondence. He would remind recipients to hold his views private. As one Union officer warned his kin, "I *can't* write what I want to, if my letters are to be put in the papers." Williams would spend the next four years sharing his opinions and judgments with blunt frankness, confessing his disappointments and revealing his hopes, compiling what a noted historian would assess as "among the best" collections of letters "by any Civil War officer," an epistler who was "incapable of dull writing."[64]

His first exposure to Civil War combat would be anything but dull.

CHAPTER 4

WILLIAMS TAKES COMMAND

S pecial Orders No. 88 was issued from the headquarters of the Army of the Potomac, Major General George B. McClellan commanding, on October 4, 1861. Among its directives was this: "Brig. Gen. A.S. Williams, volunteer service, will report for duty to Major-General Banks, commanding division, at Darnestown."[65] Williams received the order on Saturday the fifth; on Monday, he and staff set out to locate the headquarters of Nathaniel P. Banks, former Republican governor and congressman from Massachusetts, in the Maryland town some twenty miles west of the White House. On the morning of the eighth, they reached the division commander's tent around noon, dined and received orders.[66]

Williams took command of the 3rd Brigade in Banks's Division.[67] The five thousand soldiers of the brigade filled five infantry regiments, one each from Connecticut, Massachusetts and Pennsylvania and two from New York, plus an artillery unit, the 1st Rhode Island Light Artillery.[68] Banks's other two brigades were commanded by West Point graduates John J. Abercrombie, age sixty-three, class of 1822, and Charles S. Hamilton, thirty-eight, class of 1843. All three would take turns acting as division officer of the day when Banks was absent.

Headquartered nearby at Poolesville, a Union brigade under the command of Brigadier General Charles P. Stone had the same duty as Banks's Division, guarding the line of the Potomac River. Stone had Mexican-American War experience, as did a subordinate, former U.S. senator and current brigadier general Edward D. Baker. Like all but a handful of officers, they had never commanded large contingents. All found themselves leading volunteer soldiers in greater numbers than in prior wars.

Williams's brigade at Darnestown was midway between Poolesville and Rockville. All was quiet. Roads from Poolesville ran west to Conrad's (later White's) Ferry and southwest toward Edwards Ferry, crossing the Chesapeake & Ohio Canal before ending at the Potomac River. Due west, at Leesburg, Virginia, the Confederates were believed to be in force. Banks's headquarters on October 20 were at Darnestown as well.[69]

The next day, Baker crossed the Potomac with a small force and engaged Confederates at a riverside site known as Ball's Bluff. After learning of the engagement, McClellan directed Stone to "call upon General Banks, who has been directed to respond." McClellan ordered Banks to send a brigade to Conrad's in support of the action and move his others to where they could provide assistance. At 9:45 p.m., Stone telegraphed McClellan about Baker's "repulse" and severe losses, including Baker's death. He had "called on General Banks for more troops," and Banks had Williams's brigade in motion at 8:00 p.m. President Lincoln, who had named a son after Baker, was also telegraphing for information about the affair.[70]

Williams "made a forced march with my brigade" and reached Edwards Ferry before daylight on the twenty-second. En route, he was "shown Baker's full dress hat and uniform, two ball holes through the hat and several through the coat." The "corpse lay in a house nearby." On the road to the ferry, he encountered evidence of "disaster"—stragglers, many without weapons, recounting "enormous stories" of combat, as well as many ambulances with wounded. His brigade took up "a doleful position" on the muddy bank of the Potomac "crowded with arriving troops, cold rain, and high winds." They waited for daylight to cross and come to the aid of the Union troops remaining on the Virginia side.[71]

That next day, Banks crossed over without Williams. In the afternoon, the sounds of battle—the "rattle of small arms and the booming of big guns"—carried across to Williams's position: "we had a stirring sight for a half hour or so" until "all at once the fight stopped." Again he was ordered to be ready to cross, and again he was told to stand down. The same happened on the twenty-third. McClellan arrived on scene, no doubt because of the president's keen interest, and ordered a full withdrawal.[72]

Williams had heard hostile fire for the first time in this war and seen the vulnerability of a general officer. He had accomplished his mission, fruitless as it was. After the war, a book of McClellan's would praise the officers and men of Banks's Division: they deserved "great credit for its rapid night-

Edwards Ferry, Potomac River north bank. *Author's collection.*

march to the relief of General Stone."[73] And though Williams had not been engaged, he had opinions on the disaster.

First, he thought that it originated from Baker's "burning for a fight" and for glory by taking Leesburg before others could. Second, no provision was made for the possibility of retreat: water transportation was inadequate for an emergency, and Banks had not been alerted in case his assistance was needed. Third, McClellan had not been involved as a commanding general should. Altogether, it was "plainly an unpremeditated and unprepared effort." Williams also remarked about how "there is a mighty amount of stupidity" in the newspapers about what happened, the realities of the command structure and overestimates of Union strength. There had been no mention of how his troops had "assisted in straightening out the snarl of wounded men and supply trains caused by a breakdown in command leadership."

Although Williams did not necessarily agree, at least one observer believed that had the Michigander gone over, the Union could have turned defeat into victory. Banks appeared to concur in his post-action report. The debacle would heighten Congressional scrutiny of military strategy, effect the end to Stone's career and prompt skepticism about McClellan's abilities. Months later, Williams would write of how the Battle of Ball's Bluff and Edwards Ferry "haunts the souls of our chiefs." He was seeking to take the offensive but could not obtain the necessary authority.[74]

The affair proved meaningful for Williams in one other way. During the action, Union brigadier general Frederick W. Lander had been shot in the leg. The wounding caused "a slow-moving infection." The two generals would serve near each other on the upper Potomac early the next year. On March 2, 1862, Lander would succumb, leaving a vacancy in the command of his division. Oddly enough, the October surprise would elevate Williams an important notch on the command ladder, link him with a storied unit for the rest of the war and set him against a military genius whose skills would blossom in the forthcoming Shenandoah Valley Campaign of 1862. In a curious way, Ball's Bluff possessed a silver lining for one Union general.[75]

CHAPTER 5

BATTLING STONEWALL
IN THE VALLEY

O ver the succeeding months until early spring, Williams and his brigade continued to guard the north bank of the Potomac. They were posted to Muddy Branch, aptly named according to one of his regimental officers: "We are in the worst camp we have ever had. It is in a hollow, where the dampness collects, and, as we have had a great deal of rain lately, it has been a perfect bog." Moving west to a site near Seneca Creek, "both damp and without protection from the storms," was no improvement. Snow fell before Thanksgiving, converting the ground into "slosh, mud & mire" but not dampening the mood for a holiday "under canvas" with turkeys and chickens, thanks to "a big effort" by servant William Dollarson of Detroit.[76]

On December 4, Williams and his men "moved to the slopes of Catoctin Mountains, three miles west of Frederick, Md." This Christmas was the first he had not spent with at least one of his children; he wrote to Minnie that the day "has no cheerful sound, but is rather full of sad remembrances of the many, many dear ones who used to enjoy the day with me but are here no more." On January 6, 1862, his force was ordered to Hancock in Western Maryland "to resist the threatened invasion of that section" by a Confederate command under Thomas J. "Stonewall" Jackson, who had gained renown at the Battle of Bull Run in July 1861. On a reconnaissance toward Bath (Berkeley Springs, West Virginia), Williams with "other officers and an escort of only four mounted men" rode uneventfully twenty miles south into Virginia and back. It was his first venture onto Confederate soil.[77]

Efforts were underway to repair damage Jackson had wrought to the Baltimore & Ohio Railroad, a major east–west rail connection, between Harpers Ferry, Virginia, and Cumberland, Maryland. Banks sought permission to retake Harpers Ferry and then move on Winchester, thirty miles southwest at the lower (i.e., north) end of the Shenandoah Valley. "Under growing pressure from the Lincoln administration to do something," McClellan reluctantly authorized the move. To him, the objectives were limited, the enemy was too powerful to fight and the campaign needed his personal supervision. Consequently, the next months would end "without any very decisive military results." Williams complained of West Point bias against officers of his background: "I begin to think that all the prominent acquisition obtained there is superciliousness, arrogance, and insolence."[78]

After seven months as brigadier general, Williams finally faced the real possibility of combat. He obeyed Banks's order to move to Williamsport on March 1 and the next day crossed the Potomac, trudged through snow and occupied Martinsburg without opposition. On the fifth, he moved his command to Bunker Hill, meeting "slight resistance." His cavalry advance encountered a small Rebel picket in town and drove it off without loss. Williams was close by; he "got considerable of the fever of the rush and thus was one of the early ones in."[79]

Receiving conflicting reports about Jackson's strength, Williams sent a reconnaissance toward Winchester on March 7; they drove off Rebel cavalry easily and suffered three men wounded. It was first blood for his command. Williams sent Banks a detailed report, acknowledging, "If the results were not important, the effect has been to stir up the blood of the men and put them in good spirits for any work ahead." The affair convinced Williams that "Winchester was his for the taking." On the eleventh, his brigade moved to within three miles of the town, skirmishing "all day," inflicting several casualties and suffering "but one." The next day, at 4:00 a.m., he had his command under arms, and at daylight they moved forward to capture Winchester. From the Union advance could be seen a ridge offering a position for Confederate defense strengthened by rifle pits and earthworks, appearing "quite formidable." This morning, however, the works were empty of defenders—Jackson had retreated in the face of superior numbers. As Williams and his men entered the city, its civic leaders came forward to surrender and request protection. He had accomplished "an easy and bloodless victory."[80]

What followed next was an easy occupation. Williams's staff sought an appropriate home to use for headquarters, and when one female owner objected to her house being conscripted, Williams directed Wilkins to find another. Enemy sympathizers were not imprisoned, unlike the policy Jackson followed when he held the town. For Unionists and secessionists alike, Williams served as an example of fairness and leniency.[81] There was one notable exception: what to be done with the formerly enslaved.

Williams confronted the issue when eminent town citizen Robert Young Conrad paid him a visit to obtain return of two teenage siblings. Rumor had it the escapees were "working for the soldiers at one of the warehouses near the RR Depot." At the start of the war, Conrad's request might well have been honored. The war for the Union did not include a policy favoring the confiscation of Rebel "property." Developments had altered the matter by March 1862. Congress had passed the first Confiscation Act, authorizing the Union military to seize property and slaves used in the Confederate war effort. For the latter, the law provided that as to an enslaved person "required or permitted" to "take up arms against the United States" or "to work or to be employed in or upon any fort, navy yard, dock, armory, ship, entrenchment, or in any military or naval service" for the Confederacy, "the person to whom such labor or service is claimed to be due shall forfeit his claim to such labor."[82]

In a letter to Williams on March 20, Conrad "desired to be informed whether, in case of seizure of these negroes, my slaves, the military authorities will be ready to prevent any rescue by the Soldiery." Why the letter? "I called in person at your office, but was told I could not see you, nor any time fixed at which I might have the privilege." Despite lack of proof of actual involvement by Conrad's slaves on behalf of the Confederate military, Williams declined to honor Conrad's request.[83]

That day, pursuant to General Orders No. 100 of the Army of the Potomac and a corresponding order by Banks, Williams "assumed command of 1st Division, 5th Corps" of McClellan's Army of the Potomac. No increase in rank accompanied the "promotion," but it signified recognition. He now commanded three infantry brigades and five artillery batteries. The 1st Brigade of six regiments was led by thirty-seven-year-old Colonel Dudley Donnelly of New York, the 2nd Brigade of five regiments by the familiar Brigadier General Abercrombie (classmate of Joseph Mansfield) and the 3rd Brigade of four regiments by thirty-eight-year-old Colonel George H. Gordon (West Point, 1846). Williams succeeded Landers despite politicking for the position by Brigadier General Robert C. Schenck. He now commanded more than ten thousand troops.[84]

Both Lincoln and McClellan had played a role in Williams's increase in responsibility. On March 8, the president issued General War Order

No. 2, dividing the Army of the Potomac into corps. McClellan issued an order on March 13 implementing the presidential directive, prescribing that Banks's command would consist of "divisions, Williams and Shields." A grand strategy was unfolding: McClellan had kicked off his campaign to take Richmond.[85]

The bulk of the Army of the Potomac boarded ships for transport via the Chesapeake Bay to the peninsula between the York and James Rivers, a short distance from the Confederate capital. One element under Major General Irvin McDowell moved overland from the Washington defenses toward Richmond to support McClellan's right. With Jackson's withdrawal leaving the Shenandoah in Union control, McClellan ordered Banks to send one and then the other of his divisions out of the Valley east to Centerville.[86]

Williams was thus "ordered to march with all possible dispatch from Winchester to Centreville." He reached the Shenandoah River at Castleman's Ferry on the twenty-second in preparation for crossing the Blue Ridge. Then an order arrived: he must countermarch, for Jackson had advanced down the Valley toward Harpers Ferry again. Confederate strategy sought to draw troops away from McClellan's Peninsula Campaign. It worked. Reversing course, Williams's 1st Brigade reached the vicinity of Winchester on the twenty-third. Banks's other division, under Brigadier General James Shields, repulsed Jackson in the Battle of Kernstown that day. The Confederates withdrew southward, but the Union command now sought to hold the Valley. The 3rd Brigade retraced its steps to Winchester and joined the 1st in an advance to Strasburg. There it engaged "in daily skirmishes with the enemy" until March 31. Unfortunately, Williams's other brigade, the 2nd, had continued its march toward Centerville and was not within countermarching range. At month's end, the division remained understrength in the absence of one of three brigades.[87]

Banks moved farther up the Valley in early April. Williams served as the reserve during an action at Mount Jackson on the seventeenth, with Banks complimenting "his fine division" for its discipline and order. The Rebels were pursued to Harrisonburg, where Williams set up his headquarters in the Bank of Rockingham building. He supervised the employment by his quartermasters of some fifty escaped slaves. Other than his first notable illness, "a terrific cold all over," all seemed in hand. In the first week of May, tables began to turn. Jackson had been reinforced, crossed over the mountains and driven the Federals out of McDowell, Virginia, on May 8. His next move was a mystery, so Williams was ordered to send the 1st Maryland Regiment to Front Royal as a forward outpost.[88]

With Union forces in the Valley depleted, and to alleviate pressure around Richmond, Stonewall Jackson had seized the opportunity to take the offensive. His two divisions began advancing down the Valley on May 20. Banks, with about 4,500 infantry and 1,600 cavalry, realized too late his vulnerability to a much superior Rebel army. The garrison at Front Royal—Williams's Maryland detachment—suffered more than 700 casualties, primarily in men captured, when attacked on May 23. Believing Jackson might have 25,000 men, on the twenty-fourth Banks's command, "the whole under direction of Williams," headed to Winchester "in a race" to arrive before the Confederates could cut it off. To secure a safe withdrawal, Williams ordered three regiments south "to rescue the rear…and hold the enemy in check." The tactic succeeded. Covering thirty miles per day, the infantry pressed on to Winchester despite fatigue, a testimony to its leadership. More than one hundred of its six hundred wagons had been lost, but few soldiers.[89]

Williams lamented the "unfortunate policy" that had opened the door to Jackson's campaign and stripped Banks's force of sufficient strength. "We had the game all in our hands," he wrote, but now his "greatly reduced force" must be nothing but a "decoy" rather than an offensive power. He shuddered for the future, praying "God help us!"[90]

Williams posted his meager forces—some 3,600 infantry, seven regiments in two brigades, plus the 1st Michigan Cavalry Regiment and "ten pairs of Parrott guns with six useless brass pieces." He had to cover the two roads converging on Winchester from the south. A small force under Donnelly protected the left flank at the plank road from Front Royal, while the bulk were posted under Brigadier General George H. Gordon on a rise on the right overlooking the Valley turnpike. Banks had perhaps another 2,000 troops available. Williams had but a short rest in the hotel in town when "a bevy of staff officers" banged on his door to warn that "the Rebels were before us (probably around us) in tremendous force." Quickly conferring with Banks, it was decided to make a stand rather than immediately retreat. The wagons were dispatched toward the safety of the Potomac.[91]

After "a hurried cup of coffee," Williams and Banks rode together to the front just after sunrise on this momentous Sunday. The opposing artillery batteries were already engaged, and Williams's brigade commanders had made troop dispositions "as seemed most judicious with reference to our inferior numbers." The first Rebel attack on the left was repulsed, but more of the enemy appeared for a second assault. Williams rode from the right over to the left, seeing that "the case certainly looked hopeless enough" but endeavoring to strengthen the lines. As he rode back toward the right, several artillery shells "passed in most unpleasant proximity to my head." The increased fire served as harbinger for the next stage. Arrayed against the small Union garrison were Jackson's own division on the Rebel left and Richard Ewell's on the right, seven brigades and twenty-nine regiments, along with cavalry and multiple artillery batteries. Fifteen regiments confronted Williams's four on his right, and a flanking maneuver soon rendered the Union position untenable. As one regiment was overcome and retreated, the one next in line did the same. Williams sought to "fashion a new line of resistance," but the effort proved futile. A chaotic withdrawal ensued through the streets of Winchester and beyond. Williams was nearly struck by a shot from a window as he rode through.[92]

The task now was to prevent a stampede. Williams placed a battery to cover the retreat, struggled to get the infantry to form into an orderly march north to Martinsburg and positioned the Union cavalry as a screen. To keep the pursuers at bay, he periodically halted his force, requiring them to "take the back seat," and with a well-organized unit "in the rear of the main army something like confidence was kept up." A halt was called "whenever he saw the enemy prepared to dash upon the stragglers, or saw the stampede was becoming too furious." The Confederates kept up a pursuit for several miles but then broke it off. Banks's Corps reached the Potomac at several points, having become separated on the hasty retreat. Williams arrived at Williamsport and saw to crossing of the wagon train. He finally made for a small house, where a private offered him a cup of coffee, out of turn; Williams decided to take it, for he "had given my horse to a wounded soldier that afternoon." At 2:00 a.m. on Monday, the twenty-fifth, he began to get the infantry "rapidly over." By 9:00 a.m., all were safe on the Maryland side.[93]

Jackson's report paid a compliment to how Williams, though greatly outnumbered, had handled the situation: "The Federal forces, upon falling back into the town, preserved their organization remarkably well." Jackson's losses amounted to 400 men over the several days' actions; he reported 3,050 Federal prisoners. The official casualty report for Williams's Division amounted to 51 killed, 201 wounded and 1,289 missing or captured (most due to the 1st Maryland), for a total of 1,541. Cavalry losses totaled 324. Proportionately large, the numbers could have been even worse had not Williams capably managed the retreat. He chalked up the affair to War Department mismanagement, favoritism and overcaution. He had wanted to be on offense; he would have "captured all Jackson's guns and been a major general!" Donnelly hoped that his brigade had "done no discredit to the discipline attained while under [Williams's] command." A regimental commander applauded "the skill and energy of our commanding officers for the miraculous escape of our men from utter annihilation."[94]

After threatening Harpers Ferry, Jackson withdrew up the Valley to avoid being trapped by converging Federal forces. Stanton sent reinforcements to Banks, and on June 1, Williams commenced to recross the Potomac. On June 13, elements of his division had advanced to Front Royal; Williams wrote home from Winchester, since his troops were scattered between the two towns. Officers from the detached 2nd Brigade had come to lobby Banks for restoration to Williams's command. He needed such encouragement, for he remained "heart-sick" at the overall strategy in Virginia. He was further revived on arriving at Front Royal when "the men of my old brigade turned out en masse and cheered me vociferously." By month's end, Williams had 4,554 men and fourteen guns opposite Front Royal, a light division ready for action.[95]

Jackson's 1862 exploits in the Shenandoah Valley elevated him to legendary status as one of the Confederacy's top commanders. For Williams, the approbation of his men had to suffice in lieu of other recognition. Evaluating his performance under stress and anxiety, he realized that he had felt "as cool and collected as on a common march." Rather than despondence, he expressed anger that the outcome was not "Jackson and Ewell [becoming] defeated fugitives." He wondered how the fortunes of war would pivot again and told his daughter, presciently, that if Maryland were ever to suffer a Rebel invasion, it would not be directed toward the vicinity of Washington. Rather, "it will be through this valley—mark my prediction."[96]

CHAPTER 6

"FURIOUS ATTACK"

CEDAR MOUNTAIN

On June 25, 1862, Confederate forces under General Robert E. Lee began a weeklong series of attacks on the Army of the Potomac outside Richmond. The Seven Days Battles drove McClellan's army away from the Rebel capital city. McClellan urged the secretary of war on a strategy to draw troops away from Lee: "put some one general in command of the Shenandoah and of all troops in front of Washington" to lead another offensive into Virginia.[97]

On June 26, the White House answered. The president issued an order creating the Army of Virginia; consolidating the Valley forces under Banks with John C. Frémont's, McDowell's and Samuel Sturgis's in front of Washington; appointing Major General John Pope to lead it; and specifying its mission. The new command would protect west Virginia and Washington, attack Jackson's Valley force (which had now joined up with Lee), threaten Charlottesville and aid McClellan in the capture of Richmond. Banks's troops became the II Corps in the new army. Frémont asked to be relieved rather than serve under a junior officer; Brigadier General Rufus King was appointed in his place. Pope assumed command on the twenty-seventh at Washington.[98]

When Pope urged Banks to be ready to march, the II Corps commander replied that only Williams's Division was "in moving condition." It had two new brigadier general commanders, Samuel W. Crawford over the 1st Brigade and George S. Greene for the 3rd. On July 5, Pope ordered Banks to "throw forward your cavalry" to Culpeper Court House "and carefully watch the whole country toward Richmond and Gordonsville." Banks reported on the sixth that Williams had "moved forward" out of the Valley and encamped halfway from Front Royal on the seventh. Pope sought to hold Culpeper, a key station on the Orange & Alexandria Railroad, in the belief that no major Confederate force was in the vicinity.[99]

Pope's plan had everything to do with "the critical condition of affairs near Richmond"—McClellan having been pinned by Lee against the James River—"and the danger of an advance of the enemy in force on Washington." On July 20 came the first report that Rebel infantry was at Gordonsville, only thirty miles from Culpeper, followed by information that Jackson was in command and as near as Louisa Court House. Pope believed that Jackson had a force of at least thirty-five thousand. On July 30, Pope was at Warrenton and began to concentrate the rather far-flung elements of his command at Culpeper. He also began to hear that the Confederates were advancing, and in this midsummer 1862, his opponent loomed large: "Jackson was perhaps the most famous man in North America."[100]

Williams had reached Warrenton on July 11 and departed on the sixteenth. Crawford's brigade advanced to Culpeper, the remainder of the division stopping at Little Washington on August 4. On August 6, it moved out and after a march in conditions "dusty and hot in the extreme" reached Culpeper on the eighth. Crawford made a reconnaissance to Orange Court House, across the Rapidan River. He had taken more than 50 prisoners, who reported that Jackson was "in force" and that Major General A.P. Hill had arrived with 10,000 infantry. General-in-Chief Henry W. Halleck warned Pope to be "very cautious." Banks with the rest of his 8,800 effectives "marched promptly" and reached Culpeper on August 8.[101]

At 8:00 a.m. on August 9, Pope wired Halleck that the enemy had advanced "in heavy force." He expected an assault on his right but would watch for the opportunity to attack Jackson. He moved Banks's Corps forward on the road southwest from Culpeper toward a singular geographic feature called Cedar Mountain, near Cedar Creek. The landscape featured "rolling land, the ridges running northwest and southeast." Williams's Division was posted on the west of the Culpeper pike, "close behind a thick belt of timber, which crowned one of the ridges. Large cornfields and a wheat patch occupied most of the ground in front." Banks's other division posted up on the opposite side. Other corps of the Army of Virginia were stationed several miles away. Banks was instructed to defend his position if attacked. In that eventuality, Pope stated, he would bring forward all forces available. These

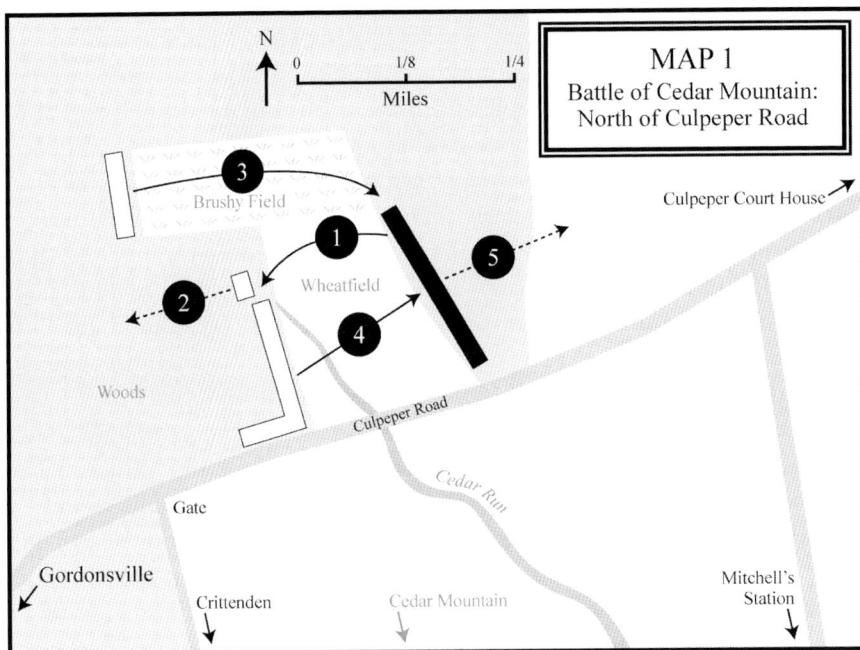

arrangements placed II Corps in the position of being alone to confront a fast-approaching, superior Rebel force.[102]

Early in the afternoon, Confederate artillery commenced firing—Williams reported that it "began soon after 2 o'clock, P.M." Rebel infantry was concealed in woods on each side of the Culpeper Road, and skirmishers began advancing toward the Union position around 5:00 p.m. followed "in strong force" by the rest of their comrades.[103]

Banks had deployed one of his two divisions, led by Brigadier General Christopher C. Augur of Michigan, on the left of the Culpeper Road. Rebel artillery had taken up position on the slope of two-hundred-foot-high Cedar Mountain, commanding approaches from the north. Williams's Division defended to the right (north) of the road. Williams placed artillery in front and awaited developments. Much of the afternoon was consumed by the Southern infantry approaching on the main road and forming for battle. Facing Banks were Stonewall Jackson's three infantry divisions under A.P. Hill, Ewell and Charles S. Winder, amounting per official records to 20,108 troops. Banks had roughly 7,600 available. Woods fringed the fields across which the two armies faced, preventing long-distance firing and requiring "that attacking units would have to come to close quarters with their opponents to gain a decision."[104]

Cedar Mountain battlefield north of Culpeper Road. *Author's collection.*

Field of attack, Williams's Division, looking northwest, Cedar Mountain battlefield. *Author's collection.*

Williams's seven regiments of infantry, 3,435 strong, enjoyed wooded cover in what he regarded as "a very strong defensible position." Given the presence "of a vastly superior enemy" and the lateness of the hour, with Pope's other elements still on the road, he was content to stand on the defensive. Instead, Williams received orders to attack with one brigade while holding the other in reserve. It was around 5:00 p.m. Crawford's 1st Brigade with six companies of the 3rd would make the difficult and gallant assault:

> *The ground was exceedingly unfavorable—across open stubble-fields, curtained in front and on the flank by dense woods.—The attacking column suffered severely but drove the enemy's advance from a half to three quarters of a mile back upon its heavy supports.*[105]

Two factors made the 1st Division attack succeed despite the long odds. Williams's assault "overlapped the left" of the Rebel line due to the repositioning of his line for better advantage. And as Crawford's brigade advanced, it struck a vulnerable point in the formation of the Stonewall Brigade (Map 1:1). In the official Confederate account, the 1st "fell with great vigor" on Jackson's left, turning it and pouring on "a destructive fire into its rear." The Federals exhibited "considerable elan and stubborn bravery" in throwing the Rebel flank into disorder (Map 1:2). As Crawford's men pushed their advance to the gate on Catherine Crittenden's farm lane, "Jackson's army teetered on the brink of disaster." His men were "back on their heels" after Williams's Division gave them "a good deal more than they could handle."[106]

Recognizing the critical situation, Stonewall Jackson waded in near the gate to stem the potential rout, attempting to draw his sword and wave it to rally his men. It had rusted from disuse. Impetuously, he unbuckled the belt and used the scabbard, sword embedded like in the proverbial stone, for the same motivational purpose, as well as to whack men back into line. His efforts alone were not the cause of the change in fortunes. The Confederate numerical advantage came to bear as more of his troops arrived and outflanked the Union line (Map 1:3). Banks had no reinforcements to turn to, and now the Rebels "could scarcely lose this battle." Eventually, as the Union attackers were driven back in the looming darkness (Map 1:4), Williams brought up the 3rd Brigade to check the enemy advance. He was gratified that "we held on till dark, though it was every moment apparent that we were greatly outnumbered." The division maintained its line until relieved (Map 1:5).[107]

Facing an "avalanche" of overwhelming numbers, Banks withdrew toward Culpeper. By 6:30 p.m. it was over: Jackson held the field. Ninety minutes of intensity had produced some four thousand casualties. It had been a bloody affair: "The engagement having been so close, in some places hand to hand, the wounds were very grave, and an unusual proportion of trunk wounds were remarked on the hospital grounds."[108]

Nightfall made pursuit impracticable. Although Banks's units "had been rather badly used up," the soldiers in the ranks had performed bravely, initially routing elements of the fabled Stonewall Brigade. According to one of the most distinguished names in Civil War historical studies, Jackson's old unit scampered, broke, ran back in disorder, fell apart twice and suffered demoralization at the hands of Williams's men. "Everywhere there was praise for the fighting, and it was deserved."[109] A battlefield marker erected for a 1st Brigade regiment, the 46th Pennsylvania, succinctly sums up its fortitude: "Charged across wheat field against Stonewall Jackson's command. Engaged, 504. Loss, 244."

The combat proved deadly beyond the rank and file, as of Crawford's eleven regimental commanders seven were killed or wounded, two captured and "every regiment but one was left without field officers." Colonel Donnelly was mortally wounded. Williams had a narrow escape as he, Gordon and other officers left the battlefield. "A hot fire, from what sounded like a regiment, was poured into our midst." Fortunately, they "were in a small hollow and the balls passed over us." None of these officers was struck or ended up captured. On the Confederate left, Winder was killed.[110]

Casualty totals amply demonstrated how hard the Union forces had fought. Losses in the 1st Division were 171 killed, 588 wounded and 453 missing or captured, for a total of 1,212. This toll formed slightly more than half of the 2,381 present for action as reported by Pope. Williams maintained his aggressive view: if reinforcements "had arrived an hour before sundown we should have thrashed Jackson badly and taken a host of artillery." He also wondered why, once thousands of reinforcements arrived to relieve his division, the fight was not renewed "as I was assured by Gen. Pope it would be by sunrise." Had it been, Williams felt "confident we should have punished them badly."[111]

He had other feelings as well. In a letter to Minnie, "my darling daughter," Williams wrote of how, during a quiet time early that fateful afternoon, he and his field officers gathered over "a good lunch of coffee, ham, etc." and reminisced about their ten months of service together. They then were "unconcerned" and unaware of what lay in store: "sorrow and misfortune seemed far away."

The letter enumerated all who had been killed or wounded or were missing, including "poor Wilkins," captured while carrying his commander's orders. Williams wrote tellingly of "the broken troops of two divisions"—as he was in temporary charge of the II Corps with Banks recuperating from a horse-induced injury. The administrative burdens, shared with but one available aide, Lieutenant Pittman, kept him "incessantly at work." They did not appear to distract him from thoughts of lost comrades.[112]

On the eleventh, Jackson withdrew across the Rapidan and concentrated around Gordonsville, not far from the James Madison home. Pope's men retook the Cedar Mountain battlefield, enabling him to claim success. Although a tactical defeat marked August 9 for the Union, the situation on August 12 appeared to show a positive outcome, though at a heavy price for the units engaged. Pope extended commendations to the "very fine" behavior of the II Corps, attesting that "no greater gallantry and daring could be exhibited by any troops." He also cited the performance of generals, naming Williams, after Banks, on the list of those who had "behaved with conspicuous gallantry." Halleck's reply telegram particularly congratulated Banks and his corps.[113]

The immediate aftermath of Cedar Mountain demonstrated that Williams had proven capabilities beyond his rank. After Banks turned corps command over, Pope issued a corresponding order placing Williams "in command of the troops in and around Culpeper." He also directed Williams to "proceed as rapidly as possible to put the corps in condition for service," regarding it as "so cut up and worn down with fatigue that I did not consider it capable of rendering any efficient service for several days." On August 15, Williams held a review of his division in order to rebuild their fitness for the next campaign.[114]

On August 18, the II Corps began a supporting role in the next phase of the Confederate campaign in Virginia. On August 28–29, Pope was defeated by Lee in the Battle of Second Manassas. Williams left Culpeper and reached Warrenton on the twenty-seventh in position to aid the Union effort along Bull Run creek, "but no order came to move nor did we hear a word from Pope." Being "off on one flank with a decimated little corps of not more than 6,000 fighting men," Williams felt "uncertainty and doubt and anxiety" concerning its chances; somehow, he "slept soundly." Ultimately, he led his hungry, tired troops into the capital defenses at Fort Albany on Arlington Heights late on September 2. Thus concluded a "terrible seventeen days" during which he and his men were under enemy fire and "incessant battling."[115]

As he learned of other losses during Pope's campaign, Williams attempted to adjust to the terrible cost of this war on leadership. Fletcher Webster, Thornton F. Brodhead and Horace S. Roberts, all from Michigan, were killed. Fifty of his friends or acquaintances were reported killed or wounded. On the one hand, Williams could react with "such is war." He also reflected on his original brigade's reductions over just one year: instead of three thousand, just four hundred remained. To this he confessed, "instead of hopeful and confident feelings we are all depressed with losses and disasters." He felt "worked to death" in what was being "called a 'brainless war.'"[116]

After three weeks of near-constant activity, Williams's force experienced a single day's rest before having to move out again. The direction this time was north. His forecast of a Rebel invasion of Maryland was materializing, and Williams had no reassurance for his daughter: "I can't tell you of the future."[117]

CHAPTER 7

ANTIETAM

BLOODIEST DAY'S COMMAND

On September 4, 1862, the Army of Northern Virginia became an invading force as it crossed the Potomac River into Maryland at White's Ferry, just upriver from Ball's Bluff. Its objectives ranged from simple to ambitious: move the war out of Virginia, secure supplies and new recruits, ally Maryland with the Confederate cause by securing its secession, secure foreign recognition for the Confederacy and pressure the Lincoln administration into negotiations before the fall elections. Victorious in the Shenandoah Valley, on the Peninsula and at Second Manassas, Lee's legions had supreme confidence as they marched toward Frederick, Western Maryland and Pennsylvania to threaten Baltimore and Washington.[118]

The units of the Federal armies of the Potomac and Virginia unified under McClellan's command; Pope went to Minnesota. Combining these two commands necessitated a reorganization, so on September 12 the president issued General Orders 129. The II Corps of the Army of Virginia reconstituted into the XII Corps of the Army of the Potomac, with a strength of approximately ten thousand. Williams remained in temporary command since "Gen. Banks seems to get sick when there is most to do." To compound matters, it was not evident where the enemy was heading. Williams reached Georgetown on September 4 and, for the next three days, was part of the slow emergence of the Army of the Potomac from the Washington defenses.[119]

By then, Banks had joined Pope on the transfer list, assigned to command of those defenses. McClellan sought deputies in the field he had faith in;

politician Banks was not his man. Brigadier General Joseph K.F. Mansfield, on the other hand, had been to West Point and served in the antebellum army. Although December would bring his fifty-ninth birthday, and he had yet to exercise Civil War infantry combat command, Mansfield had the credentials McClellan wanted. The War Department issued an order on September 8 for him to report to the Army of the Potomac. On the fifteenth, he was assigned to command of XII Corps.[120]

Until Mansfield arrived, Williams remained interim corps leader while the army searched for its opponent north and west of Washington. McClellan ordered his corps to "move with great care, feeling your way cautiously, and being always ready to concentrate." The XII Corps marched to Rockville and Middlebrook and then on the tenth to Damascus, in the advance. Despite his clothes in tatters, an influx of completely green reinforcements and lack of intelligence about the enemy, somehow Williams felt more sanguine. There could soon be a great battle, and he possessed "great confidence that we shall smash them terribly if they stand, more confidence than I have ever had in any movement of the war." When the Army of the Potomac struck next, "I think it will be a heavy blow." Despite the coming fury, he told his daughter not to "be frightened about me, but believe me, as ever, your affectionate Father, A.S.W." Before dawn on the thirteenth, the XII Corps crossed the Monocacy River at Crum's Ford and headed toward the outskirts of Frederick. Williams halted his men about one mile outside town and waited for instructions from the commanding general. This Saturday seemed no different from the days prior, a slow process of cautiously seeking for the enemy.[121]

It was early, only about 9:00 a.m., and several men of the 27th Indiana Volunteers, long of Williams's Division, prepared to rest in a wheat field near the C.E. Best farm adjacent to the Georgetown/Urbana Pike. An object under a nearby locust tree caught their attention. It proved to be an envelope, and inside were several cigars wrapped in a handwritten note.

The single-page, double-sided paper bore on its face the heading "(Confidential) Hd Qrs Army of Northern Va," a date of September 9 and designation as "Special Orders No. 191." Believing it might be important, the soldiers took the package to their sergeant, who carried it to the company commander, from where it went to the 27th's commander, Colonel Silas Colgrove. Recognizing its potential, the colonel personally conveyed the document to XII Corps headquarters and put it in the hands of the acting adjutant general. Samuel Pittman looked at it front and back; saw references to Lee's constituent forces, their locations and their objectives; and understood that he appeared to hold a Rebel operational order describing the enemy's campaign plan. It meant that Lee had divided his army into three parts and dispersed them beyond support of one another. Was it genuine?

Somehow, Pittman and his superior had been placed in a position critical to the future of the nation, "an intelligence coup unrivaled in all the war"—assuming the document really was an order from Lee. How to prove this to the typically cautious McClellan?[122]

Looking at the signature, Pittman noticed the name: "R.H. Chilton." His reaction was immediate:

> *I did at once pronounce the signature genuine....Chilton, a few years before the war, was on duty at Detroit as a Paymaster of the U.S. Army, at which time he kept his Bank account with the Michigan State Bank, and at the time I was teller of that Bank, thus paying thousands (probably) of his checks over the Bank counter that my teller's experience qualified me somewhat to judge of signatures, and that the signature on Order No. 191 was surely Chilton's.*

In an era heavily dependent on personal means of identification, when "a bank teller becomes more or less an expert as to signatures," Pittman "was able to confidently assert that I was thoroughly familiar with Col. Chilton's signature and that this was genuine."

Now it was Williams's turn in the spotlight. Pittman wasted no time and "immediately reported" to his superior, showed him the document and vouched for its legitimacy. Besides having served together through the thick and thin of their first year, the two Detroiters were friends. Brigadier General Williams knew what to do. Without hesitation, he directed his adjutant "to lose no time in placing it in Gen. McClellan's possession." As Pittman sought out a trusty courier, Williams quickly jotted a pithy cover note:

> *General*
>   *I enclose a ~~General~~ Special Order of Genl Lee Commanding Rebel forces which was found on the field where my Corps is Encamped.*
>   *It is a document of interest & is no doubt genuine.*

Telling the orderly "to ride fast," the two officers sent the important document off to the army commander.[123]

McClellan reacted by giving at least some credence to Williams's testimonial. He sent cavalry off to determine if Rebel troop positions conformed with the order. They did. Galvanized into action, possessing the key to defeating Lee piece by piece, he ordered his army to advance and engage. In a midnight-hour telegram to the president, McClellan enthusiastically wrote, "I have the whole rebel force in front of me, but am confident, and no time shall be lost....The army is in motion as rapidly as possible....I have all the plans of the rebels, and will catch them in their own trap if my men are equal to the emergency." His confidence at a peak, he ended with a promise: "will send you trophies." He repeated Williams's endorsement: in his hands was a lost Rebel operational order, "the authenticity of which is unquestionable."[124]

That night, Williams wrote to a relative in Detroit. He enjoyed "straw under a blanket! Think of that luxury!" His confidence remained; he predicted the Rebel invasion would not succeed. Perhaps he had in mind the intelligence coup, which gave his army a major advantage over a vaunted opponent, but he made no mention of the Lost Order.[125]

On the morrow, XII Corps moved out from Frederick and climbed to Turner's Gap on South Mountain, reaching the pass at midnight. Williams bedded down under a tree at 2:00 a.m. The Army of the Potomac had earlier in the day secured control of three mountain passes, including Turner's. Lee was scrambling to unite his disparate forces in time to meet the unexpected movement of the Federals. On the fifteenth, Mansfield arrived and supplanted Williams. The corps reached Boonsboro and camped east of Keedysville. Back in command of 1st Division, he slept fitfully in the house of "Mr. Nicodemus." The next day, the corps "moved up and massed behind the hills between Keidysville and Antietam Creek" near the pike that ran through Sharpsburg, knowing that the Confederates lay somewhere ahead. That night, they crossed the creek on the nearby stone bridge and marched west along the Keedysville Road to encamp on the farms of Susan Hoffman and George Line east of the Smoketown Road (Map 2:1). Had it been daylight, a woodlot known as the East Woods would have blocked their view to the south.[126]

On this eve of battle, "after a weary march," Williams halted his column and sought to arrange the troops for the next day. It required more time because of the inexperience of the five new regiments he had received. Finally, at about 2:00 a.m., he found a place to rest in the open under a rail fence. His fugacious sleep was interrupted by picket fire and by Mansfield's tinkering about the corps' alignment. Williams would never "forget that

MAP 2
Antietam:
Northern Battleground

0   1/8   1/4

Miles

N

Line

1

Hoffman →

J.
Poffenberger

2

Keedysville →

North
Woods

Smoketown Road

S.
Poffenberger

D. R.
Miller

5

3

4

Cornfield

East
Woods

Hagerstown Pike

7

Antietam Creek →

Mumma

West
Woods

Dunker
Church

6

Roulette

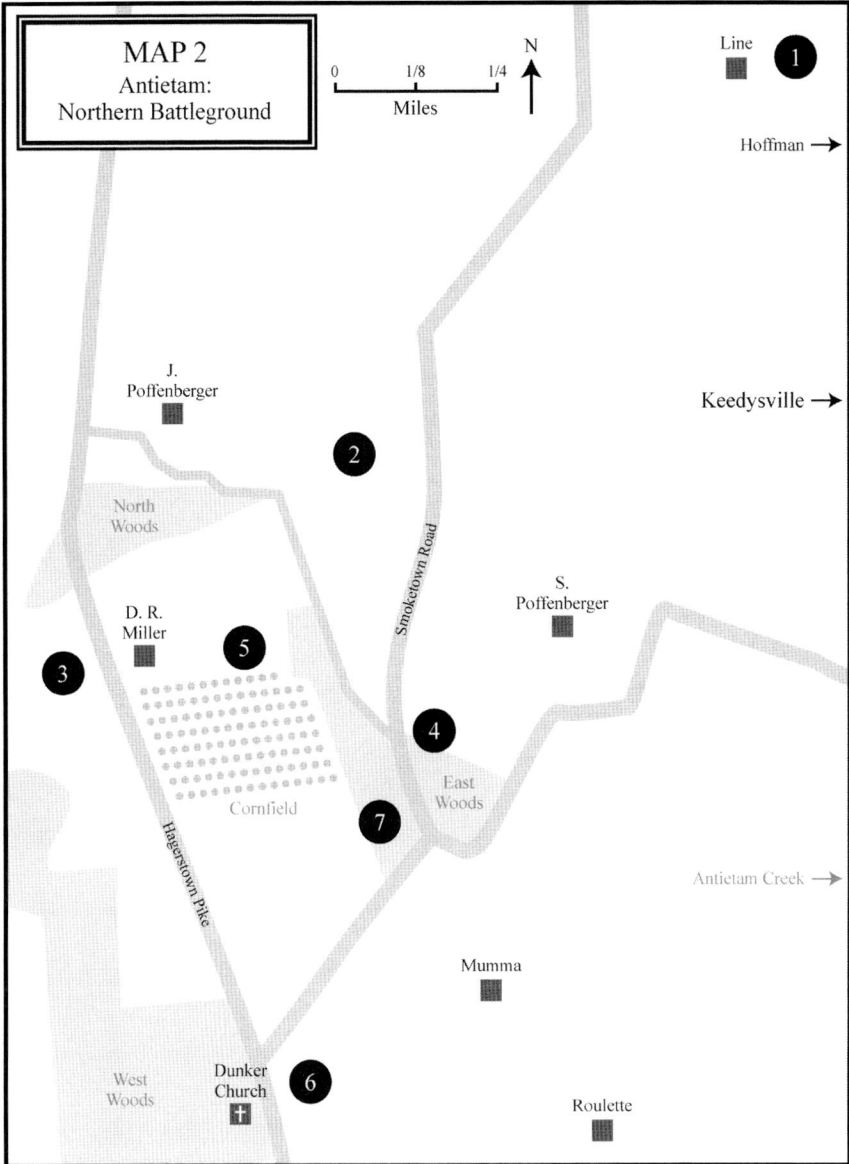

night; so dark, so obscure, so mysterious, so uncertain," his fatigue producing "a half-dreamy sensation about it all."[127]

On the farm of Joseph Poffenberger, just to the south and west, the I Corps under the command of Major General Joseph Hooker waited for daylight (Map 2:2). McClellan's plan was to attack Lee's left flank with Hooker's and

George Line Farm, Antietam battlefield. *Author's collection.*

Mansfield's corps, supported by the II Corps under Major General Edwin V. Sumner. He would follow with an assault on Lee's right with the IX Corps under Burnside and, if conditions presented themselves, pierce the center with yet another corps.[128]

Sunrise this Wednesday was at 5:53 a.m. Williams arose as the XII Corps formed into position. "By a common impulse," he would note, "our men stood to arms" in anticipation of what was to come. At the first sound of artillery fire, Williams led his men in formation south across the farm fields to the east of the Hagerstown Pike. Mansfield ordered them to march in column of companies, closed in mass. This arrangement placed the men in stacked order just paces from one another, a perfect target for enemy cannoneers. As they moved to the sound of the action, Williams received reports that Hooker had engaged all of his corps, including reserves, indicating intense fighting. He ordered the division to hasten into line of battle, lessening its exposure to artillery fire. The movement proved complicated for the many green troops in his command, but things got sorted out before encountering the Rebels. Soon a volley on his lead regiment near the East Woods caused the men to lose order again. Williams "thundered into the chaos," ignoring shot and shell to form the regiment up again. At that point, he received startling news: Mansfield had been mortally wounded, and command had devolved on him. Unlike the dying general, the Michigander could distinguish enemy fire. But Williams had never led such a large contingent, much less while in the midst of combat—a battle that would become the bloodiest day in American history.[129]

Williams did not hesitate or await orders from McClellan: "I at once reported to Major-General Hooker on the field, took from him such directions as the pressing exigencies would permit, and hastened to make a disposition of the corps to meet them." At best, Williams received "a few hurried directions" from Hooker. Replacing Hooker, George Meade also rode up to plead for immediate assistance. By then, at 7:30 a.m., Meade's 8,600-strong corps had incurred some 3,000 casualties. The I Corps, "especially his left wing, at this time seemed giving way." Positioning the XII Corps as best he could, at 9:00 a.m. Williams semaphored McClellan, "Genl. Mansfield is dangerously wounded. Genl. Hooker wounded severely in foot. Genl. Sumner I hear is advancing. We hold the field at present. Please give us all the aid you can," he urged, intent on seeking to enlist his commanding general in winning this part of the field.[130]

Across the way, Stonewall Jackson had command. His left wing strength amounted to 23,465 men before the battle commenced. The XII Corps brought into action 10,126 in two divisions. In addition to the 1st Division with its two brigades and eleven regiments, the 2nd, under George Greene, comprised three brigades of eleven regiments.[131]

Williams's first goal was to instill order. Mansfield had placed new, untrained regiments in the front line under inexperienced officers, a move designed to prevent the green troops from running away. As soon as he heard Mansfield was down, "I ordered the deployment of the old Regiments" so as to put them in the fore "and rode to the front" to provide visible leadership. Uninformed about artillery dispositions, Williams sought out and located three batteries "which were placed in position and did excellent service." And he did more than seek to hold the field. Down the chain of command came the "order for us to move forward 'with all possible dispatch,'" reported one sergeant. The units were rapidly deployed in appropriate line of battle and then moved forward to a position where "on our left and front there was a woods" and in front "a large cornfield."[132]

Williams's men made their way onto the land of farmer David Miller. It was "a forty-acre field of corn that swayed, head-high and green, in the

The Cornfield, looking south, Antietam battlefield. *Author's collection.*

September sun." On the farm's western boundary ran the road between Sharpsburg and Hagerstown (Map 2:3). To the north and south, "luxuriant clover fields" spread themselves; on the other axis stood the East and West Woods (Map 2:4). Beyond the latter, along the Hagerstown Pike, a small whitewashed one-room "Dunker" church building stood. The pastoral setting had already become blood-spattered as the men under Hooker and Jackson fought ferociously in the early hours.[133]

Under their familiar leader, both veteran and green troops of the XII Corps moved ahead, looking to press Jackson's line. Leadership of 1st Division had fallen to Samuel Crawford. The men performed well this day—under Joseph F. Knipe since Crawford disappeared. Knipe had commanded the 46th Pennsylvania and been badly wounded at Cedar Mountain. Now he became temporary brigade leader when George Gordon substituted for Crawford.[134]

Brigades from Daniel H. Hill's division advanced to secure the Cornfield (Map 2:5). Williams had the 1st Division on his left, the 2nd on his right. His intent was to "catch the Confederates in a vise and drive them back." Although he could not know the strength of the enemy ahead, "the necessities of the case were so great that I was obliged to put my whole corps into action at once." He set no reserve aside. The XII met the enemy, drove them "across a ploughed field and through a cornfield into another woods" and succeeded, in Greene's case, of reaching the Dunker church (Map 2:6).[135]

It was quite a performance for the temporary commander and the men of the corps. Williams "had hurled every unit of his command into the fray. Combined with rallied and counterattacking First Corps troops, the offensive effort of the Twelfth Corps succeeded in delivering the blow that outflanked the Confederates in the cornfield."[136]

Edwin Sumner arrived on the field with his II Corps at about 9:30 a.m. Williams "attempted to brief him on the situation. But Sumner paid little attention." He showed no interest in the XII Corps positions and failed to coordinate his attack with its commander, who had just driven the Rebels out of the farm field south of the Miller Cornfield.[137] The result was that Sumner took one of his divisions into action without waiting for the other two; he marched it into action without reconnaissance; he formed it *en echelon*, presenting a juicy target for a flank attack with no ability to respond; and the resulting "slaughter" of that division sapped Sumner's fighting spirit, prompting him to countermand any further attacks on that part of the field by newly arriving troops. Instead, he called on Williams for aid, who advanced "my wearied and hungry men" and held the field (Map 2:7).[138]

After completing the task begun by I Corps to drive the enemy from the northern part of the battlefield, Williams could point to his most advanced unit, Greene's Division, "within a mile of Sharpsburg." As the Confederates advanced after Sumner's repulse, "Greene received them with a murderous fire at a few rods distance and repulsing them with great slaughter, followed immediately into the woods around the church and held that position for over two hours." With Hooker's Corps savaged, "Fighting Joe" and Mansfield wounded and Sumner defeated, the XII Corps stood alone for precious moments on McClellan's flank. The Michigander's composed leadership meant the Union right wing "regained the wood lot and the cornfield, driving out" the men of Jackson's command. Riding "about the field with the unlighted stub of a cigar gripped in his teeth," Williams had stabilized the Union line, sent troops as far forward as the Dunker church and created potential for Federals in the center and left to drive Lee into the Potomac.[139]

The battle did not end so. McClellan continued to feed corps into action piecemeal, allowing Lee to shift his outnumbered units from one place on the field to another. At key moments, something would happen to stall a Federal attack that could have proved conclusive. At day's end, the two armies gathered themselves and waited, bloodied, for the next sunrise. On the eighteenth, they continued to pause. That night, seeing clearly the precarious condition of his army, Lee withdrew across the Potomac into Virginia.[140]

McClellan held the field and declared victory; Lincoln regarded it as incomplete since Lee's army had escaped. Still, he would make historic use of even a partial triumph. Five days later, the president issued the preliminary Emancipation Proclamation. Williams's performance had played a large role in making such action possible.

Broadly hailing Antietam as a sterling performance, McClellan's preliminary October 15 battle report attempted "nothing more than a sketch of the main features of this great engagement." Individual achievements and unit credit would have to await a later document. Still, some were acknowledged in the "sketch": the artillery as a whole, the Signal Corps (and a "Major Myers") and McClellan's staff merited compliments. Mention of corps leadership included Hooker ("his services had been conspicuous and important") and Mansfield ("the gallant and distinguished veteran"); the other XII Corps general named was Crawford (thrice). It was "Mansfield's corps" that "lost heavily," with no mention of any success. The three division commanders of Sedgwick's Corps were cited, as were those of Burnside's. Even William B. Franklin of the VI Corps received mention for having "arrived on the field" and that one of his divisions retook lost ground. Williams was mentioned, erroneously, in the capacity of commanding the XI Corps prior to the battle.[141]

The lack of recognition of the XII Corps' success was not due to any failure by its temporary commander. Under date of September 29, Williams submitted his report as "commanding Twelfth Army Corps." It was both succinct and complete as to the brave service of the officers and men under his aegis. Two of his soldiers, John P. Murphy of the 5th Ohio and Jacob G. Orth of the 28th Pennsylvania, would receive the Medal of Honor for capturing regimental flags. Casualties were 275 killed, 1,386 wounded and 85 missing/captured, total of 1,746. For his division, the figures were 159 killed, 864 wounded and 54 missing or captured, for a total of 1,077. Both amply demonstrated notable valor and sacrifice. Seeking to ensure that posterity would properly comprehend the role of his troops, Williams later wrote McClellan "to correct the corps' fighting record, how it pressed back the enemy 'and held those open fields all day, without relinquishing one inch of ground we had taken, except the woods around the Dunkard church.'" He needn't have apologized for that last point, for the "lodgment in the West Woods [was] the farthest Federal advance." Robert Gould Shaw thought so even before the battle: "Williams Division is the best I have seen—not excepting any in the army of the Potomac."[142]

Five days after the battle, Williams sent a comprehensive account to his daughters. He admitted further brushes with death, marveling at his escapes—how "a ball whizzed close" and "two or three others followed all in disagreeable closeness to my person"—how "the dust of the ploughed ground was knocked up in little spurts all around us, marking the spot where musket balls struck." He rode over the field on the nineteenth, observing the great numbers of Rebel dead, how "they lay as thick as autumn leaves," how "the number of dead horses was high" and how the detritus of battle lay "in heaps where the contest had been severest." Newspaper reports were already proving unreliable, such as that Sumner's Corps had rescued Hooker's.[143]

McClellan's initial account did not help, and his final report would not issue until August 4, 1863. It made some corrections as to Williams and the corps. By then, McClellan had been fired. He never held another command for the rest of the war.[144]

The Antietam Campaign proved momentous. The Confederate invasion failed to achieve the political goals of joining Maryland as its twelfth state and gaining European recognition. Its military goals also stood defeated. There was no prolonged sojourn in Union territory followed by a decisive victory over a McClellan-led, morale-challenged Army of the Potomac. Instead, the Union achievement meant that the war had expanded to sustain the nation's indivisibility *and* to free 4 million Americans held in bondage.

Williams expressed mixed feelings about the proclamation. He disowned a report that he had written approval of the measure. Instead, "prepared to sustain any measure I thought would help put an end to this accursed rebellion," he knew matters were yet unchanged in the South. Slaves would become free when Union arms freed them. In the meantime, he feared "promiscuous slaughter that would follow an immediate emancipation of slaves in the South." Before the war ended, Williams would regard the enslaved as better in character than poor whites and employ "contrabands" as headquarters servants. He would also persuade several of those liberated to go to Detroit—one, Phoebe Simms, he praised as "wonderfully intelligent"—so as to make a clean break from the South. One thing he did not do; it was suspected that Lincoln's action to free the slaves would result in "the resignation of a large number of officers in the army." Williams did not resign, even though his record continued to be overlooked. "My friends think I shall get a major generalship," but he knew better. "I should if I was of the regular army."[145]

CHAPTER 8

CHANCELLORSVILLE

SAVING THE DEBACLE

W illiams retained command of the XII Corps for another month after Antietam. Lincoln visited the army to gauge its temper; Williams had an informal conversation with the president and came away fairly impressed: "I had quite a long talk with him, sitting on a pile of logs. He is really the most unaffected, simple-minded, honest, and frank man I have ever met. I wish he had a little more firmness." The conversation did nothing for Williams's aspirations: Major General Henry W. Slocum, West Point class of 1852, transferred from a VI Corps division and took corps command on October 20. Williams was equally unsuccessful in obtaining promotions for some of his colonels. XII Corps advanced to the Potomac and stood post on the heights overlooking Harpers Ferry. It remained there on guard duty, occasionally on a reconnaissance, until ordered in December to serve as a reserve in covering Washington. It took position at Fairfax, Dumfries and then Stafford Court House before going into winter camp in January 1863.[146]

McClellan's replacement, Ambrose Burnside, had led the army into disaster at the Battle of Fredericksburg on December 13. The XII Corps was in reserve then but did participate in Burnside's infamous "Mud March" in January. On the twenty-sixth, Lincoln installed Major General Joseph Hooker in command of the army. His reputation was as a "fighting general," but his first task was to rebuild morale into the spring. Hooker accomplished the task through reorganization, reprovisioning and regular inspections. All 324 infantry commands were reviewed, of which 11 received high commendation; 4 were in Slocum's command, 3 associated with Williams's Division.[147]

That Williams had continued to do his duty during the early months of 1863 is significant. The lack of the army's success since September, and the Mud March in particular, led him to believe the spirits of his men were "greatly destroyed." Williams's mood was similar "amidst the trials and dispiriting circumstances that surround me." Then came word of promotions, and his name was again absent. "I have been now nearly a year commanding a division, a major general's command....How long I shall be able to hold out under this oversloughing is very doubtful." A major reason he did not quit was the love and respect of his men. They knew firsthand of his dedication and excellence, rewarding him with a ceremonial sword, ovations and support.[148]

Another effort of Hooker's to foster *esprit* was the institution of corps badges under an order of March 21. They would be worn in the center of the cap by each soldier in the ranks and on officers' hats, making unit recognition easier. For the XII Corps, the designated icon was a traditional five-pointed star, and for the 1st Division the color would be red (2nd Division white, 3rd blue). Williams embraced the move: "The insignia of our 'star' is a badge of honor we may all properly be proud of." He flew the headquarters banner for the rest of the war when in charge of the 1st Division, and the "Red Star Division" became renowned.[149]

On April 27, Hooker launched his plan to defeat Lee. He would leave a partial force facing the Confederate lines behind Fredericksburg, send most of the army west along the north bank of the Rappahannock River and bring them in on the rear and left of the Rebels, squeezing them as if in a vise. He dispatched cavalry and the V, XI and XII Corps to serve as the advance for the flanking blow, directing them to Kelly's Ford some twenty miles up the Rappahannock. Williams left Stafford at sunrise and reached Hartwood Church after a twelve-mile march. The twenty-eighth saw his division moving out at sunrise and crossing Kelly's Ford without difficulty. The combined force was put under Slocum for the potentially more difficult surmounting of the Rapidan River at Germanna Ford; thus, on April 29, Williams once again assumed command of the XII Corps while it led the way. Uncertainty lay ahead, but Williams believed that "obstacles always grow less as you approach them with confidence and vigor or with a feeling that you must meet and overcome them."[150]

The brigade of Williams's Division under newly promoted Brigadier General Thomas H. Ruger took the point for Slocum's force. Pushing the

A.S. Williams's "Red Star Division" banner. *Save The Flags, Michigan Capitol, photographer Peter Glendinning.*

few Rebels out of their way with ease, the brigade moved so suddenly that it enveloped the small enemy force controlling the Rapidan crossing. The rest of the division went over in a difficult and rocky ford, four feet deep in places with a swift current that swept some men downriver. Slocum watched in awe: "I have never witnessed a scene that tended more to increase my confidence in our troops, or that so strongly excited my admiration, than that presented by the two brigades of Williams's division in fording the Rapidan River." Once the bridgehead was secured, it took but an hour to throw across pontoons and facilitate crossing in ease by the rest of the army.[151]

On the morning of the thirtieth, the XII Corps advanced east toward Chancellorsville, a rural crossroads junction. It drew its name from the family house that "was just white pillars and red brickwork at an open clearing in the woods, with country roads converging in front of it." The bluecoat infantry brushed Rebel cavalry away near the Wilderness Tavern and reached the crossing near 3:00 p.m. Williams posted the 2nd Division

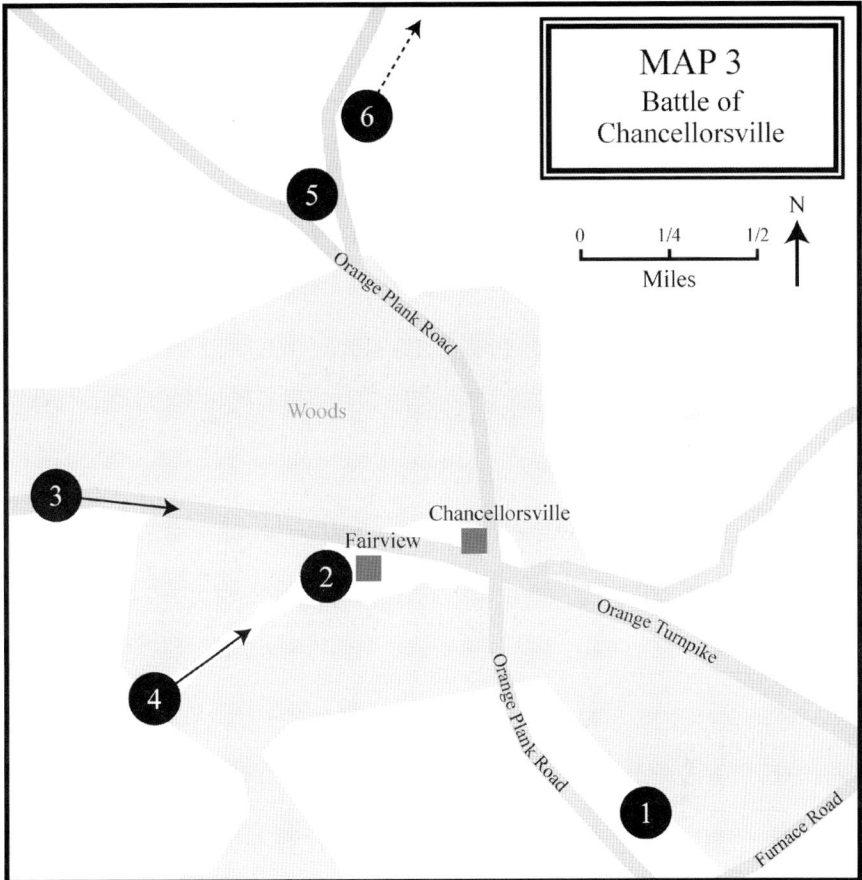

MAP 3
Battle of
Chancellorsville

under Brigadier General John W. Geary in front of the Chancellor House and his own division on its right extending west down the Orange Turnpike toward the Wilderness Church. Breastworks and barricades were thrown up to secure the line. The men had marched sixty-five miles and crossed two rivers in three days. That night, Williams slept in his tent "near the old log house on Fairview," a story-and-a-half structure south of the Chancellorsville intersection.[152]

Slocum resumed corps command on May 1, "a beautiful day," and Williams returned to division command. He reported early to Hooker's headquarters at the Chancellor House and was ordered to again serve in the vanguard for a foray east down the Orange Plank Road. He felt uneasy: "[T]here was too much boasting and too little planning; swagger without preparation." His division moved out at about 10:30 a.m. and took the left of the road, Geary's the right. Marching rapidly in the direction of Fredericksburg, the 1st Division drove enemy pickets back in spite of Confederate artillery (Map 3:1). After his men proceeded a few miles, Rebel entrenchments came into view, indicating that Williams had reached a main body of infantry. He halted and established his line for an advance in force. Hooker's plan to surprise Lee appeared on the verge of succeeding, and according to Williams, "the troops seemed never so eager to engage."[153] The quick success appeared to surprise Hooker as well.

At that moment, an order arrived directing the division, farthest in advance, to return to its position at Chancellorsville. The command was obeyed—though not without grumbling—and the retrograde movement proceeded in good order. Williams found Confederate pickets and an artillery battery threatening his old position, and his men "speedily dislodged them" (Map 3:2). The XII Corps was ordered to make secure its entrenchments, which it promptly did, in order to have them "in condition of defense." The Confederates found the XII Corps "concentrated in a position remarkably favorable" and, so far, too strong to be taken. To the west, however, the XI Corps did not secure its flank in the belief that Confederates would attack, if they did, perpendicular to the Plank Road. All this transpired because Hooker had "suspended" his attack in the hope that "the enemy may attack me."[154]

Lee indeed decided to attack. Though outnumbered and between the two halves of the Army of the Potomac, he devised a bold plan. Leaving a small force at Fredericksburg, he took the main part of his army west and then sent Jackson with the bulk of that force in a long march around to Hooker's far right.

On Saturday morning, May 2, Hooker made a tour of inspection of his right flank. Between the XII and XI Corps, a division of the III Corps manned Hazel Grove, an eminence south of the Chancellor and Fairview houses. That afternoon, around 4:30 p.m., Williams was directed to aid the III Corps when its commander, Major General Daniel E. Sickles, called for support from Hooker. Thinking that the Confederate line moving southwesterly in front of his position meant a potential retreat, Sickles moved out to engage. Hooker had an even more unequivocal view: "[W]e know that the enemy is fleeing, trying to save his trains. Two of Sickles's divisions are among them."[155]

According to a lengthy private account Williams sent soon thereafter, he "was a disbeliever in the retreat" assessment. He was so dubious that he "made Knipe send out two or three well-known scouts of his command," who reported masses of Rebels moving toward the right of the XI Corps. It was no withdrawal. Williams, satisfied that an attack loomed, "so reported to Gen. Slocum." He believed his corps commander would advise Hooker.[156]

The XII Corps reconnaissance had spied, through the extensive woods south of the Federal positions, some thirty thousand Rebel infantry on their circuitous route clockwise around the Union lines. At approximately 5:00 p.m., Jackson's shock attack fell on Hooker's vulnerable flank (Map 3:3). Union regiments that were "stronger than those of any other corps" retreated in what soon became an unchecked skedaddle. The XI Corps became a mass of "disordered and disheartened men" who were "flying in complete disorder." Corps commander Major General Oliver O. Howard sought "to check these disastrous consequences of his own neglect." Within sixty minutes, Jackson had wrecked one of Howard's divisions and rolled up and crushed the Federal right.[157]

News of the devastating assault reached headquarters, and Williams was ordered to return "at once" to his entrenchments. He directed his brigades to retire "without loss of time" and, hearing the furious din of Jackson's attack, became "apprehensive that some disaster had happened" to the XI Corps. He and his staff rode off "at full speed" and, reaching the vicinity of his former lines, found the fields "swarming with fugitives" fleeing from the Confederate blow. The army's right had vaporized. After attempting fruitlessly to rally stampeding XI Corps soldiers, Williams returned to his own troops and began to place them into position at right angles to their former line. His voice could be heard reassuring the men as Jackson's attack bore down on them: "Stand steady, old Third Brigade. Stand steady, old Second Massachusetts." The chief of artillery for the XII Corps, Captain Clermont L. Best, massed as many guns as could be found at Fairview and faced them westward. This line of artillery with Williams's men on the south of the Plank Road and Major General Hiram G. Berry's Division of the III Corps on the north presented an organized and formidable line of battle, finally halting the Confederate assault. Staff recommended Williams personally report the precarious situation to Hooker, but he "was too much of a soldier to leave his command."[158]

Slocum's after-action report revealed how important had been Williams's conduct. He had relied on Williams "to return as rapidly as possible" from aiding the III Corps so as to stem the rout of the XI Corps. "This order was promptly obeyed," and the 1st Division came back at a double-quick. Although the Rebels had overrun the right of the old trenches, Williams "at once" regained the left, formed Ruger's and Knipe's brigades to face the

Fairview house site, looking west, Chancellorsville battlefield. *Author's collection.*

Rebel onslaught and—together with Best's artillery and Berry's division—"checked the advance of the enemy" until darkness fell.[159]

The 1st Division was obliged to fight after dark when an order came, which Williams protested, to reoccupy the entrenchments west of Chancellorsville. The result was disaster to Knipe's brigade, which took many casualties and lost many captives. Williams withdrew "as best we could" to Fairview, and when the Confederates pursued "we punished them severely." He set the men to constructing log breastworks, knowing that additional assaults were forthcoming. Sickles launched a night attack to Williams's left, and his line with Best's artillery followed suit. At about midnight, the shooting died down; the cold had set in. Williams went back to the log house, warmed himself by a fire outside the hut and dozed off.[160] A few steps away, the Chancellor family cemetery signified the fragility of life.

Breakfast came before dawn, and the first of three Rebel attacks soon followed. All were repelled. To the left, however, Sickles's Division vacated the clearing at Hazel Grove in the early afternoon. The Confederates soon positioned some thirty artillery pieces and leveled them on the 1st Division

Fairview looking toward Hazel Grove, Chancellorsville battlefield. *Author's collection.*

barricades (Map 3:4). Williams undertook vigorous efforts to maintain his line despite the enfilading fire. He "remained stationary nowhere, as the changing tide of affairs kept me moving from right to left to see that all was firm and safe." An enemy shell struck directly under his horse, throwing up mud and, Williams feared, eviscerating "Plug Ugly." Not so, as both survived. He would later muse how "it seemed a wonder that anything could live on that slope and hill-brow in front of Fairview"—especially so now, when he received reports that the division had exhausted its ammunition. Williams asked to be replaced in line; Hooker said no, but Slocum approved. Not waiting, Williams sought to save his division and led the men across the Plank Road through open ground to a position where one of Hooker's aides directed a halt and to defend with bayonet (Map 3:5). "As we were suffering hugely from artillery shells...I didn't exactly see how my bayonets were to be effective." Williams reached Slocum and was ordered down the United States Ford road beyond the second line of defense. The battle continued on, though at a lower key, until after dark the division was ordered to the extreme left of the line along the Rappahannock (Map 3:6).[161]

The National Park Service today describes this combat at Fairview as "the climatic fighting of the Battle of Chancellorsville." Slocum attested to its importance: "Repeated efforts were made by heavy columns of the enemy to break these lines, but without effect; our troops held their ground with a determined bravery seldom equaled." That defense enabled Hooker to construct a secondary line of defense to the north, reposition his army and prepare to withstand assault. Only after their ammunition was exhausted did Williams's infantry retire and "in much better order than could reasonably have been anticipated." Despite losses, fatigue and hunger, they then manned the new line on Hooker's far left and awaited an attack. Thankfully, none came.[162]

Fatigue often plagued Williams. He frequently went with little sleep while on the march, on the eve of battle or during periods of heavy administrative responsibility. At the Battle of Chancellorsville, however, his exhaustion resulted in a striking scene near the Wilderness Church, described in a letter home a few days afterward:

> I fell asleep again in the shade of the church on a plank which I had given an easy inclination to on a sill of the building. My posture and an unlighted cigar in my mouth attracted the notice of a passing artist, who took a sketch of me as I slept and presented it to me on waking up. I enclose it that you may see me as reposing on the spot around which twenty-four hours afterwards lay thousands of dead and dying, Federals and Rebels, and as an interesting memento, as well as a striking evidence of how easily and carelessly the heart beats on the very eve of scenes of battle and carnage.[163]

Late on the fifth, Williams was ordered to cross to the safety of the north bank of the Rappahannock. The night was, in Williams's imagery, "darker than Erebus." These were long hours as well, for his division had to await crossing until after daylight and were next to last on the south bank. Back they went to Stafford Court House. Although he had entered the campaign with high hopes, now Williams was crestfallen. Hooker had achieved "the greatest of all bunglings in this war." On May 18, incensed about the battle and newspaper coverage, he wrote his daughters a ten-thousand-word account, confessing he was "almost melancholy" and would like a leave "to restore my spirits." Duty, however, prevented it.[164]

When casualties were tallied, Williams's Division had lost 135 killed, 801 wounded and a combined number of missing and captured of 676. Some 500 or so were due to the erroneous order late on May 1 to advance west from the strong position at Fairview. It was a sorrowful total of 1,612 soldiers, more than any other division—more than one in three in the ranks, according to Williams's estimate. Among the prisoners, again, was a wounded Captain Wilkins. According to one report, he came under guard into the presence of Stonewall Jackson fifteen minutes before the general's fatal wounding. Wilkins refused a request to divulge any intelligence other than his identity, whereupon Jackson ordered him searched. Before the directive could be carried out, Federal artillery shells began to fall on the position. Soon, Jackson would be mortally struck down.[165]

Hooker never submitted an official report on Chancellorsville. His General Orders No. 47 and 49 stand as his contemporary statements on the campaign. In the first, issued on April 30 after reaching the Chancellor crossroads, he singled out several units for recognition in making the successful flank march:

> *It is with heartfelt satisfaction the commanding general announces to the army that the operations of the last three days have determined that our enemy must either ingloriously fly, or come out from behind his defenses and give us battle on our own ground, where certain destruction awaits him.*
>
> *The operations of the Fifth, Eleventh, and Twelfth Corps have been a succession of splendid achievements.*

A later order of May 6 provided an interpretation of the defeat. Initial developments were positive: "[B]y our celerity and secrecy of movement, our advance and passage of the rivers were undisputed." Again, the XII Corps, with Williams on the point, came in for praise. Although they had not accomplished "all that was expected, the reasons are well known to the army." Glossing over the debacle on the right, Hooker opined that "we have added new luster to [the army's] former renown."[166]

For some, the assertion bore truth. Williams had, until the moment the hammer blow fell on the XI Corps, done all that had been asked. His was the leading element across the Rapidan and then in the Union flanking force before the recall. He had stopped Jackson's attack. He had fought off multiple assaults the next day until ammunition ran out. He had anchored the left flank of the army on the riverbank, maintaining a key link in the defensive chain. And he had, perhaps, made possible the Rebel volley that, in some histories, is credited with dooming the Confederacy.

According to Major John Bigelow's detailed 1910 study of the battle, it happened like this. Around 9:00 p.m. on May 2, Jackson was continuing to order his men forward, including those under the command of General James H. Lane. The colonel of the 128th Pennsylvania Infantry, 1st Brigade, 1st Division, XII Corps, approached the Rebel line to locate the former trenches of his unit. He was taken captive. Another Federal officer, "probably General Knipe, rode up in the woods…and called out for General Williams, commanding his division." Some of Lane's men fired at the voice, and Union troops fired back. More Confederate infantry responded, as did more Federals. An orderly with Jackson's party, which was out in front of the Rebel lines, went ahead and incurred more hostile fire. Jackson turned his horse back toward his troops, and the scouting party began to hurry west. The "thumping of hoofs" and "clanking of sabers" in the darkness, coupled with the previous volleys, gave the nearby Confederate regiment "an impression in the line that a charge was about to break upon it" from the Union side. They let loose a volley, and it "was fearfully effective." Stonewall Jackson was hit; he would be carried to the rear and then moved to where he might recuperate. Lee "did not believe Heaven would deprive the South of a man whose services were essential to victory." Jackson died on Sunday, May 10. Williams had never been intimidated by his opponent's reputation; now he would outlast him.[167]

Although he came across far less as an Old Testemant prophet, the Union general with whom Stonewall contended, here for the fourth and last time, still had God's work to do.

CHAPTER 9

GETTYSBURG

HIGH TIDE AND LOW CREDIT

PART 1: ANCHORING THE FISHHOOK

The ignominious outcome at Chancellorsville portended poorly for Union arms in the East that summer of 1863. Lee again took the initiative in June, launching his second invasion of the North. As in the year before, the Confederate leader stole a march on his Union counterpart. Lee's main body slipped away into the Shenandoah Valley and marched toward the Potomac and into Maryland. Once Hooker gained an appreciation of his opponent's whereabouts, he ordered the Army of the Potomac northward to shield Washington. On June 13, the XII Corps started for Dumfries; Williams's Division moved from Stafford. The corps reached Dumfries on the fourteenth and Fairfax Court House on the fifteenth. On June 17, it camped just northeast of present-day Reston. Leaving Fairfax at daybreak, the men breakfasted at Hunter's Mill and halted before noon because of the heat—ninety-nine degrees in the shade. Williams noted that the dry grass in the fields and woods caught fire and filled the air with smoke. They reached Leesburg later that day.[168]

On June 26, before daybreak, the XII Corps broke camp and began to cross one of the pontoon bridges laid across the Potomac at Edwards Ferry. The 2nd Division crossed first, followed by Williams and the 1st Division. He recalled well how to here he had "made my first march in October 1861." Twenty months later, prospects seemed much worse. The corps with artillery and ambulances moved up the Potomac to Trammelsburg and Point of Rocks, Maryland. On June 28, it reached Frederick and on the twenty-ninth marched eighteen miles to Taneytown and Bruceville. On the thirtieth, it concentrated twelve miles forward at Littlestown just across the Mason-Dixon line in Pennsylvania, where Slocum ordered a halt. Here the 1st Brigade of the 1st Division "came in proximity to the enemy," which fled as the division double-quicked through the town. These moves were part of Hooker's design to interpose between Washington and the Army of Northern Virginia. But Hooker had resigned on the twenty-seventh, and on the twenty-eighth, Major General George Meade accepted command of the Army of the Potomac. The development renewed in Williams a more confident attitude. He "rejoiced at the change of commanders" and believed "we shall at least do enough to preserve our honor and the safety of the Republic....God save our Republic!"[169]

As Meade took over, Lee had moved from Maryland into Pennsylvania—where, precisely, the new commander was ignorant. Late on the thirtieth, Meade wrote from his Taneytown headquarters what became known as the "Pipe Creek Circular." He announced to his subordinate commanders a policy not "to assume the offensive until the enemy's movements or position should render such an operation certain of success." Rather, the army would form line of battle along the general confines of Pipe Creek in northern Maryland. Various responsibilities were apportioned: "General Slocum will assume command" of two corps, including the XII.[170]

Events quickly overtook Meade's strategy. Early on July 1, Union cavalry and Confederate infantry clashed west of Gettysburg; soon more infantry from both armies, including the Union I and XI Corps, reached the field and went into action on the far side of the town. Williams's Division "marched at daylight" to Two Taverns, five miles southeast of Gettysburg, "where the sound of cannonading first reached" units of the XII Corps. After stopping here in late morning, "information was received of the engagement...with the enemy beyond Gettysburg. The division moved rapidly up the [Baltimore] pike." As the 1st Division, in the lead, approached a stream known as Rock Creek (Map 4:1), Williams received orders "to occupy an eminence a mile or so east of Gettysburg" known as Benner's Hill. Taking this height would gain command of the Hanover Road and eastern approaches to the town. It would create a Union stronghold on the left of Lee's forces, which were driving the two other Union corps into and south through Gettysburg.

By this time, Williams had taken command of the corps because Slocum had implemented the Pipe Creek directive to assume overall command

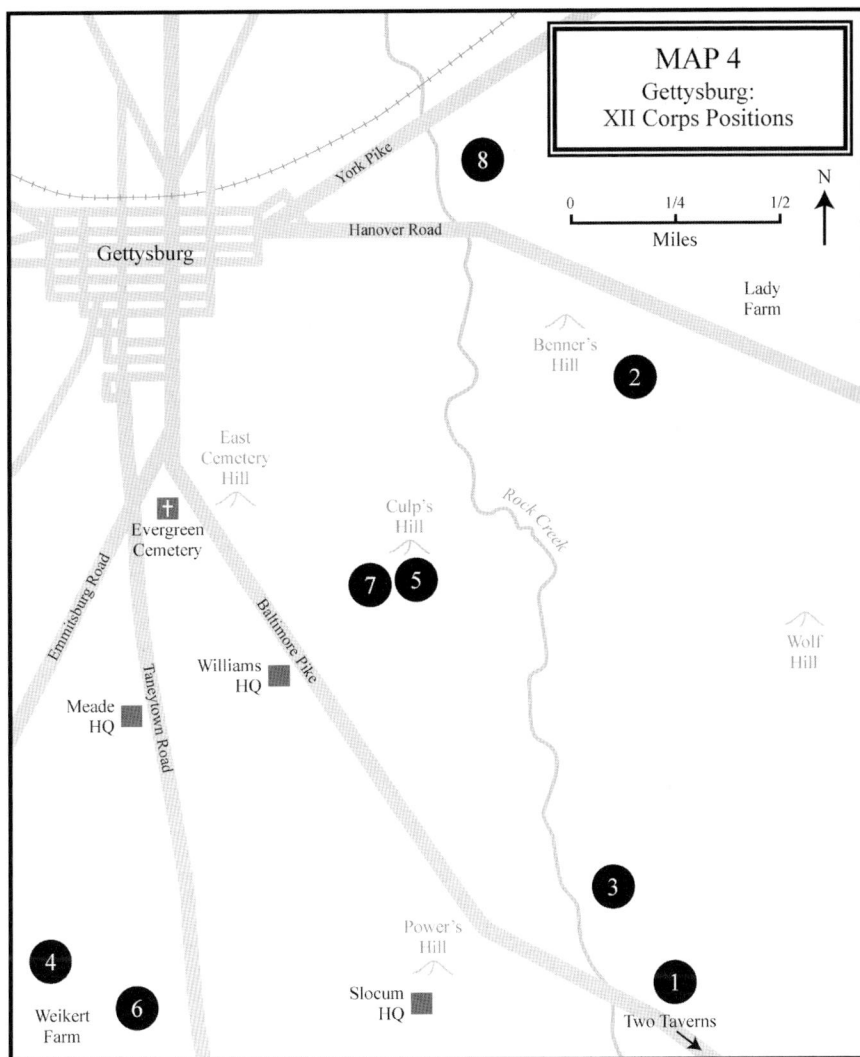

MAP 4
Gettysburg:
XII Corps Positions

of the two corps on the right wing of the army. Accordingly, Williams dispatched a 1st Division brigade under Ruger to take the hill (Map 4:2). Ruger's men followed a cross-country path toward the Hanover road, shook out into formation and began to move up the elevation. Confederates were seen above them on the hilltop. Elements of Williams's command climbed to within three hundred yards of the crest.[171]

Colonel Silas Colgrove of the 27th Indiana, which led the advance, detailed the movement: "[W]hen within about 2 miles of Gettysburg the [3rd] brigade filed to the right, leaving the [Baltimore] pike, and proceeded

Benner's Hill, facing southeast. *Author's collection.*

about 1 1/2 miles, apparently with the intention of flanking the enemy's left." Upon arriving at the bottom of the hill, "the brigade was halted in a piece of woods," and skirmishers moved to the front and right, "who soon reported the hill in our front to be held by the enemy's mounted skirmishers." Colgrove advanced his regiment in line, with his skirmishers "well to the front." By the time the regiment had reached "the foot of the hill, my skirmishers had nearly reached the crest of the hill occupied by the enemy, who had retired as my skirmishers advanced."[172]

In a private letter written five days later, Williams described how close his soldiers had been to a feat that might have completely altered the next several days. He had accompanied the detachment, and when the 27th Indiana moved to the base of the hill, the general went along. In the woods Colgrove described, Williams "went forward himself to reconnoiter," without staff, "reached the ravine at the bottom of the hill" on foot and "from behind a tree" observed "Rebel cavalry on top, but no infantry." The key position was patently within his grasp, and he "determined at once" to take the hill. Ordering Colgrove "to advance at double-quick" and surprise the Confederates, the unit was charging halfway up the slope when a courier arrived from Slocum. He handed Williams an order directing withdrawal. A letter of November 1865 echoed this chronology and further revealed that Williams had planned to bring up his artillery, position it on the crest and "open on the enemy's masses" near the town.[173]

Williams had nearly achieved "the purpose of getting on the [left] flank of the Confederate army" and becoming the anchor of the Union right. But the Union positions to the left of the hill had crumbled. The Army of the Potomac had lost the town and was reassembling on hills to its south. Williams confirmed that "a brigade was advancing up the hill to the assault" when, "to preserve our communications," he was ordered to withdraw back toward the Baltimore Pike (Map 4:3), "as our forces had retired behind the town, which had fallen into the hands of the enemy."[174]

Despite the movement, which surrendered Benner's Hill, the show of force had proved beneficial. Ruger would report, "The appearance of the division in this position at the time it occurred was apparently a timely diversion in favor of our forces, as the farther advance of the enemy ceased."

Confederate accounts corroborated the effect of Williams's movement. Command on this part of the field was under Richard Ewell. Jubal A. Early led one of his divisions, and he received a message from troops on his left while riding into Gettysburg: Federals were approaching on the York Road, the artery just north of Benner's Hill. The only Union troops nearby were Williams's. This worrisome intelligence required an alteration in any plan to proceed immediately to the heights south of town. Consequently, "Ewell decided to postpone any action" until Jackson's division, now under Edward Johnson, arrived on scene. By the time that transpired, it was too late in the day for an advance.[175]

The events here on July 1 have long been fodder for alternative historical interpretation. If only Ewell had pressed forward in the style of Stonewall Jackson, goes the logic, he would have secured the two positions, Cemetery Hill and Culp's Hill, which controlled the Union right. In his classic biography of Lee, Douglas Southall Freeman lamented that "by his delay" Ewell had forfeited "the key to victory" at Gettysburg. A classic study of the battle, however, endorsed the school of thought that the Federals had something to do with the eventual outcome. In this magisterial analysis, Ewell's judgment took into appropriate account the rumors, reports and "alarms" that Union troops threatened his left. Had Ewell decided initially to attack, "he could very well have found himself suddenly ambushed by Williams." A division of the XII Corps *had* posed a danger, and Ewell *had* to ascertain whether Williams threatened the Rebel flank.[176]

As for the whereabouts of the other XII Corps division this Wednesday, Slocum had ordered Geary forward to Gettysburg. Leaving one brigade in reserve, at around 2:00 p.m., Geary reported to Major General Winfield S. Hancock, overall field commander pending Meade's arrival. Hancock ordered Geary to "the extreme left" of the Union line, with the need for troops there being "imperative" because of "the unprotected condition of his left flank along Cemetery Hill." Geary's force arrived at 5:00 p.m. and occupied a line connecting with I Corps on the right and on the left with "a range of hills"—Little and Big Round Tops (Map 4:4). Night came without a Rebel attack.[177]

On the Union right, the 1st Division went into position along the Baltimore Pike west of Rock Creek "and bivouacked for the night." Williams made his headquarters here, west of the Pike, north of Slocum's headquarters and northeast from Meade's.[178]

Waking at daylight on July 2, Williams sought to exercise command over both XII Corps divisions. He did not yet know the location of Geary's. He placed his own on Culp's Hill. At 8:00 a.m., Brigadier General Henry H.

Farm field site of Williams's headquarters per the *Official Records. Author's collection.*

Lockwood reported for duty with two large (six-hundred-plus) units, the 1st Maryland Infantry, Potomac Home Brigade, and the 150th New York Infantry. Because Lockwood would rank Ruger and for sake of flexibility, Williams kept this command under his own "watchful" control and denominated it the 2nd Brigade. Geary and the 2nd Division went into position, with Greene's 3rd Brigade on the left and the 2nd Brigade on its right. Williams arranged the 1st Brigade of the 1st Division next, then the 3rd Brigade and Lockwood's Brigade anchored the right of the corps, covering "nearly a mile of front." The V Corps linked up on Lockwood's right; later in the day, it would be ordered to the Union left. The I Corps manned Cemetery Hill to the left of the XII Corps; the anchor on the army's right was secure.[179]

Williams deployed his men "along the crest of a rocky and wooded ridge of moderate elevation, running in irregular shape in a southeasterly direction to Rock Creek," the center of which was known as Culp's Hill (Map 4:5). He "ordered at once a breastwork of logs," which the men threw up within two hours. They used felled trees, cordwood, rocks and earth and formed their defense along the entire crest. "A thick stone fence parallel to the ridge, less than 50 yards behind it, furnished an excellent cover" for the second line of defense. The topography was very steep on the left and then diminished to a gentle slope on the far right.[180]

The position of the Army of the Potomac resembled an inverted fishhook with the curve at Culp's and Cemetery Hills and the shank running down Cemetery Ridge to Little and Big Round Top. For much of this second day, the Rebels undertook to assault the Union left. To Williams's left, Confederate infantry attacked Cemetery Hill during the afternoon with artillery support from opposite the XII Corps. Around 4:00 p.m., Williams placed in an open field on his left two artillery units: three ten-pound Parrott guns of Knap's Independent Pennsylvania Battery and one section of twelve-pounder Napoleons of the 5th U.S. Artillery. He wanted them to focus on an eight-gun Confederate battery posted on a hill opposite; "in about thirty minutes" their accurate fire forced its withdrawal. It was the latest example of his sagacious use of artillery.[181]

On the Union left, matters were not so positive. Confederates had nearly taken Little Round Top, unmanned for a time after Geary had been ordered to the right. In an area marked by a peach orchard, Sickles had advanced his III Corps in repetition of the maneuver at Chancellorsville. He met with devastation. Meade urgently called for reinforcements to hold on to the ground so critical to that end of the line. Once again, troops from Williams's command were to be hurried where needed.

At 5:00 p.m., Williams received an order from Slocum to go to the aid of the beleaguered Union left. He took the 1st Division and Lockwood's Brigade, ordering Geary's Division to stay and defend Culp's Hill, relying on the entrenchments and hilltop position to make up for the reduced number of defenders. To one keen Confederate, "[t]his was, perhaps, the strongest part" of the Union line—if properly manned. "Williams exchanged parting words with General Slocum" and ordered the 2nd Division "to cover the line on entrenchments thus vacated." Slocum agreed but then apparently "reneged." He sent Geary to follow Williams, reserving only Greene's brigade of 1,400 men to hold the entire Culp's Hill line. Slocum would insist that he had followed Meade's directive to send everyone available and that, on his own authority, he had kept back a remnant. "There is no evidence for this claim," wrote one historian, and it contradicted Williams's account.[182]

Williams led his men "with all possible dispatch, under a severe artillery fire, following as nearly as possible the direction of the heavy firing." Lockwood had the advance west on Granite Schoolhouse Lane and left onto the Taneytown Road, then across to the George Weikert farm lane (Map 4:6). Beyond here the III Corps had been wrecked, but fortunes had since recovered when other Union elements counterattacked. Williams arrived on Cemetery Ridge and followed the signs of battle and the sound of infantry volleys. An artillery officer he knew "rode rapidly towards me begging for assistance": his battery, with no infantry support, had lost several guns to the Rebels. Williams ordered one of Lockwood's units "to pitch into the woods" ahead between the Weikert and Peter Trostle farms without delay to recapture the lost cannons. Rushing forward, the 1st Maryland swamped the Rebels in their front, and they abandoned their treasure. Williams positioned his other brigades and went forward to determine next steps, satisfied that his "division completed the repulse" of the enemy here. Because of the fast-falling darkness, he found the action "was really over." Meeting a jubilant Meade, the new commander confirmed the successful holding of the Union center.[183]

Williams may have played an additional role here. According to one member of the 3rd Michigan Infantry, as the III Corps desperately held on, "getting on top of a round hill, an officer rides up, General Williams of Michigan, and begs of us, for God's sake, to form a line right there." Falling into line "in an instant," the regiment poured volleys into the enemy until they faltered, commenced "to skedaddle" and retreated—"all of them up and dust."[184]

George Weikert house and farm lane, the Union left-center. *Author's collection.*

Not all of Williams's force saw action, but all were soon needed on the right. Geary and his division had left Culp's Hill; inexplicably, they marched south on the Baltimore Pike away from the path of the XII Corps. After helping stabilize the center, Williams led his force back in the darkness and, to his astonishment, discovered that Rebels had seized two-thirds of the Union breastworks.[185]

Greene's brigade ended up with the task of holding Culp's Hill alone. He extended his line to the right, stretching it thin and hoping that the entrenchments would aid in the defense. Not long after, pickets sent word that Rebels—Johnson's division of 5,837 effectives—were advancing in heavy force. "In a short time the woods were all flecked with the flashes from the muskets" of the brigade skirmish line; "for half an hour they obstructed the enemy's approach." As the Confederates neared the Union line, "now was the value of breastworks apparent, for, protected by these, few of our men were hit, and feeling a sense of security, we worked with corresponding energy." The Union line had been well chosen, as it "ascended a broken and rocky slope toward our left, and presented

Meade's headquarters, the Leister house. *Author's collection.*

a steep wall of rock toward the enemy." Still, Johnson's attack enveloped the brigade's right flank and "entered the breastwork beyond our line, and crumpled up and drove back, a short distance, our extreme right regiment." Darkness and reinforcements from Cemetery Hill checked further advance after a three-hour firefight.[186]

Williams could not immediately tend to the problem. Once again, he was ordered toward the army's left, this time to attend a council of war at Meade's headquarters in the Lydia Leister farmhouse on the Taneytown Road. All corps generals attended, along with Butterfield, chief of staff, and Warren, chief of engineers. After discussion of the two days' battle and the army's condition, three questions were put to the group. Each man answered, in reverse seniority. Pencil-written "Minutes of Council, July 2d, 1863" listed the questions: "1. Under existing circumstances is it advisable for this army to remain in its present position, or to retire to another nearer its base of supplies? 2. It being determined to remain in present position, shall the army attack or wait the attack of the enemy? 3. If we wait attack, how long?" Under "Replies," each participant's answers were recorded. As the most junior member, temporary II Corps commander Brigadier General

Scene of the council of war, July 2, front parlor of Leister house. *Author's collection.*

John Gibbon went first. Next in line came Williams, whose answers were: "1. Stay. 2. Wait attack. 3. One day."[187]

Three days later, Williams wrote to explain his votes. Waiting one day made sense, as "we had but one single day's rations" for some, but not all, of the army. Fodder for horses and mules was in short stead. Ammunition was needed. Rail connections did not exist for rapid supply. As for staying and remaining on the defensive, his experience these two days had proven that the Army of the Potomac could hold its own.[188]

The votes of remaining generals tracked those of the initial pair. For the next two, Major Generals David B. Birney and George Sykes, their answers were summarized as "Same as General Williams." After all tallies, Meade announced the army would stay, and the meeting broke up.

Returning to the right, Williams made arrangements to take back his breastworks "speedily" early on Friday. He positioned artillery to concentrate fire on the Rebels; after a fifteen-minute barrage, the infantry would make its assault (Map 4:7). The troops who had vacated the lines were staged in open fields by the Baltimore Pike. At 3:30 a.m., Williams lay down for "a half hour or so of sleep on a flat rock sheltered by an apple tree."[189]

At 4:00 a.m., the Union artillery opened fire. At the prescribed fifteen-minute mark, it ceased, signaling the time for the infantry assault. But the Confederates responded with their own attack on Greene and Geary, "conducted with the utmost vigor." Ewell had reinforced Johnson and doubled his forces to bring equal numbers to bear. Seven hours of continuous combat ensued. The difference in the outcome: "Williams' well-conceived battle plans were much more efficiently executed than his opponent's." The XII Corps, aided by a few I and VI Corps regiments, regained its entire line of entrenchments and drove Johnson's force, including the Stonewall Brigade, "back of the position originally held by him." More than five hundred prisoners were captured "besides several thousand stand of arms and three stand of colors." By noon on this third day, the Union right had once again been secured. Along with it, "the vital Baltimore Pike, the army's main line of supply, just a few hundred yards behind Culp's Hill," remained safely in Union possession. Disaster had been averted.[190]

Even while engaged in securing his lines on the right, Williams managed to send reinforcements to the Union center when Lee unleashed what became known as Pickett's Charge. He dispatched Lockwood and a brigade of the 1st Division. Their assistance, as it developed, was not required. Late the next day, the Fourth of July, a defeated Confederate army retreated toward Virginia. Williams advanced to Rock Creek as soon as such reports reached him and then sent a brigade with Slocum to reconnoiter east of Gettysburg (Map 4:8).[191]

According to recent histories, "sterling individual performances marked the three days" and helped gain the Union victory. Among them was Williams's—he had taken the XII Corps "from Slocum's palsied hands." Although Greene came in for plaudits, overall it was Williams "who deserved the recognition for establishing the line, placing troops where needed, and reacting to the exigencies of the moment."[192]

The Army of Northern Virginia, seventy-five thousand strong, embarked on the Gettysburg Campaign full of confidence, assured of its commander's superiority. Lee had outmatched McClellan on the Peninsula, Pope, Burnside and Hooker in turn. Lincoln's promotion of Meade on the eve of battle betrayed the instability in the Union command. If Lee could defeat Meade and continue his almost unbroken string of victories, the way lay open to Philadelphia, Baltimore or Washington, and "a successful battle in Pennsylvania would have secured Southern independence."[193]

In three days of battle around Gettysburg, the Union had triumphed. Though initially driven through town, the Army of the Potomac held the high ground and sequentially defended its flanks and center. Only six days promoted from corps command, Meade and his generals—apart from Sickles—overmatched their Confederate counterparts. One of those generals, again pressed into corps command as a battle began to unfold, performed as capably as any. One of the army's trophies was the flag of the Stonewall Brigade, captured by the 60th New York of the XII Corps. Later that July, an ebullient Williams wrote home that "there never was a better army."[194]

As Lee retreated toward Virginia, the Federals cautiously pursued. Meade convened another council of war, on July 12, which concluded with a decision not to immediately attack, enabling the Army of Northern Virginia to recross the Potomac and extend the war. Williams did not attend; on that date, Slocum was back as XII Corps commander. The campaign that involved the "high water mark" of the war had ended.[195]

Williams reported casualties for the XII Corps: 204 killed, 812 wounded and 66 captured or missing, for a total of 1,082. The 2nd Division incurred 540 of that total, the 1st Division 533. On the other side, Johnson's division suffered 1,728 in losses, a casualty rate of 29.6 percent.[196]

From mid-July through late September, Williams and his men would march, camp and occasionally fight in small but always dangerous skirmishes. Meade and Lee jockeyed for position, neither much interested in initiating a battle. One day near the Manassas battlefields, Williams came upon an English cotton broker at his "splendid country place." He became the guest of Mr. Green and "his stout and very ladylike wife." The couple "was very pleasant, setting out his good things with capital whiskey and ice water! Altogether I was sorry I could not stay longer." Although he could not know it, Williams did not have a much longer stay in the Army of the Potomac.[197]

Part 2: The Battle for Credit

Not many months passed before Meade's performance at Gettysburg became a very public controversy. First came a joint resolution of Congress, approved on January 28, 1864, bestowing credit not just on Meade but on two other generals for their roles in the campaign: Hooker for covering Washington and Baltimore from Lee's invasion and Howard (with Meade) for defeating the Rebel army. The remaining "officers and soldiers" of the Union army—without specific names—were extended gratitude in general.[198]

Next came proceedings even less charitable to the Union chief. Early in 1864, the council of war on the night of the second day became the subject of a Congressional inquiry. Meade appeared before the Joint Committee on the Conduct of the War to explain whether he had planned a retreat rather than stand and fight. He denied any such intent, explaining that the Pipe Creek Circular had been but a contingency plan. A week later, the *New York Herald* published a letter from "Historicus"—Sickles writing under a pen name—attacking Meade's veracity and putting into sharper issue whether the unauthorized advance of the III Corps had aided victory or risked the army's survival. Lost in this controversy was that Sickles's actions had prompted the withdrawal of Williams's force from Culp's Hill, jeopardizing the Union right flank. Meade wrote to the council participants, including Williams, seeking concurrence in his version of the July 2 conference. The disputation put sharp focus on the impact of the council of war.

The controversy still rages. Citing comments by Meade, his directive that a withdrawal plan be drafted, the fragile condition of the Army of the Potomac and the godsend of a scapegoat in Sickles, two prominent modern historians argue that Meade convened the council at the close of the second day's fighting because he was "looking for an affirmation for a fallback." The outcome? "He did not get it." Rather than counsel a withdrawal, the generals (including Williams) collectively voted to stay; "this was not the conclusion Meade had wanted." In 2018, bestselling author Ron Chernow agreed: Meade "had wanted to withdraw before Pickett's Charge but was overruled by his generals."[199]

Another analysis devoted wholly to the controversy takes the opposite view. Assessing the evidence, this military history concludes that "we can see quite clearly that Meade never did intend to retreat from Gettysburg unless Lee forced him." Sickles and other generals with grievances against Meade—Butterfield, Doubleday, Pleasanton and Slocum—unjustly marred Meade's reputation by not coming to his defense.[200]

One of those with a grievance, but who nonetheless sided with Meade, was Williams. Despite no longer being under his command, Williams promptly (within two weeks) answered Meade's March 10, 1864 request for validation with a confirmatory account. Not so Slocum: he let Meade be attacked before the Joint Committee and in the press without answer. Both subordinates felt aggrieved for the same reason: Meade's official account of the battle, already influencing popular understanding of the battle, had done them injustice. Slocum was mentioned only once in the October 1 report, virtually in passing. Williams's name appeared not at all.[201]

Perhaps worse, Meade had given prominent play to the contributions of several other infantry generals. Of those voting in the council of war, singled out for favorable comment were Birney, Doubleday, Hancock, Howard, Brigadier General John Newton, Major General John Sedgwick, Sykes and Brigadier General James S. Wadsworth. Gibbon, the first to vote, was mentioned for being wounded. In fact, only two officers at division level or above, Slocum and Williams, failed to receive any real notice.

Did they have only themselves to blame? Slocum submitted his report to Meade on August 23, three days after being requested and a full month before completion of the October 1 report. It was a rather full account encompassing all of the forces Slocum had directed. It also included a map showing the XII Corps in action on the right flank, distinguishing the document from other reports. Ironically, it positioned Slocum's, Meade's and Williams's headquarters all within range of one another. That, however, was the only mention of the Michigander's name.[202]

As for Williams, he submitted *two* post-action reports, one as division commander and one as temporary corps commander. Both were in response to Meade's request of August 20. Both went to Meade's assistant adjutant general. Both were written on August 22, a day before Slocum's. One was a "report of the movements of this division"—the 1st Division, XII Corps. The other was "the report of the part taken by it"—the "Twelfth Army Corps"—from the general on whom "the temporary command" of that unit "devolved upon me from July 1 to 4, inclusive." Altogether, both documents comprised nearly three thousand words, with the corps report twice as long as the division's.[203]

Less than a month later, on September 12, Williams sent in another report to Meade's headquarters "in reply to circular of September 11." He reported no artillery pieces "lost or captured during the recent campaign by this command." Which command? That of "Hdqrs. Twelfth Army Corps."[204]

Two months after Meade's report became public, Thomas Ruger submitted his Gettysburg report—the part played by the 1st Division while under his command—to Williams through Pittman. Williams forwarded it to Slocum on December 26, taking the occasion to note "certain errors and omissions" in Meade's report that "do much injustice to some portions" of the XII Corps. It was a lengthy list. Meade had bestowed credit inappropriately, omitted notice of gallantry by certain units of the corps and repudiated "most of the material statements of my report as temporary commander of this corps." Williams was "at a loss to comprehend (when all other corps sending supports to the left are especially named) why the 12th Corps"

Monument to 1ˢᵗ Division, XII Corps, Culp's Hill. *Author's collection.*

received no credit. Overall, he was "at a loss to conceive from what source Gen. Meade derived his information"—clearly not from Slocum's report or either of Williams's. Finally, he made one directly personal point: Meade's report "carefully names all general officers temporarily in command of corps," including one who exercised such authority for less than six hours, but "suppressed" his role during the entire three days. Because he knew Meade as a gentleman and meritorious officer, Williams had read the October 1 report not with contempt but "with a mixed feeling of astonishment and regret." Posterity, he feared, would never know the extent to which the XII Corps and its commander had contributed to victory in the most important and well-known battle of the war to date.[205]

Slocum forwarded this documentation to Meade on December 30, along with his own letter respectfully asking for revisions. Meade responded on February 24, 1864, by submitting the tardy Ruger material to "be placed on file as part of my official report" with the War Department. He went on to "embrace this opportunity to make certain corrections and alterations" in that report. Nearly eight months after the battle, he finally confirmed the XII Corps had been under temporary command of Williams.[206]

Meade also wrote to Slocum explaining "that what has occurred"—the slighting of the corps and its officers and men—"was the result of accident and not of design." He frankly admitted "palpable error, which I am utterly unable to account for." He also pleaded self-defense as if channeling McClellan, claiming that his report "only pretends to be a general statement of the battle" written "very hurriedly." He extended Williams an oblique apology on his complete omission: "This I very much regret, particularly on account of the good opinion I have always entertained for that officer, and the personal regard from long acquaintance which rendered him the last man in the army I would intentionally wrong." It is doubtful that the "Old Snapping Turtle," West Point 1835, ever elsewhere confessed such error or so candidly.[207]

Apologies mattered not. Being overlooked in Meade's October report deprived the Michigander of a powerful case for promotion. Brigadier General Williams had once again performed with aplomb at a critical juncture possessing high stakes. Meade could have served as a patron. Instead, he failed to exhibit a key trait of a good leader: apportioning credit to subordinates. By the time the record received partial correction— insufficient to remedy the damage—Williams would be gone from Meade's influence.[208]

A number of silent sentinels mark the battleground at Gettysburg these many years later. Many memorialize individuals, primarily generals. Meade has a monument; Sickles has his; so, too, Geary, Greene and Slocum among those on the right flank. Like Meade's and Slocum's statues, those for

Road sign, Culp's Hill. *Author's collection.*

Hancock, Howard, John F. Reynolds and Sedgwick are equestrian. Warren's has become an icon, located on the summit of Little Round Top to denote his quick action to save the Union left.

The temporary commander of the XII Corps, one of the saviors on the Union right, is not completely ignored among the tableaux found there. The Slocum Avenue roadway takes the visitor to an observation tower at the summit of Culp's Hill, providing vistas over Gettysburg to the mountain range beyond. From that lofty viewpoint, it is all too easy to overlook a road sign so far below. That marker identifies a shortcut for those hurrying, who might only seek to view the Slocum and Geary statues and avoid unecessary time on the most famous of American battlefields. There is so much else to see. It could hardly matter whether this one-third mile of asphalt has been named for anyone.

CHAPTER 10

TO THE RESCUE

GREAT TRAIN RIDE

The Union Army of the Cumberland suffered disaster in mid-September 1863 at the Battle of Chickamauga, Georgia. A costly error by its commander, Major General William S. Rosecrans, opened a gap in the Union line just as twelve thousand soldiers of Confederate general James Longstreet's Corps, transferred via an eight-hundred-mile train ride from the Army of Northern Virginia, attacked with gusto. Only due to an audacious holding action by Major General George H. Thomas did the Federals survive. Retreating into Chattanooga, the Union army found itself besieged and its supply line choked off by the Army of Tennessee under Braxton Bragg.

Alarming telegrams arrived in Washington. From Charles A. Dana, Stanton's aide, came word on the twenty-second that Rosecrans might abandon Chattanooga unless amply reinforced "within one week." James A. Garfield, Rosecrans's chief of staff, telegraphed that "we can stand here ten days if help will then arrive" and "if we hold this point we shall save the campaign, which will be great gain even if we lose this army." Rosecrans messaged Lincoln requesting "all re-enforcements you can send hurried up." On September 23, Dana wired, "[N]o time should be lost in rushing twenty to twenty five thousand efficient troops." The situation was precarious. Stanton replied that "every nerve is being strained to strengthen Rosecrans and his gallant army." Chattanooga was "a critical rail hub" and a base for advancing to Atlanta and into the breadbasket of the Confederacy. Additionally, its surrender "would be a political disaster in states such as Ohio, Pennsylvania, and New York, states with imminent elections."[209]

Stanton's assurance was genuine. Late on September 22, he had convened an urgent strategy meeting. Seeking Lincoln's attendance, Stanton asked presidential aide John Hay to fetch the president. "As it was the 1st time Stanton had so sent for him," Lincoln knew the news must be very bad. Though "abed," he rose and rode to the War Department. The midnight debate produced a bold decision. Believing reinforcements from the Western Theater unavailable, the need would be met by transferring units from the relatively inactive Army of the Potomac: "the 11th and 12th Corps were selected for the purpose, Hooker to be placed in command of both." Stanton made the proposal; Lincoln, though skeptical that rail transportation could carry so many so quickly, approved.[210]

At 2:30 a.m. on September 24, Stanton wired Meade to confirm his need for the XI and XII Corps. No, Meade replied, but withdrawing the XII Corps would be difficult since it, including Williams's Division at Kelly's and Raccoon Fords, picketed the Rapidan River at the front. Stanton escalated "to the President. He directs that the Eleventh and Twelfth Corps be immediately prepared to be sent to Washington." Meade obeyed: "Cars for the Twelfth Corps, 10,600 men should be sent to Brandy Station." He ordered Slocum to fall back, prepare rations and take the rails to Alexandria: "[T]he utmost promptitude and dispatch must be shown in executing this order, and the troops be kept on the march if necessary all night." Williams dashed off a quick note to his daughters from Raccoon Ford about orders to be ready to move, destination unknown, but thinking an attack on Lee must be imminent.[211]

That day, the War Department assigned Joseph Hooker to command of the XI and XII Corps. He received presidential authorization "to take military possession of all railroads, with their cars, locomotives, plants, and equipments, that may be necessary for the execution of the military operation committed to his charge." Hooker advised Rosecrans that he was on his way and issued directions to Slocum. The XII Corps marched to Brandy Station and then to Bealeton Station. On the twenty-sixth, at 2:45 p.m., the corps still awaited cars. On the twenty-seventh, at 4:00 p.m., Washington was advised that part of the corps had "gone forward," and at 10:00 p.m. "the whole force, except 3,300 of the Twelfth Corps, is now moving." On the twenty-eighth, at 9:50 p.m., Stanton received news that "the whole force has gone forward."[212]

Williams and his infantry rode on the Orange & Alexandria Railroad, crossed the Long Bridge over the Potomac and changed engines from the military railroad to the Baltimore & Ohio at New Jersey Avenue station. The

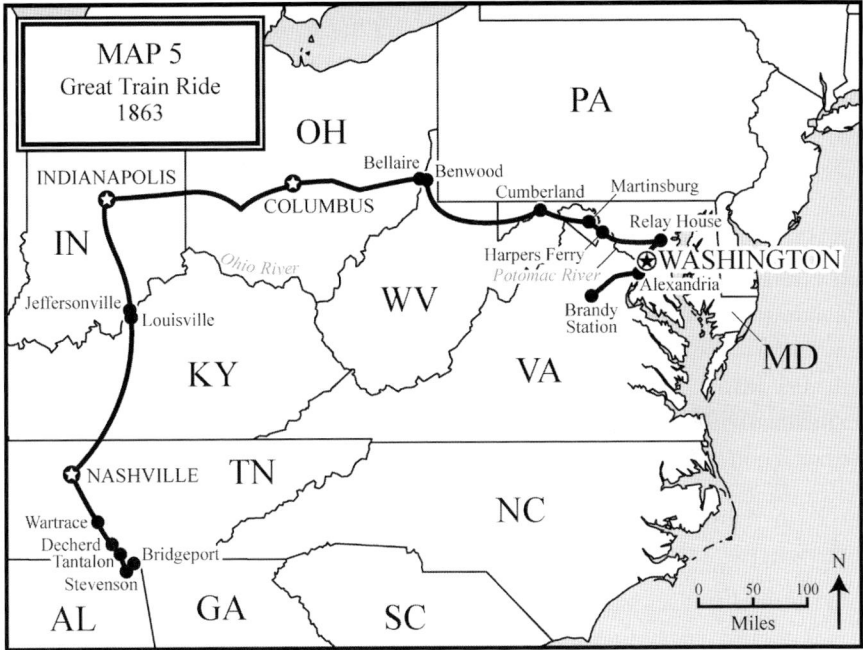

MAP 5
Great Train Ride
1863

route from Washington went north to the Relay House outside Baltimore, thence west to Harpers Ferry, Cumberland and Benwood on the east bank of the Ohio River. Early on the twenty-seventh, all troops transferred across to Bellaire, traveling over the Central Ohio Railroad to Columbus and then to Indianapolis on the Columbus & Xenia and the Indiana Central Railroads. They took the Jeffersonville Railroad from Indianapolis to Jeffersonville, went across the Ohio by ferry again and began arriving at the Louisville depot at 4:00 a.m. on the twenty-ninth. While here, Williams enjoyed a quick visit with daughter Minnie; coming after two years apart, it left him "low-spirited after parting." The Louisville & Nashville Railroad carried the forces to Nashville, where, at 4:40 p.m. on October 2, Hooker wired Stanton that "the Twelfth are now passing through this city." The final leg came on the Nashville & Chattanooga Railroad. At 10:30 p.m. on September 30, the first troop trains reached Bridgeport, Alabama, the terminus of the journey. The leading regiments of Williams's Division arrived on October 2.[213]

Williams, his division and the rest of the two corps "completed their twelve-hundred-mile journey in eight days." It was no mean feat: "[T]he obstacles were daunting—the troops had to cover 1,233 miles, including crossing the Appalachian Mountains and fording the Ohio River—making the successful move a tour de force of military organization." Their 150 four-horse teams, 156 two-mule teams and 75 two-horse ambulances trailed but would soon arrive on succeeding trains. The odyssey was only possible because of a remarkable achievement: "8,000 Negroes hastily changed the gauge of the Louisville & Lexington." The Federals had crossed the unbridged Ohio River twice, changed trains numerous times and kept order and fighting trim over days and nights of almost uninterrupted pace. Nothing like it had ever been achieved: "It was an extraordinary feat of logistics—the longest and fastest movement of such a large body of troops before the twentieth century."[214]

Hooker reported the XII Corps strength as "aggregate for duty a force of 9,245. These numbers will be increased somewhat." His military district embraced the vital supply line of the Nashville & Chattanooga from Wartrace, Tennessee, to Bridgeport. The XII Corps's first assignment was to guard the line from Wartrace to Tantalon, a distance of many miles. The XI Corps protected the rails on to Stevenson, Alabama, a short distance from Chattanooga. Williams's men settled in for guard duty, unsure of its challenges. One was the command of the corps. Slocum had tendered his resignation rather than serve under the architect of the Chancellorsville fiasco. Hooker ordered Daniel Butterfield to take charge, and Williams obeyed his instructions to leave Murfreesboro for a rendezvous south. Confusion ensued. After Slocum was assured a transfer, he again exercised command, leaving Nashville and reasserting his leadership when Butterfield relinquished it on October 9. Williams had his 1st Division headquarters at Decherd, Tennessee. Knipe and the 1st Brigade were also based there, while the headquarters of the 3rd Brigade under Ruger were at Tullahoma.[215]

Guard duty involved several kinds of work. One was construction. Williams advised Slocum two weeks after disembarking that the railroad lacked essential protections: "As soon as I can get tools I shall begin work at the several important points, on such small defenses as seem necessary. There are some very feeble, badly-located works at most of the bridges and trestles. I will make a detailed report of them." It had proved easy for saboteurs to interrupt rail service, for the "monstrous line" of three hundred miles that crossed numerous streams and valleys had many weak points. Guerrilla forces and Rebel cavalry played havoc. Williams had choice words about the inhabitants, regarding "the 'poor white trash'" as "vastly inferior to the Negro." For Confederate prisoners shipped north, he thought them "dirty, destitute, and diabolical." Tullahoma he found "dolorous."[216]

Williams's official duties involved commanding the Military Sub-District No. 1, Defenses of the Nashville and Chattanooga Railroad. He had known hostilities with irregular troops in the Mexican-American conflict, an experience that assisted his administration here. Although assigned a frustrating duty, Williams did not treat the population under his control with contempt or oppression. By contrast, his successor, Major General Robert H. Milroy, also a veteran of Virginia campaigning, carried out a "blood and fire" program against civilians. One of the most notable features of the N&C fell within Williams's jurisdiction, the 2,200-foot-long Cowan tunnel south of Tullahoma, which repeatedly became the target of sabotage. He moved his headquarters to the town to be in a more central location. Aside from having to be "constantly in motion" along his ninety miles of track, he made the time useful by reading Dickens and military treatises such as "Kinglake's Crimean War."[217]

Another challenge involved rivalry between troops who had served in this theater and the newcomers from the East. Williams issued an order noting "a decided lack of harmony" that "has nearly resulted in a collision between small parties of the respective commands." He called on the soldiers to cultivate "a spirit of at least apparent harmony." Failing such cooperation, he vowed to arrest anyone in uniform, officers included, should they persist in disharmony.[218]

The Lincoln administration had its sights fixed on the true adversary. On October 16, U.S. Grant took command of the Military Division of the Mississippi with the goal of relieving Chattanooga and defeating the Confederate Army of Tennessee. George Thomas replaced Rosecrans as commander of the Army of the Cumberland. From Louisville, Grant traveled over the same rails as had Williams and his men, stopping at Tullahoma en route to Chattanooga. A number of soldiers and officers gathered at the depot, hoping to see the Union general who had yet to lose a battle. When the diminutive man in his faded coat appeared, those of Williams's Division reacted: "[T]he sight of this plain, unassuming Western man, with his Western ways, brought our hearts right up into our throats. We cheered with a wild abandon, Bless God!" They knew well how a western leader could perform.[219]

Grant spent his first full day at Chattanooga on October 24, ordered a new supply line opened to connect with the railroad to Nashville and made plans to attack. The Union troops replenished their supplies and morale and readied for battle. Hooker received orders to move to the south side of the Tennessee River with the XI Corps and one XII Corps division, the other to remain and guard the Nashville & Chattanooga. On the next day, Williams's 1st Division was specified for that guard duty. It would be absent from the

Battle of Chattanooga in late November, a stunning victory that catapulted Grant into command of all the armies of the United States.[220]

Williams and his men had enabled both outcomes. Although it was unsung duty, they had "preserved the vital supply line that they had helped reopen." Williams bragged about their stalwart protection of "every bridge, station, culvert and water tank." They had constructed fortifications "at all exposed points." And they had fought the difficult fight against guerrillas, repairing damage and effectively keeping the railroad in nearly continuous operation. The western veterans came to appreciate their comrades from the Army of the Potomac. Leading the fighting men in the ranks were officers, including Williams, who were "first-rate soldiers."[221]

CHAPTER II

TAKING ATLANTA,
SAVING A PRESIDENCY

As Grant became general-in-chief of the U.S. Army, his close colleague Major General William T. Sherman succeeded to overall command between the Mississippi River and the Appalachians. While Grant transferred to Washington, Sherman began to follow Grant's directive to defeat the Army of Tennessee and inflict as much damage as possible on Confederate war resources in its interior. From early 1864 into September, the opposing forces would maneuver over hundreds of miles of hilly and mountainous terrain crisscrossed by waterways and festooned with deep woods and forests. Before the campaign began, Williams enjoyed his one and only leave from the front: a thirty-day sojourn in Detroit between December 28 and January 27. The respite fortified him, and he soon would write, "God prosper the right and let it come."[222] More combat loomed.

On Thursday, April 27, 1864, Sherman ordered consolidation of his dispersed armies of the Cumberland, Ohio and Tennessee at Chattanooga. Williams brought his division together at Bridgeport on Sunday, May 1, and to Lookout Valley two days later. It was now a constituent of a new organization, the XX Corps of the Army of the Cumberland, and commanded by Joseph Hooker. Williams disliked losing the old designation, but he took comfort in commanding his two familiar 1st Division brigades plus another from the XI Corps under Colonel James S. Robinson, as well as the retention of the "Red Star" designation. On May 6, all Union forces near Chattanooga stepped off into north Georgia. In their path lay ridges, hills and mountains; a rather sparsely populated countryside; and difficulty

Brigadier General A.S. Williams with the Red Star Division hat. *Library of Congress.*

of movement given the lack of good roads and rail routes. They also faced General Joseph E. Johnston, a careful, conservative leader whom Grant and Sherman regarded as "the most skillful opponent they faced during the war." The Army of Tennessee "was a tough, confident army" of some seventy thousand effectives.[223]

Sherman's strategy rejected frontal assaults in favor of maneuver, aiming to force Johnston back to Atlanta. Johnston planned to make Sherman pay for mistakes, attacking when he held the tactical advantage despite overall numerical inferiority. The line of the Western & Atlantic Railroad to Atlanta would form the axis of movement by the two armies.[224]

Williams's Division moved "without halt" and reached Ringgold, Georgia. Continuing to march forward, on the night of May 10 it reached and occupied Snake Creek Gap. The rail line weaved across Chickamauga Creek and over slight rises before entering the passage into the first ridge east of a town appropriately called Tunnel Hill, then paralleling the high ridges to the west. Johnston's army occupied "a strong position" around nearby

Western & Atlantic Railroad line completed in 1850, Tunnel Hill, Georgia. *Author's collection.*

Resaca; the Gap was to its northwest. On the thirteenth, Williams rejoined Hooker's command and the other XX Corps divisions, now commanded by Geary, Butterfield and Major General L.H. Rousseau. Williams's unit was the largest at 6,715 effectives.[225]

Sherman sent a contingent south to cut the Confederates off below Resaca, while the rest of his force pressed "at all points." In the afternoon of Saturday, May 14, having changed front to the east in support of Butterfield (Map 6:1), Williams's Division received a summons to aid Sherman's left flank north of Resaca adjacent to the W&A several miles away. "Taking the double quick," the division arrived "just before sunset" where Major General David S. Stanley's division of Howard's IV Corps was being

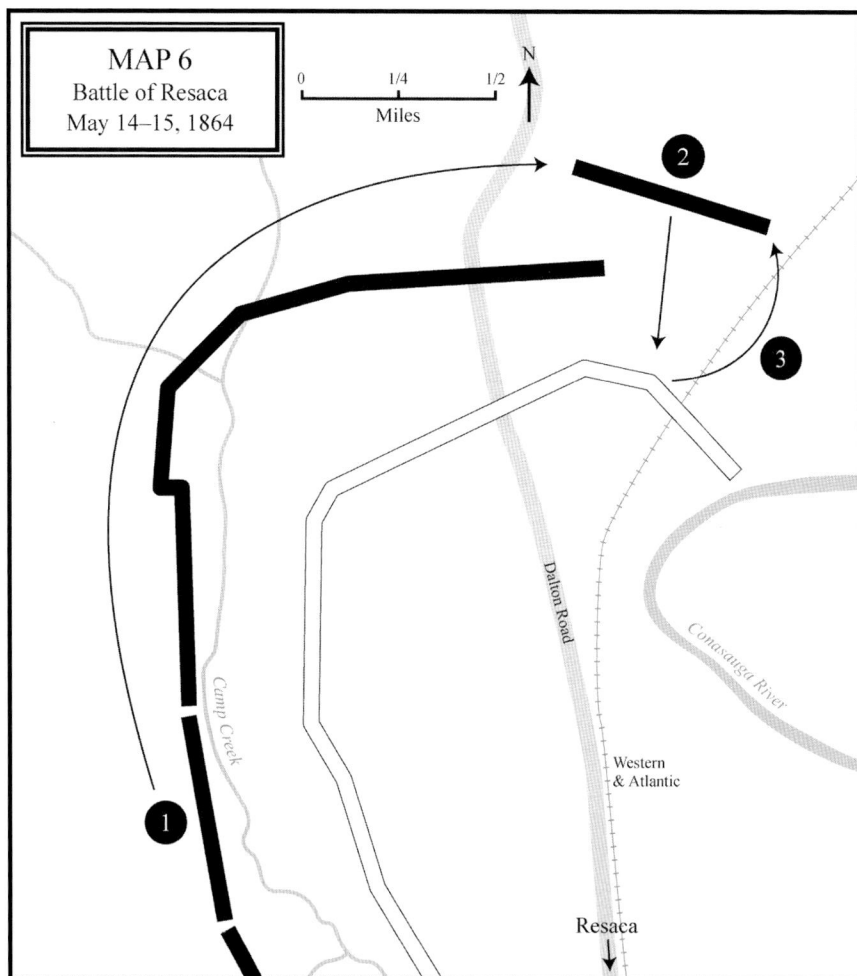

MAP 6
Battle of Resaca
May 14–15, 1864

0   1/4   1/2
Miles

N

Dalton Road

Conasauga River

Camp Creek

Western & Atlantic

Resaca

seriously pressed by a Confederate assault (Map 6:2). For Williams's men, it was a first opportunity to demonstrate their mettle to westerners in a volatile combat situation.[226]

Their position was a wooded ridge facing Confederate defenses on "high chestnut hills." Williams deployed the lead brigade, Robinson's, on the left and prolonged the line to the east with the others. In their front, one of Stanley's batteries with a small infantry detachment faced the Rebels. They had arrived just in time:

> *Scarcely was Robinson's brigade in line before numerous fugitives from our own troops came pouring in confusion over the open in front, followed by the exultant enemy making confidently for the battery. After a fruitless effort with my staff officers to rally and organize the fugitives, I sent orders to them to clear the front, and rode back to bring forward Robinson's brigade....Robinson moved with great promptness down the steep wooded ridge side, crossing a difficult creek at the foot, and, changing front forward on his right regiment in good order, he opened in volley upon the astonished enemy. They fled in greater haste than they had advanced, and in fifteen minutes not a rebel gun was heard in the valley.*

Williams's men had "rescued" the battery.[227]

The next day, Williams received orders to continue protecting the left flank, the corps having joined him, as Sherman advanced. Williams moved "toward the menaced point" of a Confederate attack from two divisions of John B. Hood's Corps (Map 6:3). Carefully posting his men, placing artillery where "I deemed the key point" and throwing up "slight breast-works," Williams "deployed in a single line":

> *The enemy massed his forces in the woods near the railway, which was distant from 300 to 600 yards from the different portions of my line. Advancing under cover as far as practicable, he attacked the whole line with great vigor and apparent confidence. The attack was received with perfect steadiness and repulsed with ease. The assaults were renewed three separate times, and each time with signal failure. My line in no part was shaken or disturbed, and we literally had no skulkers.*

Ruger's brigade charged and captured the flag of the 32nd/58th Alabama and 125 infantrymen.[228]

Eastern edge, Resaca battlefield. *Author's collection.*

These performances in the two-day Battle of Resaca inspired "strong confidence and good-will" among the western veterans. The Confederate attack on Stanley's division caused it "to stampede from the field, and only the timely arrival of [Williams's] Division prevented a rout from occurring on the Federal left flank." For Williams, it was "a feeling closely cemented by the subsequent events and occurrences of the campaign." Here also came the first instance where Williams acknowledged in writing that his men called him "Old Pap." The nickname arose as they saw their commander "right amongst us" in combat. They also revered him for his concern for the wounded. After a previous battle, he had visited the division hospital and "saw and talked with every man." It took Williams hours to succor the many hundreds, and such solicitude inspired mutual affection. Division losses here totaled 417 men: 48 killed, 366 wounded and 3 missing.[229]

Johnston withdrew from Resaca that night, escaping an envelopment. Sherman pursued. Several points were reached at which a battle seemed likely, but each time the Rebels retreated, especially as Sherman threatened flanking movements to cut them off from their line of communication to Atlanta. Each time, marching through Calhoun and Cassville, crossing the Etowah River, Williams had his troops readied for battle.[230]

On May 25, west of Marietta, the division reprised its performance on a hot Wednesday afternoon. Initially directed to "take position in advance of Dallas," Williams received an order "to countermarch and move as rapidly as possible to the support of Geary's division." Thomas was seeking to stem Johnston's assault by his entire force; Howard did not answer the call, but in Williams was "found a more willing accomplice." Reversing "with all haste," the 1st Division "after a rapid march of over five miles, came up with Butterfield's and Geary's divisions massed on the road toward New Hope Church, and passed to the front." Hooker ordered an attack on enemy entrenchments through "dense woods and under growth" over "rough and stony ground." Williams's men, in three lines, "without sufficient halt to recover breath, moved promptly in advance for a mile and a half, driving the enemy before us and forcing back his strong skirmish line and heavy reserves at double-quick." Recognizing their fatigue, Williams relieved each front line by passing the next to the advance and preserving "excellent alignment." He followed "just behind the leading line." The Confederates took refuge in their entrenchments, and the Federal line "forced its way close up the enemy's works." Darkness and a thunderstorm ended the affair; they were then relieved. Losses here in the Battle of New Hope Church were 102 killed, 639 wounded and 4 missing, for a total of 745.[231]

After successfully exploiting open gaps in the long, tall ridges that marked the landscape south of Chattanooga, Sherman had now engaged Johnston on the "flatter terrain covered with dense vegetation" south of the Etowah River, marked by "rugged roads, few farms, and almost a trackless forest." The armies continued to maneuver with skirmishes keeping them in contact.[232]

On June 22, Johnston took up a defensive position anchored by Kennesaw Mountain to guard the Western & Atlantic Railroad at Marietta and the thirteen miles behind it to the Chattahoochee River. On that Wednesday, the lines of the two forces faced west (Rebel) and east (Union). A space opened near the farm of Peter Kolb along the Powder Springs and Marietta Road. Schofield's Army of the Ohio lay to the south and west, Hooker's XX Corps occupied hills to the north. Williams's infantry now numbered 271 officers and 4,331 enlisted men. On a slightly northwesterly line extending from the road, he posted, in order, Ruger's (2nd), Knipe's (1st) and Robinson's (3rd) brigades. The farmland in the division front had been cleared and "extended about 1,000 yards east to west, and a couple of miles north to south." Around 3:00 p.m., Hooker advised Williams that Johnston "was massing in his front." The division prepared for battle.[233]

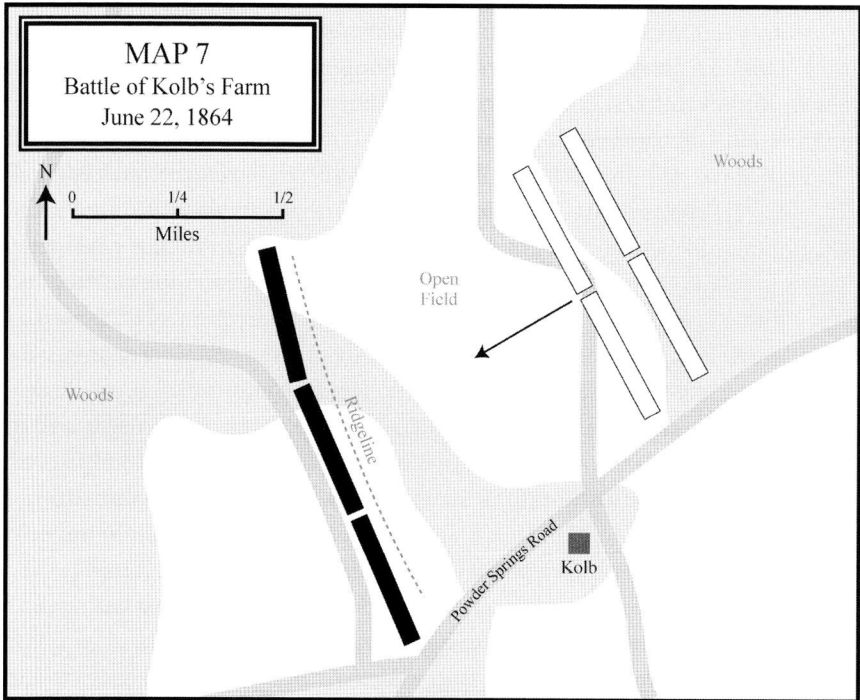

MAP 7
Battle of Kolb's Farm
June 22, 1864

N

0   1/4   1/2
Miles

Open Field

Woods

Ridgeline

Woods

Powder Springs Road

Kolb

Sherman summarized what unfolded: "[T]he enemy (Hood's corps with detachments from the others) suddenly sallied and attacked. The blow fell mostly on General Williams' division…yet when he reached our line of battle he received a terrible repulse, leaving his dead, wounded, and many prisoners in our hands." Williams had positioned his artillery in the intervals between brigades, and he ordered it to "shell the woods briskly" while the Rebels were still organizing their assault. They pushed out "in one large column closed in mass" and came bravely forward. Reaching the range of Williams's infantry fire, "they were at once brought to a stand and rapidly dissolved into a rabble of fugitives." Retreating to shelter, the Confederates continued to demonstrate as if to attack again. It only served to "excite the derisive yells and jibes of my men." Williams believed enemy losses exceeded 1,000 men from his "wall of flame." His stood at 130.[234]

His opponent, Hood, had "believed he was onto something." After several previous assaults had been cancelled as the armies jockeyed, and with two enemy regiments having advanced and withdrawn in his front here, Hood sought to reclaim "his reputation as an aggressive commander." This advance, made without reconnaissance, resulted in a repulse with heavy losses. It also soon led, oddly enough, to Hood's promotion.[235]

Sherman made his own unsuccessful major assault on June 27 at the Battle of Kennesaw Mountain. Williams had made his headquarters in the Greek Revival antebellum plantation house of former Georgia governor Charles J. McDonald and held his troops in readiness for an order that did not come. On July 3, Williams advanced and took part in maneuvering that pursued Johnston as he withdrew south. Reaching the Chattahoochee River, Williams "got a dim view of our main objective point—the city of Atlanta!" When the XX Corps crossed the river on the seventeenth, Richmond reacted.[236]

On July 18, Confederate president Davis sacked Johnston and installed Hood as commander of the Army of Tennessee. Hood's penchant for aggressiveness prompting the change, he did not wait long to again evidence the trait. Thomas began crossing his army over Peach Tree Creek early on July 20. The IV Corps took up its position on the left, the XIV Corps on the right and the XX Corps in the center, with Williams's Division on its right. Seeking to catch the enemy with his back to the river, Hood launched a terrific assault on the XX Corps with two of his corps. Three Confederate divisions confronted Williams, who had received no word of their approach. The day was hot, the men had crossed the creek early and marched under "a bright, hot sun." Williams allowed them, thanks to his corps commander's "nonchalance," to stack muskets and rest.[237]

The assault fell first to Williams's left on the IV Corps. Forewarned by "the sound of heavy infantry vollies, rolling in increasing volume," Williams "firmed up his position to get ready for trouble," double-quicking his three brigades into position just as a Confederate division got "within point-blank range" before the 1st Division could be sighted. At first, the battle went the Rebel way. Surprise on their side, the Confederates threatened to envelop Williams on each flank thanks to ravines that prevented the Federals from digging in. Despite taking fire as they deployed, the 1st Division "poured in a disciplined fire" that halted the enemy. The Confederates pressed a second assault along Williams's entire line. He maneuvered troops to reinforce the line where most needed. Well-placed Federal artillery played havoc, and soon it was the 1st Division that had the upper hand and flanked the Rebels. The Confederates "encountered a terrible enfilade" from the Union positions. "The musketry along the Red Star line was furious and well sustained. Some of the men loaded and fired so fast that their rifles became overheated." Finally, "after three hours of desperate fighting the enemy retired discomfited and beaten." Much credit went to Williams's artillery dispositions and its "furious cannonading, which all will remember who heard it." Williams suffered the most losses in the Battle of Peach Tree Creek, 600, in the XX Corps total of 1,700. The Confederate losses amounted to 25 percent of those engaged.[238] Hood withdrew into Atlanta.

Two days later, the XX Corps crossed past empty Rebel fortifications to within two miles from the center of Atlanta. The day was marked by the death from sharpshooter of Major General James B. McPherson, commander of the Army of the Tennessee. Sherman commenced siege operations, and the XX Corps occupied positions on either side of the Western & Atlantic northwest of the city. Though under fire, the men constructed "a continuous line of strong earthworks" close and parallel to the Confederate fortifications. The Union trenches were in some cases within one thousand feet of the Rebels' and were sixteen feet thick at the base, four feet high on the enemy side and seven feet wide, with logs perched on wood blocks at the top.[239]

On July 27, Williams once again assumed temporary corps command. Sherman had designated Oliver O. Howard to replace McPherson rather than the XX Corps commander. Hooker asked to be relieved, citing that Howard was "his junior"; the War Department acquiesced. At Thomas's request, Sherman sought appointment of Slocum to replace Hooker, which was approved. Slocum was then at Vicksburg. The same day all of this transpired, an order issued from Thomas's headquarters that Williams "will succeed" temporarily to the corps command. Before Slocum arrived on August 28, Williams led the 13,524-man corps, implementing the theater commander's strategy. To secure his communications, Sherman ordered the XX Corps back to the Chattahoochee. As his main supply line, "it was imperative that he maintain firm control of the railroad bridge" across the river.[240]

Sherman also had his focus on Hood's communications. If he could sever them, the Rebel defense of Atlanta would become untenable. From its position seven miles northwest of the city, the 1st Division heard "violent and repeated" explosions within Atlanta before dawn on September 2. Receiving an order at 2:30 a.m. to "send out as soon as possible a reconnoitering party," Williams dispatched three regiments before daylight arrived. They discovered that a portion of another division had entered the evacuated city. Williams sent in more troops, and the whole division soon entered Atlanta and occupied the trenches on the northeast side of the city. Williams rode through the Rebel works "full of queer sensations and exciting emotions," trying to grasp the achievement. The military evacuation meant the mayor had to surrender the city, and the XX Corps had the honor of receiving it.

Slocum took full possession on the third; at 6:00 a.m., Sherman telegraphed the news to Washington.[241]

Only ten days earlier, Union fortunes had appeared so bleak that Lincoln penned a memorandum, and then asked his Cabinet to initial it sight unseen, stating "it seems exceedingly probable that this Administration will not be reelected." Sherman had not yet bagged Hood or Atlanta; Williams's former comrades in the Army of the Potomac had not defeated Lee. If Southerners "could hold their own, continued stalemate could actually mean victory for the Confederacy." Lincoln knew this, knew that the people of the North were war-weary.[242]

> *Then fate stepped in. Like a moving hour hand on a clock of doom came news flung world-wide, news setting crowds of Northern loyalists to dancing with mirth and howling with glee, news centering about one little dispatch wired to Washington by Sherman[,] September 3: "Atlanta is ours, and fairly won."*[243]

In Richmond, the mood changed as recorded in the journal entries of a Confederate official. September 1: "The intelligence from the North indicates that Gen. McClellan will be nominated for the Presidency....Our people take a lively interest in the proceedings of the Chicago Convention, hoping for a speedy termination of the war." September 2: "It is reported that a battle has occurred at Atlanta, but I have seen no official confirmation of it." September 3: "There is an ugly rumor on the streets to-day—disaster to Gen. Hood, and the fall of Atlanta." September 4: "Atlanta has fallen, and our army has retreated some thirty miles; such is Hood's dispatch, received last night." September 5: "The loss of Atlanta is a stunning blow."[244]

On November 8, Lincoln won reelection. Williams had not hesitated "to say that if I was at home I should vote for 'A Linkum' and his party." The reelection meant there would be no McClellan victory, no negotiated peace between two separated nations, no retreat from emancipation and no abating to press the struggle for the Union. The president acknowledged military contributions that had bent history's arc:

> *The national thanks are herewith tendered by the President to Major General William T. Sherman, and the gallant officers and soldiers of his command before Atlanta, for the distinguished ability, courage, and perseverance displayed in the campaign in Georgia, which, under Divine favor, has resulted in the capture of the city of Atlanta. The marches, battles, sieges,*

and other military operations that have signalized this campaign must render it famous in the annals of war, and have entitled those who have participated therein to the applause and thanks of the nation.[245]

Those "gallant officers and soldiers" included the 1st Division of the XX Corps and its commander, A.S. Williams, also interim corps commander and battlefront officer. Narrowly, he was not among the reported 2,276 casualties. Riding over a battleground meant grieving: "I feel nothing but sorrow and compassion" seeing a blue jacket "lying stretched in the attitude that nobody can mistake." He cheered at the valorous performance of his soldiers, "constantly on the *qui vive*," in battle behaving "splendidly," always fighting "without skulkers," the "paper collar soldiers" now known to comrades as "iron clads." That such troops were led by "Old Pap" speaks volumes.[246]

CHAPTER 12

MAKING THE SOUTH HOWL

During the occupation of Atlanta, Sherman maintained secrecy about his upcoming plans. On November 8, he told his men that they were about to undertake "a special purpose" known only to higher authorities, involving a "long and difficult march" to a new base. Williams wrote about "rumors." The next day came Special Field Orders No. 120, dividing his force into two wings, with Howard in command of the Right Wing and Slocum the Left. The army would proceed along four distinct routes; two corps in each wing would march separately. Special responsibilities were placed on their commanders: in addition to properly managing the wagon trains, to them alone was "intrusted the power to destroy mills, houses, cotton-gins, &c." Liberated "Negroes who are able-bodied and can be of service" could be "taken along."[247]

Williams's part in the occupation had involved administrative work, since one of his officers served as commandant of the post. He also needed to obtain sustenance for human and beast, and some hostile operations continued, usually to repel "feeble demonstrations" by small Rebel parties. Other corps pursued Hood's forces. The two months of garrison duty proved rather tedious with interruptions in the supply line to Nashville and plenty of rain. He looked forward to another campaign, now to commence.[248]

The tedium ended on November 11. Williams was placed in temporary command of the XX Corps, part of the "Left Wing, Army of Georgia," commanded by Slocum. He likely had mixed emotions: promised promotions had never materialized, but his earnestness "to see the end" and refusal to

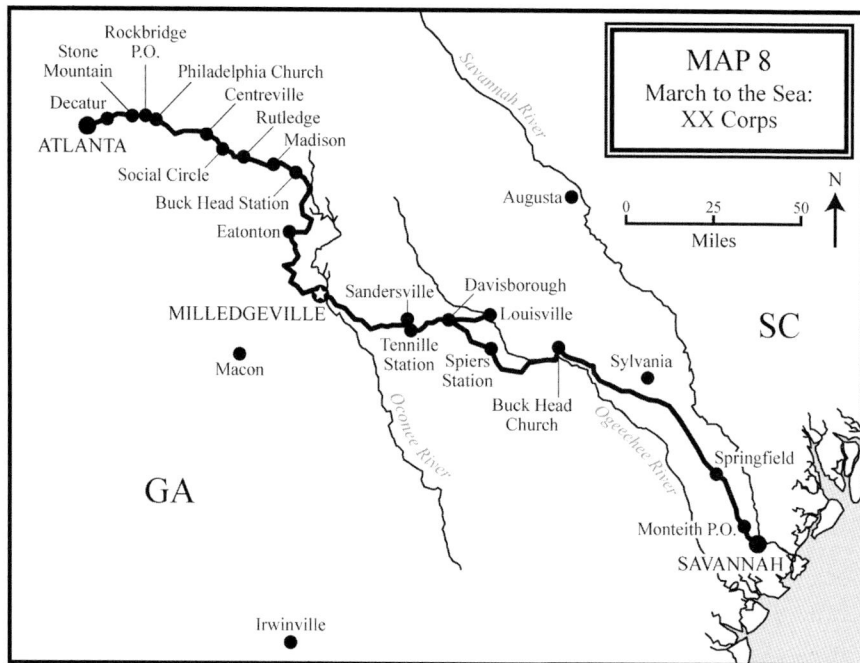

MAP 8
March to the Sea:
XX Corps

resign had been rewarded with a front-row seat on the war's longest and most storied campaign. On the morning of November 15, Williams and his three divisions—the 1st under Brigadier General Nathaniel J. Jackson, the 2nd commanded by Geary and the 3rd by Ward—marched out of Atlanta, with one conspicuous absence: the faithful Samuel Pittman had gone home. Behind lay a hollowed-out hub, "the city's military assets in waste." The XX Corps route went through Decatur, and they camped the first night along the Georgia Railroad south of the Stone Mountain rail station. The next day involved departing from the rails, crossing the Yellow River and using the historic Hightower Trail (a Native American trading route) before, on the seventeenth, passing by Philadelphia Church and reaching Centreville (now Jersey), Georgia.[249]

Thousands of Union soldiers camped out around the small farming village with the lead division, Geary's, moving east onto the Dalley Plantation. Accompanied by wagons, artillery and a growing number of formerly enslaved persons, the Federals "were pleased to rest in an area with little danger and sufficient water." Deep wells, including one in the village center, proved the main source. Here began the practice of fanning out into the countryside to obtain sufficient foodstuffs and livestock as rations for this half of the Left Wing.[250]

Sherman's secrecy initially paid dividends. As the wings followed separate routes to the southeast, Davis, Lee and Hood were perplexed about their destinations. Southern newspapers confidently predicted calamity for Sherman. The folly of cutting loose from a secure base was a "prodigious design" that the people of Georgia could defeat by withdrawing food and forage, blocking roads and burning bridges and repeating what Napoleon's army encountered on its devastating retreat from Moscow. Confederate senator Benjamin H. Hill told his Georgia constituents, "You have now the best opportunity ever yet presented to destroy the enemy....Every citizen with his gun, and every negro with his spade and axe, can do the work of a Soldier. You can destroy the enemy by retarding his march. Georgians, be firm!" Once, Williams had agreed with such predictions: "The history of war proves that an united people can in the end overwhelm any superior invading force if acting purely on the defensive." He did his best now to disprove that maxim.[251]

On Friday, November 18, advance elements of the XX Corps entered Social Circle, Georgia, the rail center of Walton County via the Hightower Trail. The Georgia Railroad facilities had been destroyed during an earlier raid, so Williams's men contented themselves with foraging and appropriating foodstuffs. The enslaved population greeted the soldiers; nearby, a host of exiles from Atlanta were inhabiting boxcars. At noon that day, the first of Williams's three divisions marched east on the Trail into the town of Rutledge. Geary's detached division torched the railroad facilities—depot, water tank, warehouses and track—before continuing on. The column of fourteen thousand infantry stretched for two hours over ten miles. The last unit departed Rutledge before sunset; the XX Corps encamped that night just west of Madison on the railroad. Williams would report that on this third day after departing Atlanta "supplies for man and beast became abundant."[252] His men no longer needed to rely on the provisions they carried; there would be no supply line, for the troops were living off the country.

Before daylight on the nineteenth, Geary's division passed through Madison. Williams rode in with the other two; soon, the depot, warehouses, switching station, cotton gin, clothing factory and stores were ablaze, along with the courthouse "and, in the most symbolic action, the town slave pen." Madison's stately homes, however, were spared. As rain fell and the Union forces departed, Geary marched east toward the Oconee River. Ward and Jackson moved south on the Eatonton Road a few miles.[253] Geary's division burned the railroad bridge over the Oconee on the twentieth and then marched south to rejoin the main body.

The immediate objective of the Left Wing was Georgia's state capital, Milledgeville. By marching consistently eastward until passing Madison, Williams made it seem as if his goal might be Augusta. Late afternoon on Tuesday, November 22, the advance entered the capital city limits "to the cheers of local African Americans." Ascertaining no Confederate defenses, the column formed into line, unfurled flags and marched to the center of town, passing the statehouse and Capitol Square while bands played "The Battle Hymn of the Republic." Detachments fanned out into the countryside. With the weather cold and rainy, most fences and outhouses became tinder for warming fires. Despite the virtually complete stripping of all materiel that could support military purposes, the XX Corps burned only two houses in town and only the arsenal and magazine among the public structures. Destroyed were thousands of muskets and accouterments, lances, cutlasses, ammunition, powder kegs, artillery rounds and primer boxes. Railroad property, as usual, was wrecked. Some soldiers engaged in a mock legislative session and voted to repeal the Georgia ordinance of secession adopted here in January 1861. Black residents from all over the area flocked into town, overjoyed with their freedom. As of the twenty-fifth, Williams's troops had moved on to their next objective. This day also marked the first real skirmishing as they drove off Confederate cavalry attempting to impede the march.[254]

On Saturday, November 26, Williams's force "rapidly" entered the town of Sandersville. One division encamped in a meadow across from Woodlawn Terrace. Sherman made it his headquarters for the day and then moved out to join his Right Wing upon learning that it, "marching from the southwest, had come abreast the Left Wing near Tennille along the line of the Central of Georgia Railroad." Before leaving, he ordered the Washington County Court House burned since Confederate cavalry had used it as shelter from which to fire on Union troops entering the town. Sherman did not thereafter travel with the XX Corps; its leaders were trusted to do the right thing. Continuing the march south, Williams directed the divisions of Geary and Jackson to Tennille, where they arrived the same day. They destroyed the depot, several warehouses, numerous cotton bales and the rails to Davisborough. The 1st Michigan Engineers & Mechanics played a key role in this deconstruction.[255]

Ward's division approached the west bank of the Ogeechee River at noon on Monday the twenty-eighth. They were fired on by Confederate cavalry from the east bank after the Rebels burned the bridge crossings. The other two divisions destroyed sections of the railroad near Bartow southwest of

Louisville before crossing the Ogeechee on November 30 several miles south of the town. As the Union infantry converged on Louisville, no Confederate military defended it. After ransacking all of the stores, a building was fired and several were destroyed in the center of town. Between the twenty-eighth and December 1, the Left Wing encamped in and around the community.[256]

From the twenty-seventh to the twenty-ninth, Williams's force destroyed the Georgia Central railroad and bridges from Tennille to the Ogeechee River, "including the long railroad bridge over that stream, by the First and Second Divisions and Michigan Engineers." The 3rd Division marched via Davisborough across the Ogeechee and Rocky Comfort Rivers and encamped near Louisville. On the thirtieth, the 1st and 2nd Divisions moved up the Ogeechee to a partially destroyed bridge, which was easily repaired. The XX Corps then encamped three miles south of Louisville.[257]

On Friday, December 2, the corps bivouacked around Big Buckhead Church northwest of Millen, while the other Left Wing corps camped across the creek. Williams and XIV Corps brigadier general Jefferson C. Davis "supposedly met inside the church the following morning with Left Wing commander Major General Henry W. Slocum to review plans for the continuation of their march."[258]

The route of the corps thereafter "was down the peninsula between the Ogeechee and Savannah Rivers, following the Louisville and Savannah road." After the encampment at Buck Head Church, each day saw more progress toward Savannah: on the third to Horse Creek (likely where today it is crossed by Georgia Route 21 east of Millen), on the fourth using the same road to Ogeechee Creek, on the fifth into Sylvania, on the sixth near Cowpens Creek north of Shawnee, on the seventh at Jacks Branch just west of Springfield and on the eighth near Eden (Cross-Roads). It had taken six days to traverse the sixty miles from Millen. Williams blamed the slower pace on how "the roads between the creeks and ponds, though apparently of sandy and substantial character, proved to be upon a thin crust, which was soon cut through by our long trains into the deep quicksand, requiring miles of corduroy." Additionally, "at several of the swamps the enemy had attempted to obstruct our march by felling timber."[259]

Williams now turned the troops eastward. They marched from Eden toward where the Augusta & Savannah Railroad and the railway from Charleston neared each other. The location was close to Monteith Post Office (or Station), just north of present-day Port Wentworth. Williams's move could prove key to the successful conclusion of the campaign, for "the fate of Savannah depended entirely on maintaining the integrity of the

Charleston & Savannah Railroad." Before long, both wings of Sherman's force had come up on the Rebel defenses of the city.[260]

With such stakes, it proved no surprise for the XX Corps to find that Confederates had felled trees to obstruct the Union advance. Further, "two small earth-works…with a single gun and about 400 infantry was making a show of stopping our march." Williams ordered Jackson's Division to confront and capture the Rebel force. Seeing the overwhelming Union numbers, the Confederates abandoned their position. Union losses were "one man killed and four wounded."[261]

The following morning, December 10, the corps moved toward Savannah down the Charleston railroad, "destroying some miles" until reaching the Confederate line of defenses "behind swamps and artificial ponds." Williams ordered the men to encamp but not before, during the afternoon, "a party of foragers, with some cavalry, succeeded in bringing to and capturing, near the foot of Argyle Island, a rebel dispatch boat, called the *Ida*, having on board" a staff member of General William J. Hardee, commanding the Confederate defenses. Argyle Island lies between the Middle and Little Back Rivers in the low area drained by the Savannah River.[262]

Arrival on the outskirts of Savannah presented Sherman with a key decision: fight or demand surrender. He chose the latter and waited for Hardee's reply. If capitulation did not follow, the Union armies would attack:

> *Reconnaissances during the week since the investment of the Confederate line had disclosed a number of points where it was vulnerable….Alpheus Williams reported that while there were very few assailable positions on the Confederate right the confidence of his men in taking them was "perfect and/earnest." One of General Williams' brigade commanders believed that the works in the vicinity of the Augusta Road could be easily carried.*[263]

Williams established the line of the XX Corps from the Savannah River to the area where the two railroad lines joined, connecting to the XIV Corps. Over the next days, he edged his main line toward the Confederate works and made preparations for assault "by close reconnaissances, construction of light bridges, and experiments with balks of the pontoon train and fascines of straw and cane for bridging canals." Artillery was placed in "strong field-works," some within 150 yards of the Rebel entrenchments. Williams's action in placing Carman's brigade on the South Carolina side, threatening the one escape route from Savannah, would compel Hardee to abandon his planned defense of the city.[264]

On that Tuesday the twentieth, Confederate fire from their works and gunboats in the nearby waterways "was unusually heavy and continuous." Williams received reports that the barrage was covering for columns of Rebels crossing over to South Carolina as if evacuating the city. The movements continued into the night. He instructed his division commanders "to keep on the alert and press their pickets closer to the rebel works, but the enemy, intending to abandon his heavy guns, kept up a fire until the moment of quitting their defenses." At 3:30 a.m. on Wednesday, Geary reported that one of his brigades had entered the abandoned Confederate main lines. Williams immediately ordered an advance by additional units, and by 6:00 a.m. Geary's entire division had entered Savannah. Williams gave him the honor of assuming command over the city. Sherman was away. He had gone to Hilton Head, planning on how take the city by force.[265]

On December 22, Sherman telegraphed his famous message to Lincoln presenting, "as a Christmas gift, the City of Savannah" along with assorted military prizes. The president replied, "My Dear General Sherman: Many, many thanks for your Christmas gift, the capture of Savannah....Please make my grateful acknowledgments to your whole army, officers and men." A shorter commendation arrived soon from Grant, who opined that the fall of Savannah "must tell upon the people of the South."[266]

It did. On December 19, President Davis had advised Lee that the fall of Savannah was imminent. "I cannot realize the consequences," he agonized. Lee's reply must have been sobering: evacuating Savannah would enable saving troops, rather than surrendering them, and enable concentration of forces to block Sherman's next move. Savannah could not be saved. Davis did not respond. His military subordinates did, beginning to plan on how to defend South Carolina, should that be the next Union target. At the moment, Hardee's available force, he reported to Davis after the evacuation, amounted to just over nine thousand soldiers.[267]

Just over a month had been required to march three hundred miles to the sea, following all kinds of roads and the routes of rail lines, to take Georgia's vital port. During the campaign, the XX Corps incurred 12 killed, 88 wounded and 165 missing—most likely captured when they wandered too far afield. As for the plunder by the corps, recorded were: 71 miles of railroad destroyed; 600 horses and 1,720 mules taken; some 3.3 million pounds of corn foraged and nearly 2 million pounds of fodder; and innumerable bales of cotton burned. Williams had helped achieve Sherman's twin objectives, to "make Georgia howl" and to capture Savannah. Yet another unanticipated outcome was also realized.[268]

Sherman's two wings, by force of opportunity, had become an army of liberation. Thousands of escaped slaves accompanied the army into Savannah, many with the XX Corps. Williams's report evidenced an admiration for their unbridled passion to be free and his candor about the limits of the aid he could provide.

> *Negroes of all ages and of every variety of physical condition, from the infant in its mother's arms to the decrepid old man, joined the column from plantations and from cross-roads, singly and in large groups, on foot, on horseback, and in every description of vehicles. The vehicles were discarded, as obstructing the progress of our very long column. Beyond this no effort was made to drive away the fugitives. The decrepid, the aged, and the feeble were told of the long journey before them, and advised to remain behind.*

Few did. He estimated that from six to eight thousand fugitives joined his column, all told, and "something over 2,500 reached our camp before Savannah." Most of them "were, on account of scarcity of subsistence, placed in colony on the Coleraine plantation, on the Savannah River, and plentifully supplied with rice, and occasionally with beef." Able-bodied males took on work for the army. Eventually, the entire community was assigned to the protection of the quartermaster department. An additional four to five hundred "found employment as officers' servants and teamsters for the Government."[269]

In stark contrast stood an earlier incident during Sherman's march at Ebenezer Creek. XIV Corps commander Davis ordered the pontoon bridge over the creek dismantled before a huge number of fugitives could use it to cross. "In their fright" at being left to the devices of the pursuing Confederate cavalry, some tried to swim across but drowned. After a report on this inhumanity made its way to Halleck, he made Sherman privy to what he called the "Inevitable Sambo" problem in a private letter; he also suggested that Sherman do more to provide escapees a safe haven in Savannah. Davis justified the matter as a military necessity, Sherman backed him and Stanton let the matter pass. A contemporary order by Davis suggests a less than justifiable explanation: "Useless negroes are being accumulated to an extent which would be suicide to a column which must be constantly stripped for battle and prepared for the utmost celerity of movement." No similar order is found for the XX Corps.[270]

The presence on his staff of a Detroiter might have reinforced Williams's more compassionate approach. William Dollarson had been with Williams since he first assumed command in October 1861. Dollarson's "cooking apparatus" had kept his general alive and well for more than three years in the field. "Uncle Billy" had become Sherman's nickname to his troops, but Williams had his own in the person of a camp cook who was as faithful to the cause as the officer he served. Dollarson had aided the efforts of Seymour Finney, innkeeper and Underground Railroad conductor, before the war; as part of Williams's command, he had aided many more to gain their freedom.[271]

Antebellum Georgia's population of 1 million residents included nearly 463,000 enslaved persons. A twentieth-century Georgian would place the contributions to liberty of Union generals like Williams into perspective. They neither returned the slave to master nor withdrew the mantle of protection; rather, they "enabled the Negro to play a significant role in his own liberation." Such leadership, given the times, exhibited spiritual values as well: it "resurrected and restated the principle of equality upon which the founding of the nation rested."[272]

The occupation of Savannah proved an enjoyable sojourn. He found the city "charming and the weather superb." Williams stayed at the home of Richard A. Cuyler, president of the Central of Georgia Railroad. He was one of the Union leaders responsible for damaging the railroad, causing it to

Sherman reviewing his army, Savannah Customs House. "Among the mounted officers... are Gen Williams." Artist William Waud. *Library of Congress.*

lose more than one hundred hundred miles of track and much rolling stock. Perhaps because Cuyler was an in-law of the Sibley family of Detroit, he nonetheless extended his hospitality to the general: "Good wine of very old vintage abundant, and altogether it was a delightful winter residence. We had the grandest reviews, and by common consent the 20th Corps waxed them all." Sherman had ordered reviews of the various corps as a way of celebrating their triumph. The first occurred on Christmas Eve; during the next week, the XX and remaining corps had the same honor. As reported in the *Savannah Republican*, "The review of the 20th Army Corps on December 30 with the 'prancing steeds, gaily caparisoned,' the 'battle scarred colors' and 'superb bands' presented 'a kaleidoscopic picture which words cannot paint.'" Williams wrote home of his pride over the appearance his corps made. "Hundreds of officers have told me it was the finest and most splendid review they ever saw. Gen. Sherman confesses it was the best of all."[273] The militia man had apparently won over a West Pointer.

CHAPTER 13

THROUGH THE CAROLINAS TO THE GRAND CONCLUSION

As 1865 dawned, Sherman set his sights to link with Grant to defeat Lee around Richmond. The first phase was to "undertake at one stride to make Goldsborough," North Carolina, a rail junction less than 150 miles from Petersburg, Virginia. Cutting loose from Savannah to march northward would mean traversing some of the wettest and most difficult terrain yet encountered. A conventional supply line would again be abandoned. In Sherman's way were troops under P.G.T. Beauregard, Hardee, Braxton Bragg and Wade Hampton, with Joseph Johnston taking overall command to block Sherman's path.

Williams remained in command of XX Corps. The continuing assignment meant that he had shown Sherman his capabilities, and he now possessed a second star for his shoulder bar—on January 12, he was notified of appointment by the president as "Brevet Major General." Receiving a brevet meant a virtual promotion and no additional pay. While other nominations cited "long and continued services" and "special gallantry," his was bestowed "for marked ability and energy, &c." The appointment was confirmed by the Senate on February 14 as part of a mass set. The Valentine's Day gift did not assuage his feelings of injustice and insult. Williams regarded the brevet as "valueless" except as it gave him command stature "in my own corps." Otherwise, he wrote his daughters, "I would send it back."[274]

Planning ahead, and despite that newspapers had done him few favors, Williams extended a "kind invitation" to Charles Coffin of the *New York Journal*: "Come with me, you will see high old times, I reckon. My soldiers

Brevet Major General A.S. Williams. *Library of Congress.*

are crazy to get into South Carolina." On New Year's Day he transferred one of his three divisions across the Savannah River toward Hardeeville. The campaign launched on January 17, per Sherman's orders, when Williams maneuvered the XX Corps out from the city's defenses. The 1st and 3rd Divisions "stepped foot on the *sacred secesh* soil" of South Carolina and moved to Hardeeville, while the 2nd Division had to follow firmer roads up the Georgia side of the Savannah River to opposite Purrysburg. The country was "low and swampy, covered with pine, gum, and cedar" woods, the weather cold. On the twenty-ninth, a skirmish ensued with Rebel cavalry. By February 2, the two divisions with Williams had moved to Robertsville and on to Lawtonville for a skirmish with Confederate infantry and artillery. Williams had the Rebels flanked and driven off. For three of the next four days, it rained while the corps continued its northward course. On the tenth, the lead elements reached the Edisto River after Geary's division arrived; on the twelfth, the Confederates were again driven back; and on the fifteenth, the corps neared Lexington just west of Columbia. "Slight skirmishing with the enemy" took place daily.[275]

In their path stood the capital city of South Carolina, the "fountain-head of rebellion." On the seventeenth and eighteenth, much of the town went up in flames. Williams had dispatched the 1st Michigan Engineers & Mechanics to Columbia per orders, the regiment having rejoined the corps on the tenth. Williams did not take part in the destruction. On the day after Columbia burned, the mayor of Charleston surrendered his city to Union forces, and the U.S. flag again flew over Fort Sumter.[276]

Williams moved his force to Winnsborough on February 21. Approaching the town, "several buildings were seen to be on fire." Williams hurried forward a brigade to extinguish the conflagration, "which, after much effort, was successfully accomplished." From here the corps turned to the northeast and reached Chesterfield on March 2. It had yet another minor encounter with Rebel forces, driving them "on the double-quick" through town and securing two bridges over the waterway beyond. As the corps crossed into North Carolina on the seventh, a fellow Michigander bade "goodbye land of secesh. Your country is now nearly desolate." There was a more lenient attitude in a state that had seceded in May 1861.[277]

On the eleventh, the XX Corps reached Fayetteville "after long and weary marches." Although the March to the Sea was already gaining almost mythical status, Williams regarded this campaign as "more arduous, weather worse, and roads infamously worse." His corps had corduroyed an estimated one hundred miles of road. A silver lining was the "little fighting" experienced over the last month. His health remained "excellent. No exposure seems to affect me." He sent love to uncles, aunts and cousins and affection to his daughters. The army marched "in review order" through the city and crossed the Cape Fear River en route to Goldsboro. Confederate forces had departed north toward Raleigh. Sherman took the opportunity to forward refugees of both Caucasian

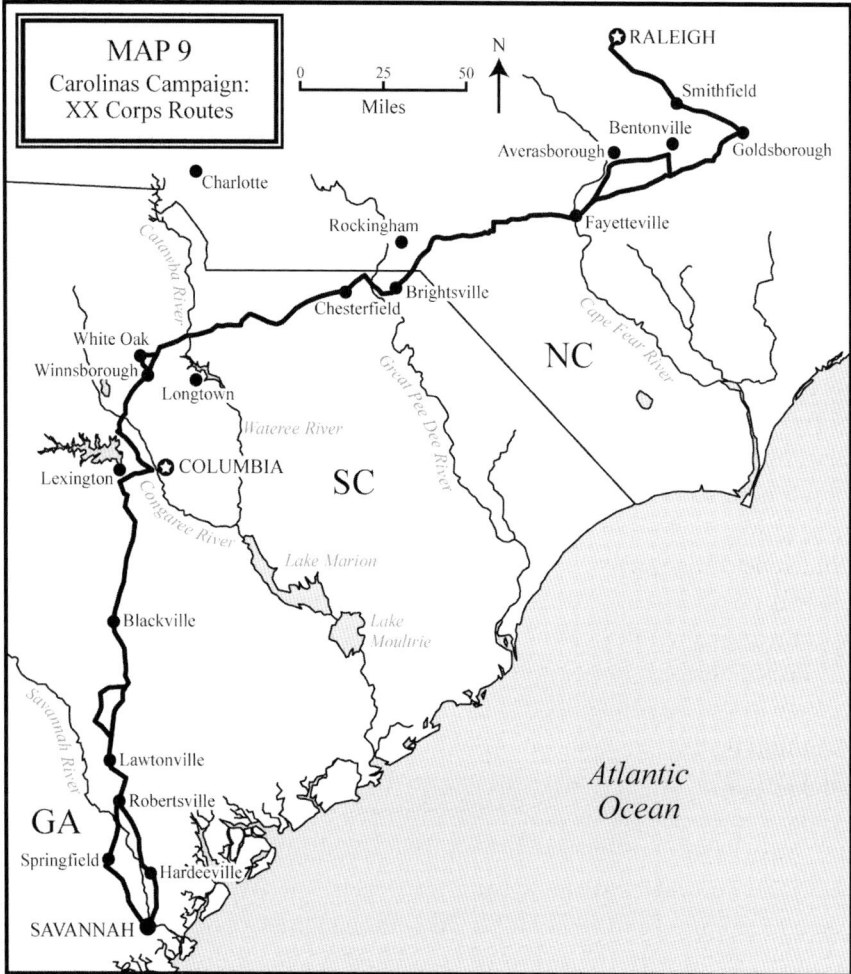

MAP 9
Carolinas Campaign:
XX Corps Routes

With modern features.

and African lineage on to the seacoast. An estimated twenty-five thousand were transported.[278]

On March 15, Hardee with six thousand infantry blocked the road to Raleigh and entrenched twenty miles north from Fayetteville. Union cavalry advanced and engaged the enemy, but Rebel artillery checked further progress until infantry arrived. The following morning, Confederate infantry attacked in force and threatened to turn the Union flank. At 7:30 a.m., Williams received a message that aid was urgently needed. He immediately directed the corps ahead about five miles and formed Ward's division in line of battle across and to the left of the main road, Jackson's division to the right (Map 10:1). Williams's troops "arrived on the field just in time to stem the Confederate attack." He would report that Selfridge's brigade "was severely attacked while moving into position by a large force of the enemy attempting to turn our right. He handsomely repulsed the attack." After reconnoitering, Ward's division was ordered to feel toward the left and find the enemy's flank. Union artillery "vigorously shelled" the Confederate breastworks. The 1st Brigade of Ward's division located Hardee's right, "charged down the line on a double-quick" and drove the Confederates "out at a run."

Williams then ordered his whole line to advance against the enemy, who were attempting to form for a stand in a second line (Map 10:2). The Confederate force "was pursued as rapidly as the miry nature of the ground would permit for about a mile." At this point stood a line of strong entrenchments "behind swampy and partly overflowed ground" with flanks anchored on waterways. Williams ordered a careful advance; "the rebel skirmishers were rapidly driven into their works and our line pushed up to within a few hundred yards." Here he received an order to await reinforcement before making a full assault. The next morning, "it was discovered that the rebels were gone."[279]

Williams took pride in how the XX Corps had performed in the Battle of Averasborough. Casualties were 56 killed, 378 wounded and 51 missing, for total losses of 485. He estimated Confederate losses of more than 800. The "stubbornness of the Confederate resistance," though, should have served as a warning to Sherman.[280]

On Sunday, March 19, Williams was ordered to protect the army's rear. Information reached him that the XIV Corps "was seriously engaged with what was then supposed to be a large cavalry force supported by a large body of infantry." Next came an "urgent message" from Slocum to come forward. Williams ordered Jackson's division up and rode toward the front. Soon, "having ridden far in advance of his troops," he met a courier from Slocum and received orders to hurry up his whole command—the Rebel infantry had seized the initiative. He quickly ordered Ward's division forward. "All the troops moved rapidly" into position toward the left of the XIV Corps. Williams then received reports that "large bodies of the enemy's infantry were moving to our left and were within a mile of the field upon which our trains were parking." Unexpected disaster loomed, as it had so many times while with the Army of the Potomac.[281]

Williams "galloped back" and ordered units to the front immediately; the Confederates were pressing in "a final effort to break the Union line." They

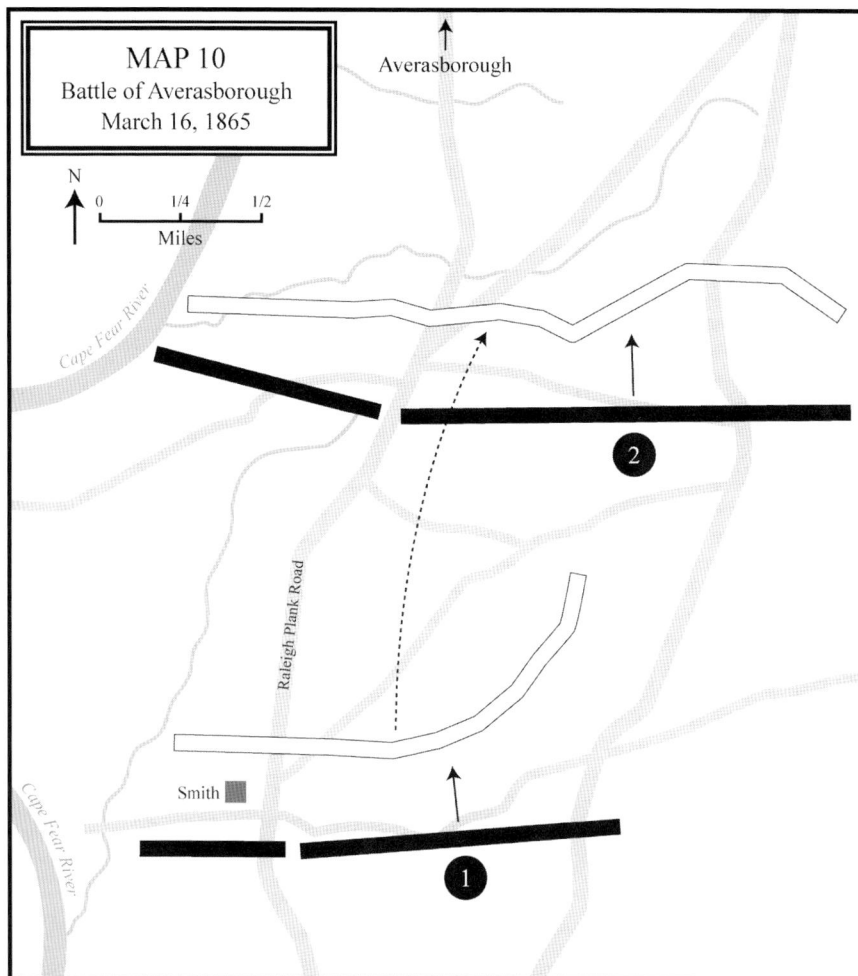

MAP 10
Battle of Averasborough
March 16, 1865

N

0   1/4   1/2
Miles

Averasborough

Cape Fear River

Raleigh Plank Road

Cape Fear River

Smith

2

1

"fell in overwhelming force upon Robinson's three regiments," his others being elsewhere, in the "last grand charge of the Army of Tennessee." Warned of a flanking movement, Williams ordered Selfridge's brigade into line, with Robinson in reserve. Ward's brigades were ordered to prolong the line to the left and angled "so as to oblige the enemy, evidently bent on attacking, to draw out and weaken his line in seeking our flank." Artillery was placed characteristically in commanding positions. The Confederates attacked but were "driven back in great discomfiture by the artillery and the infantry" fire. Five more Rebel assaults were made, and repulsed, until darkness fell. Williams was able to send another brigade of Ward's division to aid the XIV Corps; while on the way, it struck a Rebel column and drove it back.[282]

XX Corps losses in the Battle of Bentonville were lighter than in the previous engagement: 14 killed, 168 wounded and 52 missing or captured. It had performed well again, having "stemmed the movements of Johnston's troops" and providing time to bring superior numbers to bear. Sherman analyzed his opponent's strategy in a communique to Slocum: "Johnston hoped to overcome your wing" before the rest of the Union forces could concentrate, but he failed. Much of the credit was due to Williams "for speeding his two XX divisions and three artillery batteries to the front" and swiftly and effectively stemming the tide.[283]

On March 24, the corps arrived at Goldsborough, now under Federal control, and passed through the town in triumphant order of review as per custom. Its appearance conveyed the many miles of hard marching now behind them. Williams wore a coat torn "and badly patched," a vest having but two buttons, a hat "lopped down all around" and trousers that had darkened. His men had dealt with bad roads, a lack of provisions, rain (one-third of the time) and cold. They had laid many miles of corduroy roads and put down and taken up pontoon bridges across various waterways, destroying miles of railroad and thousands of cotton bales. They continually forced back Confederate forces, whatever their size, whether cavalry or infantry. Williams recounted a typical setting:

> *Behind Moccasin Creek, a broad swamp, heavily tangled with trees, brambles, and bushes, full of pitfalls and badly overflowed, the enemy had torn up the bridges over two unfordable channels into which the creek divides itself at the crossing. Several hundred rebels under cover kept up a severe fire upon the roadway and across the swamp. The skirmishers of Selfridge's (First) brigade (One hundred and twenty-third New York, Col. J.C. Rogers) spiritedly dashed into the swamp and, advancing through deep water and strong entanglements, drove back the enemy, so that the bridges were promptly relaid and the whole division placed in camp a mile north on Atkinson's plantation before nightfall.[284]*

It was as simple as that.

Goldsborough meant the close to this phase of Sherman's plan. It meant other endings. Nearly 600 of the 2,000 fugitives who had followed the XX Corps were sent to the Atlantic coast and freedom. The corps had suffered 1,121 casualties during the two months of the campaign, 88 of whom had been killed. And the months-long tenure of its leader was over.[285]

Williams would no longer lead the XX Corps. On April 1, Sherman promoted Major General Joseph A. Mower to the post. Just ten days before, Mower had made an "impromptu," unauthorized, uncoordinated and ultimately unsuccessful attack near Bentonville; the affair obviously was no disqualification. Like Williams's other superiors, Sherman never offered a criticism or negative comment. Williams reassumed yet again command of the Red Star Division. He shared his reactions in a letter home: although he had "lost the corps again" he was going "back to my division without grumbling." This latest demotion had been cushioned by a formal audience by his brigade commanders, who "announced that they spoke the wishes of every officer and man in the division that I would resume command." The replacement of "the popular and solid" Williams by Sherman's "pet" had caused a great stir in the ranks. Williams was also bolstered by learning that Richmond had been evacuated when Lee pulled out of its defenses. The war appeared to be reaching its climax.[286]

Sherman had hoped to join Grant and defeat Lee together. Williams shared that notion and feared Lee and Johnston would unite and bring on yet more bloodletting. The 1st Division led the way when the Army of Georgia moved out for Raleigh on April 10, seeking to press Johnston before any such rendezvous. Hard work remained; the division "skirmished all day" and waded across a swamp up "to their arm-pits" in order "to get possession of the bridges that had been thrown into the creek." Here, with perhaps only a few more days until war's end, Williams did not relent in leading from the front: "I got into a very hot place on one of the bridges."

On the twelfth, word came of news Williams had only imagined: the surrender of Lee's army to Grant at one of the typically "dilapidated" Virginia courthouse towns, this one named Appomattox, he had years ago denigrated. As Williams passed by his commander, he heard his name called out—Sherman "grabbed my hand and almost shook my arm off," exclaiming how Johnston's and the war's days were numbered. Williams "expressed a pretty large sized 'Laus Deo' at the prospect of an early end of this great Rebellion and a return to my family." He yearned for nothing more than "quietude and repose." Only Johnston's army interposed.

The 1st Division reached the Dix Hill institution for the care of the mentally ill outside Raleigh on April 13. After proceeding "through the city in review order," Raleigh became their final wartime encampment. The vaunted Army of Northern Virginia having capitulated, Johnston soon surrendered. Sherman formally reviewed the corps on April 21, with Williams's Division in the lead as it stepped through the city center. The ceremony marked its latest achievement, helping defeat an army under Joseph Johnston that, though smaller in numbers, "was larger, better equipped, and better supplied" than many histories describe. Its morale also "remained surprisingly good" despite the odds, supply problems and Union successes. Lee—not Johnston—had surrendered his army first.[287]

Although other Confederate forces remained under arms and President Davis was a fugitive, Sherman was directed to bring his army to Washington. Williams and the 1st Division stepped off for their final trek on April 30 at 5:30 a.m., one without expectation of hardship or hostilities. On May 11, the XX Corps reached Richmond, and Williams's Division led it through the city, crossing the James River pontoons at noon "and marching through in column, with colors displayed and bands playing." They passed Libby Prison and Castle Thunder, two prisoner-of-war sites and the state capitol, as well as through the principal streets. At long last, Williams had entered the Confederate capital, his fifth of the Southern states.[288]

On May 15, the division marched through the area known as the Wilderness toward a special destination. At Chancellorsville, it "halted for three hours upon the battle-ground to enable the officers and men of the division to visit the scenes of that memorable contest in which most of the regiments took part." Four days later, it reached the outskirts of Alexandria and encamped. A "Grand Review" had been scheduled for May 23 to fete the Army of the Potomac, with a second on May 24 to honor Sherman's forces. The route would be from the Capitol down Pennsylvania Avenue past the White House reviewing stand and before the eyes of the president, the Cabinet, Grant, Sherman and other dignitaries. Williams and much of his division were entitled to participate on either day, but Wednesday would be their moment. How would they appear compared to the men in Eastern blue?[289]

Williams wrote to his daughters to deprecate the whole idea of the event. It would only be, he foretold, a "tramp of masses, all looking alike, for hours and hours, till everybody will be tired to death of seeing soldiers." His own unit would probably not make the reviewing stand until midnight. He was war-weary, and he forbade their coming—"you'd be bored to death," he asserted, "as we shall all be tired to death." He had been overlooked for a promotion he deserved probably "about the fortieth time"; likely no one would care whether he and his men even participated.[290]

Northern newspapers covered the festivities in great detail, none exceeding the *New York Herald*. Although a frequent administration critic, with the war won even the *Herald* now celebrated. A subheadline enumerated the "heroes" who had conquered Georgia and South Carolina, featuring Sherman and including Williams. After reporting on Sherman, Slocum and Mower, the scribe turned to the commander of the 1st Division and his 4,800 "stout men," describing how they had come "steadily down" the avenue in good order. He also described an amazing show of respect by their comrades in the Eastern army. Potomac veterans paralleled the 1st Division's cadence all along Pennsylvania Avenue in the same way they had "followed at militia musters when they were boys, admiring the men who wore 'Red Stars.'" The ranks in Williams's Division were "as straight as the front of a wave, and their solid tramp resembled the regular strokes of a beetle." Accompanying their "Pap" with "glistening guns, new flags and red stars," the unit ended up "carrying off the palm for best appearance in all the two days' show."

Williams was portrayed as "a grand old son of the State of Michigan," known by nearly everyone in the Army of the Potomac by virtue of their common experiences "on all its famous fields prior to September, 1863." He had "passed all the military grades" by commanding units from brigade up through corps—whatever duty required. In a display of fondness that surpassed that for any other general on either day, Williams "was vociferously cheered and loaded down with bouquets till he had no hands to wave his acknowledgements." The journalist found himself moved. "I will be bound," he wrote, about how Williams and his "old tried troops" shared a special bond.

This account found echo in a portrayal by Frederick W. Swift, former captain of the 17th Michigan Infantry:

> *Meade, Sherman and Logan were accorded tremendous ovations, their horses decorated with wreaths, a sea of handkerchiefs waving frantically. Every throat sends out its shouts. Every eye beams and sparkles! There is no diminution of enthusiasm although three mortal hours have been consumed by the "Army of the Tennessee" in passing by. But listen! why that great outbreak of applause? this redoubling of the cheering? Why that commotion in those banks of humanity? It did not seem possible that the cheering along the avenue could be any more vociferous or any more enthusiastic than heretofore, but it is! The explanation is easy—for there comes the man, the best loved man of all! General Alpheus S. Williams! "Old Pap" as all the boys loved to call him….How like a soldier to the manner born he looks as he rides steadily along under the headquarters flag of the "Red Star Division." Wreaths of flowers are thrown over his*

Grand Review "during the passage of the 'Red Star' Division," May 24, 1865. *Library of Congress.*

horse and over those of his staff. He is deluged with bouquets and so are
they. Ah! this is a proud day for the Old Hero....Who shall wonder then
at the frenzy of this vast crowd, for here comes General A.S. Williams—
Michigan's Military Idol! [291]

Yet another observer chronicled this special reception. Slocum's entourage
had "received a continuous ovation throughout the entire route," and "the
Army of the Tennessee received generous applause." The crowd, however,
waited in anticipation for another sight. At first glimpse "of General Williams
and the men with the old star badge," the veteran bystanders "sent up a roar

Grand Review, "Units of 20th Army Corps," May 24, 1865. *Library of Congress.*

of enthusiastic greeting that did not cease its tumultuous volume until the last regiment of the corps had passed."

Williams's post-review letter to his children struck a different tone from the "bored to death" missive. The day had been "a great success," and he wrote with pride of the appearance of his men. He admitted receiving "whole armfuls of bouquets" and much adulation. He also told of how "hundreds of Michiganders" had sought him out on the streets of Washington. The Grand Review had proved to be quite grand, indeed.[292]

On May 27, Williams authored his final wartime report. He waxed nostalgic about the 1st Division having "sploshed" over "greasy" roads and completed "the great circuit" from the banks of the Rapidan via railroad

1st Division, 20th Army Corps

James Loven
Brevet Brig. Gen. J.L. Selfridge
Comd'g 1st Brigade
(Col. 46th Penna.)

Alpheus Starkey
Brevet Maj. Gen. A.S. Williams
Comd'g 1st Division

Wm.
Brevet Brig. Gen. W. Hawley
Comd'g 2d Brigade
(Col. 3d Wis.)

Brig. Gen. J.S. Robinson
Comd'g 3d Brigade
James Sidney

A.S. Williams, commanding 1st Division, XX Corps, with brigade commanders J.L. Selfridge, J.S. Robinson and W. Hawley. MOLLUS–Mass Civil War Photograph Collection, vol. 54. *U.S. Army Heritage and Education Center, Carlisle, Pennsylvania.*

to Tennessee and on to Savannah, Raleigh, Richmond and "back to the precise spot it left, a little over a year and a half ago." He confessed satisfaction about May 24: "It was a day, if memorable to the great throng of citizens, not less so to our returning soldiers, for the vastness of the concourse, the cordial and enthusiastic welcome and greetings, and the great gratitude and joy for the restoration of peace and the felicitous reunion of the victorious Armies of the Republic." The report concluded with special recognition of his brigade commanders, Robinson, Hawley and Selfridge.[293]

Williams and his command moved on after the parade to west of the Baltimore Pike near Bladensburg, Maryland, on "Hoover's Farm."[294] On June 4, he was assigned command of a Provisional Division of veteran XX Corps units. On June 6, he said farewell to his beloved Red Star Division.

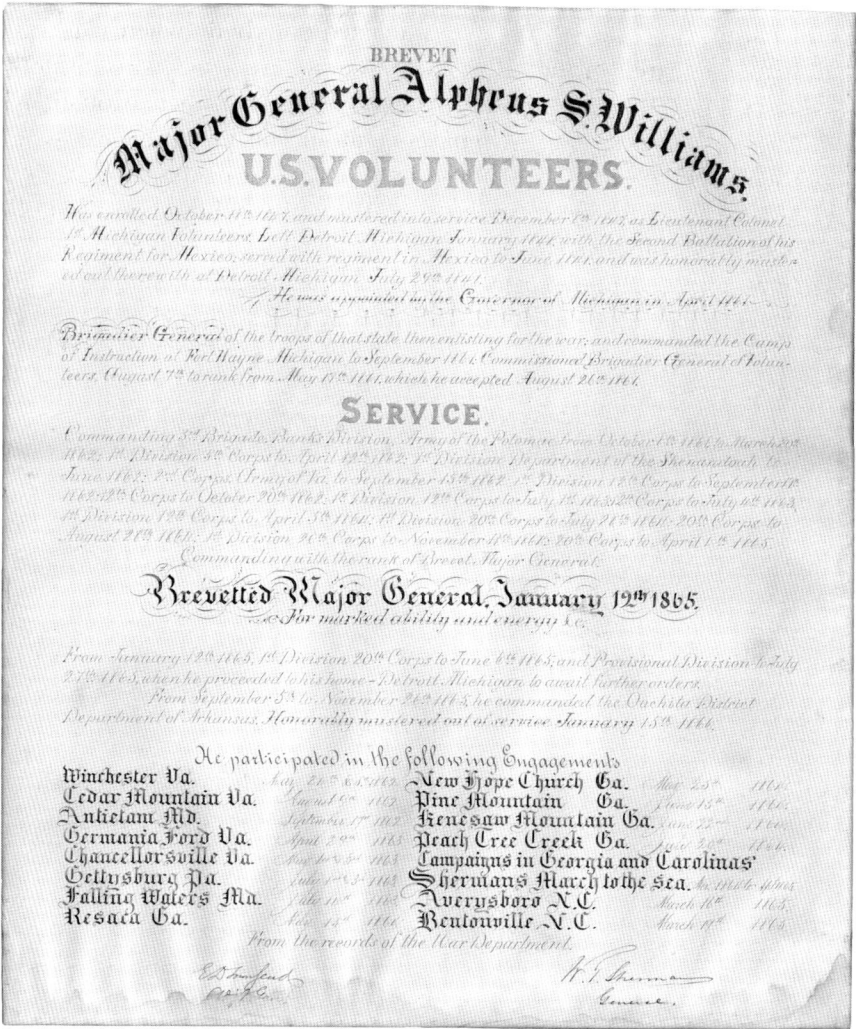

Certificate of Military Service, Adjutant General's Office, U.S. War Department, 1866. *Detroit Historical Society.*

His new command left for Louisville on the eighth, becoming part of the Army of the Tennessee under Major General John A. Logan.[295]

Regard for the campaign through the Carolinas was soon eclipsed in American memory by Appomattox and Lincoln's assassination. Sherman complained that it undeservedly took a back seat to the march through Georgia. He lamented to his brother, "[N]o one ever has and may not agree with me as to the very great importance of the march north from Savannah.

The march to the sea seems to have captivated everybody, whereas it was child's play compared to the other." Confederate eyewitnesses—Johnston and Hardee—held such a view. During the April 1865 surrender negotiations near Raleigh, Johnston told a Union general, in Hardee's presence, how his colleague had telegraphed that Sherman would be unable to cross the South Carolina wetlands and reach Columbia. When Johnston learned of the Union army's progress "at the rate of a dozen miles a day or more, and bringing its artillery and wagons with it, I made up my mind that there had been no such army in existence since the days of Julius Caesar."[296]

One of Sherman's key legates had been "Old Pap" Williams.

CHAPTER 14

SERVING IN THE RECONSTRUCTION SOUTHWEST

W ithin a week after the Grand Review, U.S. Grant ordered a massive reduction of the United States military. Units were rolled up, soldiers mustered out and general officers "whose services can be dispensed with" were ordered to their homes. Some generals of volunteers were being retained. Age fifty-four, uncertain of prospects and with "a paucity of pecuniary resources," Williams had a serious need to remain in uniform. Having been "miraculously kept from harm" for the last four years, perhaps he had been spared to further serve his country.[297]

On the Fourth of July, Williams began mustering out his regiments and sending them home from Louisville. The next day, Sherman—now in command of west of the Mississippi River—wrote to Grant on behalf of certain favorites:

> *There are several of the general officers that I want to serve all I can....I want Maj. Gens. John M. Corse, Charles C. Walcutt, and A.S. Williams retained. They are most valuable officers, and I beg you will assign them to me to be retained till the proper time for them to seek new commissions in the future army.*

The War Department responded on July 21: Williams would be assigned to Sherman's military division, reporting to Major General Joseph J. Reynolds, existing commander of the Department of Arkansas. He was to report to Arkansas under General Orders No. 130 of July 28, 1865.[298]

Two days earlier, the *New York Times* had reported on the "Progress of Reconstruction in Arkansas." The state had been the ninth to join the Confederacy, seceding in May 1861. "Events have conspired favorably," the *Times* noted hopefully, "for the early rehabilitation of the State in the Union." Violence had abated, Confederate leaders were now loyal and the only impediment to the economy was an inadequate transportation system. Given that "the State is so peaceable—the State Government so complete—acquiescence in, and support of all the authorities so universal," full restoration into the Union could be imminent.[299]

Williams received a delay in his report date until September 9, providing a month's respite in Detroit. During his stay, he formed part of the greeting committee along with Mayor Kirkland C. Barker, U.S. Senator Zachariah Chandler and General Orlando B. Willcox when U.S. Grant brought his family to Detroit. The Grants traveled through Canada and crossed into Michigan at Port Huron. The committee came up by train the night before and escorted its distinguished guests back to Detroit on Saturday, August 12, using the same Grand Trunk Railroad line. The train arrived at the Detroit depot, located at Atwater and Brush Streets, around 11:00 a.m. to the cheers of huge throngs. The leave also enabled him to join a distinguished board of directors spearheading the effort to erect a Civil War monument in the city. Seven more years would be required to complete the project. Arkansas would rejoin the Union in only three.[300]

At the end of the war, Williams spoke of how he thought Reconstruction would be difficult: "[T]here will be the great swell of the storm for years to come." When he arrived in Arkansas, the duty proved more of a challenge than the *Times*'s report suggested. Guerrilla warfare was not extinguished. The U.S. Freedmen's Bureau had opened its office to work on behalf of the formerly enslaved; their relations with former owner-planters would be a challenge. A peace council convened in August with Confederate Indian nations to resolve their postwar status, and Colonel Ely S. Parker of Grant's wartime staff participated. Although many Union troops had been demobilized, the 57th U.S. Colored Troops continued in service as a garrison at Belle Point near Fort Smith.

Williams first assumed command of a district headquartered in Camden and then moved to Little Rock. He no longer commanded a division of veterans who revered his leadership; frequent altercations with civilians resulted in numerous courts-martial. Unlike during the war, Williams was frequently ill and felt a growing discontent. He saw his colleagues returning to civilian life—Slocum in September. Staying in the army might have been a mistake. Irene's upcoming nuptials only added to his homesickness.[301]

When the Congressional Joint Committee on Reconstruction held hearings in early 1866, witnesses testified to the successful reinstitution of law and order. Others asserted that it was premature to restore the state to its former relations in the Union. Since the process of Reconstruction commenced during the war, truth lay on both sides of the question. A new Arkansas Constitution abolished slavery but also "sought to bar additional blacks from entering the state."[302]

By then, Williams no longer wore a uniform. A few months proved to be the duration of his postwar military career. He left for Detroit on January 9, 1866, on a twenty-day leave. While at home, an order issued honorably mustering him out as of January 15. His name came first on the list of brigadier generals whose time had elapsed. The order failed, however, to refer to his status as *brevet major* general.[303]

In March, Williams was in New York City, "the center of everything," looking for opportunities since he saw "nothing promising in Detroit." He went to Deep River in May, confessing, "I really have lost all energy and spirit." Thanks to his political credentials, he received an appointment in July from President Andrew Johnson to serve on a commission dealing with Missouri war claims. In April, Congress had authorized a commission of three appointees to fix the federal obligation to reimburse Missouri's government "in enrolling, equipping, subsisting, and paying" state forces that acted "in concert with the United States forces in the suppression of the rebellion." The commissioners' pay was fixed at ten dollars per day of actual service.

Williams began service on the commission "in the latter part of July" and worked into December. His efforts frequently went well into the night. The commissioners looked into "voluminous vouchers" and supporting testimony presented to support the state's request for nearly $7 million in recoupments, ranging as low as $50 per claim. The documentation went into detail "as to companies, regiments, troops, etc." Williams stayed to the end of the year in order to wrap up the commission's work, although another federal post, even farther south, was in the offing.[304]

Reconstruction of the South would prove to be as difficult as, and longer than, the war itself. Williams received two trans-Mississippi assignments during the initial eighteen months, neither of which brought him involvement in the sharpest conflicts. As a War Democrat, he was a candidate for presidential appointment. Party affiliation, however, would not prove immediately helpful in Michigan.

CHAPTER 15

CANDIDATE, DIPLOMAT, CONGRESSMAN

P olitics in America and in the Wolverine State during 1866 were highly contentious. President Johnson became at ever more bitter odds with the Republican-controlled Congress after overrides on two key vetoes of legislation aiding freed persons. The Fourteenth Amendment began its journey to passage as the Joint Committee on Reconstruction devised a plan to supersede the president's. When Michigan Republicans met in August in Detroit, they nominated incumbent Henry H. Crapo as their candidate for governor, given his staunch opposition to Johnson's programs. Democrats met on September 5 and nominated Alpheus Williams for governor and John G. Parkhurst for lieutenant governor.[305]

Both standard bearers were Civil War veterans. Parkhurst had commanded the 9th Michigan Infantry and received a general's commission, demonstrating solid military credentials. Williams's four-year record was well known. Notable military candidates for the party emerged in other states, such as Winfield S. Hancock, Thomas Ewing Jr. (Sherman's father-in-law) and Williams's old XII Corps comrade Henry Slocum. Williams was one of six ex-soldiers who would face off against five statewide soldier candidates advanced by the Republicans.[306]

The key issue in the campaign was "control over Reconstruction and the fate of American freedom." Republicans argued that the Democratic platform sustained the return of secessionists to power. Democrats contended that their opponents embraced despotism and urged voters to "stand by the Constitution." Williams signed a public letter calling "for a moderate and conciliatory Southern policy" but, per custom of the period, did not campaign. When the votes were tallied in November, Crapo had trounced Williams 59 to 41 percent, with a margin of 29,038 votes out of 165,000 cast. Besides Wayne County, which he carried 6,299 (55.5 percent) to 5,054 (44.5 percent), Williams won only nine others. His worst showing was in Manistee County, where he polled not a single vote. It would be the worst defeat for a Democratic candidate in the 1860s. His statewide total of 67,708 votes represented 6,500 fewer than received in 1864.[307]

Several factors contributed to the defeat. Chief was Johnson's ever-eroding popularity: "During the two months between the [Republican] convention [on August 30] and election President Johnson's influence perceptibly weakened, and the Republicans came out in greater strength than ever" to vote for anti-Johnson candidates. The president actively campaigned, breaking with tradition, and a September visit to Michigan backfired. The midterm canvass "was in fact a referendum" on the administration. Republicans emerged with a two-thirds majority in both houses. A year prior, Michiganders saluted Williams on the streets of the nation's capital. A year afterward, they rejected their "military idol" at the ballot box.[308]

The electoral loss left Williams very low. Neither Irene's marriage to William J. Chittenden on January 18 nor Mary's marriage to Francis U. Farquhar, Union officer and gentleman, on November 14 alleviated his dejection. Father bared soul to daughter in a soberly frank letter as the month closed:

St. Louis, Nov. 30th, 1866

My Dear Daughter:
It gives me great pleasure to learn from your letter of 21st that my first one to you, as a married woman, *did not distress you with its sadness. I suppose I ought to have written you in a cheerful vein; but some how I could not get the feeling up. The event conjured up the memories of the sainted dead, as well as those of the early and happy days of my living children; when we had a home, saddened now and then and by sorrows and bereavements, but for the main part cheerful, happy and blissful. You were all too young to appreciate the great loss of your most excellent and matchless mother; while my heart was greatly consoled and my sorrows lessened by the affectionate, cheerful, dutiful and happy children, that Providence had left to my sole care and keeping. Still, no one knows, how heavy my heart grows when these anniversary days, holidays and family occasions bring back strongly the memory of that sainted wife and mother. Her love for her children was*

a part of her pure nature; and when any of them are made happy I cannot but reflect how her loving heart would have rejoiced with them; how proud she would have been to have seen them grow up to maturity, full of her own native goodness and worthy of that almost celestial love she had for them. The longer I live the more strongly and frequently these thoughts and reflections occur to me. Perhaps as we grow older the mind becomes more retrospective; for the future has little of promise.[309]

With his daughters now married and his son in Philadelphia, "Old Pap" no longer found solace at home.

Williams's recompense for his gubernatorial effort was a consular appointment. In July, the Senate had rejected a North Carolinian to the post of minister resident to the nation of Salvador (today, El Salvador). On August 16, Johnson gave Williams a temporary appointment to the post, providing a sinecure. Once the election was settled, the president formally nominated him on December 12, 1866. Accepting the post, perhaps chiefly for the $7,500 annual salary, Williams put his affairs in order, prepared another departure from Detroit and sailed to Central America, where he presented his credentials on January 21, 1867. His nomination was reported out of committee favorably in February, and he was confirmed by the full Senate on March 2.[310]

The position of representing his nation largely involved protecting U.S. trade. Salvador's principal exports were coffee, cotton, indigo, sugar and tobacco. The population of 750,000 was less than that of Michigan, which by 1870 would increase to more than 1 million. The "propensity for strife among Latin American nations" meant the likelihood of contending with political instability. His role would be to avoid entanglements, counsel measures to promote peace and ensure that American interests were protected and advanced. His performance, proving up skills at diplomacy, won plaudits from the Salvadoran government.[311]

In November 1868, voters nationwide went to the polls. Republican Ulysses Grant defeated Democrat Horatio Seymour and was sworn into office on March 4, 1869. On October 27, Williams's nearly three-year mission ended when President Grant's appointee, Brevet Major General Alfred T.A. Torbert, arrived to assume the post. Williams returned home to mourn his granddaughter and to top her grave with a child's marker on which was inscribed "our little Laura." He also found that his home had named a street in his honor. He appears to have resumed the legal profession. Able to participate more in veterans affairs, he became a member

"With the sincere regards of A.S. Williams, Taken at San Salvador, June 30, 1868." *Burton Historical Collection, Detroit Public Library.*

of the Society of the Army of the Cumberland in 1870 and volunteered to be on the local organizing committee for the 1871 reunion in Detroit. As committee chairman, he was privileged to offer a welcome speech to his old comrades. Although Williams was available for another run at the governorship, Democrats chose former Grand Rapids mayor Charles C. Comstock. Incumbent Republican Henry P. Baldwin won reelection.[312]

The election of 1872 again found Williams on the political sidelines. Grant trounced Democrat Horace Greeley, and Republican John J. Bagley won the gubernatorial race by nearly the same margin over former Republican Austin Blair. Instead, Williams was spending time in Salt Lake City on business. Unlike the Democratic platform four years earlier, however, the 1872 document did not lead off with a call to restore southern states "to their rights in the Union." Instead, its first two planks spoke to a new kind of national society that the Civil War had produced:

We recognize the equality of all men before the law, and hold that it is the duty of the Government in its dealings with the people to mete out equal and exact justice to all, of whatever nativity, race, color or persuasion, religion or politics.

We pledge ourselves to maintain the union of these States, emancipation and enfranchisement; and to oppose any reopening of the questions settled by the thirteenth, fourteenth and fifteenth amendments of the Constitution.

Such a shift could pave the way for Union veterans in the Democratic Party to achieve electoral success.[313]

Williams had, by the fall after the election, turned to other campaigning. On September 6, 1873, he married a widow, Martha Conant Tillman. Her first husband, James W. Tillman, was a prominent Detroit furniture dealer and Republican politician, as well as an officer in the Michigan Lancers. He had died prematurely in 1867. She was a patron of the arts and a fellow member of the First Presbyterian Church—perhaps where the two became close. Williams's age was recorded as sixty-three and hers as forty-seven, with his occupation as "Gentleman," on the marriage papers.[314]

Just before the wedding, Williams finished completing an official record of his wartime experiences. In April 1872 and June 1873, the War Department wrote surviving Union generals to request a supplement to its military history from March 1864 on, which had been the end date of an earlier request. Williams prepared a detailed 114-page report, in his own handwriting, and sent it off to Washington in August. Publication of such official wartime records enabled him to quote from—and occasionally challenge—accounts by his peers. He included a commentary on his January 1865 "honor": "a promotion that placed me junior in brevet rank to four fifths of the Brigadier Generals (my juniors) who were then serving in the Army of the Potomac."[315] Setting history straight was important.

Buoyed by these developments, in 1874 Williams again stepped forward as a candidate for office. Relying on his evident local popularity, he ran for the seat in the U.S. House of Representatives from the 1st District in Detroit. In the November 3 election, he emerged victorious, garnering a comfortable majority with 10,848 votes (54.82 percent) and defeating the incumbent Republican, Moses W. Field, who received 8,892 votes (44.94 percent). Where the previous Congress had a solid Republican delegation from Michigan, Williams became one of three Michigan Democrats elected to the 44th Congress.[316] He would take his seat on March 4, 1875. That same year, his commander in the Western Theater published two volumes of personal reminiscences—and in doing so ruffled feathers among former Union army colleagues, including Williams.

In Sherman's *Memoirs* on his life and career, he insisted the writing came from a subjective point of view, without aid, and not from a historian's perspective: "What is now offered is not designed as a history of the war, or even as a complete account of all the incidents in which the writer bore a part, but merely his recollection of events."[317] Not all of his comrades accepted this caveat. Later in 1875, Henry V. Boynton, Washington correspondent of the *Cincinnati Gazette* and future chief historian at the Chickamauga and Chattanooga National Military Park, published an extended critique.[318]

Boynton sought "to show wherein the Memoirs…fall short of presenting the correct history of many great events of which they treat." He pledged "no intention to underrate the great and brilliant services" that Sherman had performed but simply "to correct error and do justice" to the many who had been injured, including "associate generals." One of Boynton's chief beneficiaries was George "Pap" Thomas, who he felt had been demeaned and, having died in 1870, was no longer able to correct the record. He did not address the other "Pap," who was mentioned by Sherman in the second volume on six occasions. Williams did regard himself as among the aggrieved.

That grievance was addressed, though, not through any public vehicle. Rather, Williams apparently capitalized on a request for assistance from Lieutenant Colonel William F. Fox, veteran of the XII and XX Corps, who was compiling the first history of that organization for publication.

Mustering his considerable writing skills, Williams delivered a pointed, detailed yet balanced criticism of Sherman's *Memoirs*. Relying on independent sources of evidence, he demonstrated that the Army of the Cumberland, and the XX Corps particularly, engaged in actions as bloody as the Army of the Tennessee, Sherman's obvious favorite among his commands, which benefited in the *Memoirs* from "palpable" and unnecessary "partiality." Union casualty returns comprised one documentary source; another was Joseph Johnston's *Narrative of Military Operations*, published in 1874. By citing Johnston's versions of events, Williams chronicled the fierce nature of the battles his men had fought and the sometimes superior

"Hon. Alpheus S. Williams of Mich." *Library of Congress.*

Confederate force that fought them. Where Sherman overlooked the XX Corps, or belittled action with a bloodless term like "noisy" (akin to "sound and fury signifying nothing"), Johnston's account told more complete narratives that did justice to his Union opponent's performance.

In his commentary, Williams credited Sherman with a special genius and as, "in many respects, the ablest" army commander. But he felt "virtually stigmatized" by the *Memoirs*, such as by inserting William Ward in his place and then highlighting service by other temporary corps commanders. He was particularly rankled by Sherman's explanation for Mower taking over corps command in April 1865. Sherman said he was "one of the boldest and best fighting generals in the whole army." He expected "a most desperate" final battle with a combined Rebel army under Johnston and Lee. The obvious implication was that Williams had to be replaced for lacking such martial traits. The fact that Mower was of higher rank, Williams complained, should have been enough of a rationale in the book. Instead, the denigration of Mower's predecessor (Mower was also called "rash") was "gratuitously and purposely offensive." Overall, Williams lamented that Sherman had failed to fashion "a grand comprehensive record" on the order of great military histories, like that of Wellington, or that treated with fairness all those who had served under him. Three years later, unaware of Williams's unpublished critique, Sherman spoke of how the Michigander had been "eminently an officer of action."[319]

Williams turned to creating a new record rather than solely safeguarding an old one. The 44th Congress assembled in the Capitol at noon on Monday, December 6, 1875, for its 1st Session. The roll was called, and the first name announced for the Michigan delegation was of Alpheus S. Williams, 1st Congressional District. Soon after came William B. Williams of the 5th Congressional District, presenting an opportunity for confusion as to their respective identities—although they were from different parties. U.S. Grant was at the halfway point of his second and final presidential term. Congressmen John R. Lynch (Mississippi), Robert Smalls (South Carolina), Josiah T. Walls (Florida) and other African American members also answered the roll.[320]

The House of Representatives held a historic session that day. While the Senate remained Republican-controlled, Democrats enjoyed a majority in the lower chamber for the first time since before the Civil War, 182 to 103. They elected the Speaker of the House, Michael C. Kerr of Indiana. Some seats were disputed, but not Williams's. His first recorded roll call vote came in regard to such a dispute. The next day came the drawing for seats by lot, an especially important moment because a member's desk served as his office. Williams took seat 53 East, in the fourth row near the south side of the chamber. He found familiar faces: Nathaniel P. Banks of Massachusetts, James A. Garfield of Ohio, John H. Reagan of Texas, Alexander Stephens of Georgia and Fernando Wood of New York, all prominent Civil War personages. He took up residence in the National Hotel, at Pennsylvania Avenue and 6th Street NW, later moving to the Congressional Hotel. His private secretary was Harry Tillman, his second wife's son.[321]

The Speaker named Williams to the Committee on Military Affairs and to two Select Committees: one "for the Centennial and proposed National Census of 1875" and the second on Texas Frontier Troubles. He was also appointed as a visitor to the U.S. Military Academy and served in 1876, truly an ironic role given his experiences with the school's graduates. Williams offered twenty-eight bills, one resolution and four joint resolutions this session. The House acted favorably on several having a military character, including a private pension bill for a soldier of the 130th Illinois Infantry. It was not the only example of Williams's legislative activity on behalf of the military. After the deaths of George A., Thomas and Boston Custer at Little Bighorn in June, he offered pension bills for the late general's parents, Emanuel and Maria, and for Libby Custer. In the widow's case, he spoke for and helped secure passage during the day of the bill's introduction. For the grieving couple, he invoked the House's sympathy and cited how their welfare could no longer be sustained by "those noble, I may say heroic, sons, who have fallen in the service of their country." Among his measures on civil affairs were to authorize construction of railroad bridges across the Detroit River and for "construction of a light-station on the northern point of Belle Isle, Detroit River." He also introduced a Constitutional amendment to address corruption in the federal government.[322]

The work of the committees also provided opportunity for positive contributions. In *Report No. 1 by the Select Committee on the Centennial*, Williams and colleagues bucked the precedent of the several prior sessions, calling on Congress to support the 1876 commemoration with an appropriation of $1.5 million. He also saw passage of his resolution to permit the use of government tents and equipage by veterans of the Wars of 1812 and with Mexico who would attend the exposition. On the Committee on Military Affairs, his work included examining individual cases in line with his experience in adjusting Missouri claims. Among these was a petition by Marine Corps veteran John News to enter the Soldiers' Home in the nation's capital, a bill for the relief of ex-prisoner of war Samuel Greek and the issue of reimbursing several cavalrymen for the loss of their private property the year before in Texas.[323]

On August 15, 1876, he spoke on the floor in support of a bill to amend the internal revenue laws and, more particularly, vowed to seek amendments on behalf of domestic cigar manufacturers, whose products suffered from unfair foreign competition. Detroit was home to major cigar producers, and his cigar use provided a personal interest. Williams coupled this advocacy with criticism of bureaucratic enforcement of the existing regime:

> *To these unwise provisions has been added by the administrative department of the Government a system of regulations in some instances arbitrary and despotic, the enforcement of which is confided to agents whose actions are not unfrequently controlled by interested motives or governed perhaps by some spasmodic impulse or idea as to the obligations of his official duty.*

His proposed changes would favor "home manufacture," increased domestic employment and more tax revenue to the federal government.[324]

The 2nd Session began after the controversial presidential election of 1876. While Democrat Samuel J. Tilden won the popular vote against Republican Rutherford B. Hayes, disputes over Electoral College returns from multiple states meant neither candidate could be certain of a majority. Convening on December 4, 1876, the 44th Congress—Williams included—found itself embroiled in the greatest national election crisis since 1800. To eliminate partisanship, a bill to create an independent electoral commission was offered. The Senate passed the measure on January 25, 1877, and it came before the House the next day. Inauguration day, March 5, was just over a month away. After debate came the vote and passage by a margin of 191 to 86 (14 not voting)—Williams stood in the affirmative to create and rely on the commission to settle the matter.[325] President Grant signed the bill into law.

The commission process did not match Democratic expectations, for all disputes were resolved in favor of the Republican position. The final electoral tally, therefore, would be 185 to 184 in favor of Hayes. Unless both houses overruled the commission's decision, it would become final and make Hayes the nineteenth president of the United States. Some Democrats sought to overturn the outcome. Williams faced a choice: side with party or sustain the commission and enable a timely inauguration. He had voted for the commission bill in hope that the body would impartially adjudge the popular and electoral vote totals. The partisan outcome left him disappointed. Still, he brooked no partisanship by his side of the aisle. "Shall I stand excused while voting for dilatory motions intended practically to nullify a law of Congress," he asked in remarks on the House floor, "and to place the Government of the Republic in a state of chaotic uncertainty?" He had only one answer:

> *Neither my conscience nor my judgment allows me to be a party to such a fatal measure. I shall therefore continue to vote hereafter as I have done heretofore, against all motions plainly dilatory and intended to obstruct a completion of the presidential count by the commission established by law. I leave it to the people to apply the remedy in future elections.*[326]

A modern-day chief justice of the U.S. Supreme Court judged that "realistic threats of violence" helped persuade Congress to pass the Electoral Commission law, and the outcome may "have saved the nation from…a situation fraught with combustible uncertainty."[327]

The election held one important bright spot for Williams: he had been returned to Congress, the only Michigan Democrat to have success. Although his vote tally increased substantially, his margin had decreased. In the canvass on November 7, 1876, Williams received 14,471 votes (50.53 percent) to 12,417 (43.36 percent) for Republican Henry M. Duffield. The Greenback Party candidate tallied 1,736 votes (6.06 percent); 12 went to the Prohibition Party candidate. Democrats still held the majority in the House of Representatives but by a margin of 155 to 136.[328]

The national platform on which Williams ran in 1876 built on the evolving changes from the previous two. This document had a greater emphasis on the need to eliminate government corruption, a theme lingering after eight years of the Grant administration, and to institute civil service reform. It sought to capitalize on Republican control of the national government during the Panic of 1873 and the ensuing economic slowdown. And it repudiated Republican attempts "to light anew the dying embers of sectional hate between kindred peoples once unnaturally estranged but now reunited in one indivisible republic, and a common destiny." Such tenets harmonized with the Michigan congressman's long-standing views.[329]

Williams took a new position on the House floor for the 1st Session of the 45th Congress. He was in seat 64 East, in the fourth row one aisle off the center. His assignments were the Committee on the District of Columbia, where he became chairman, and an appropriations committee on U.S. Post Office expenditures. Once again, he took quarters at the National Hotel.[330]

In December 1877, Williams found himself in a power struggle on the floor of the House with Benjamin Butler, Republican congressman from Massachusetts and former major general in the Union army. Williams sought expeditious consideration of a bill to prohibit embezzlement in the District of Columbia; Butler objected, asserting that proposed criminal penalties required the bill to be referred to his Judiciary Committee. In a parliamentary maneuver, Williams moved to amend Butler's motion and have the bill referred to his own Committee on the District of Columbia. Butler argued he had not yielded the floor for such a motion. Williams persisted, and the House voted, approving his motion 116 to 45 and referring the bill to his committee.[331]

Based on his activity as reported in the *Congressional Record*, Williams would become more active and more prominent on several significant initiatives as the calendar rolled over to 1878.

In his chairmanship of the District committee, Williams brought measures forward to provide for the public good, and he actively guarded its jurisdiction. In March 1878, he managed for passage a bill authorizing employment of those less fortunate "in the work of filling up, draining, and placing in good sanitary condition the grounds south of the Capitol along the line of the old canal." Such proposals arose on a day set aside for consideration of District business in the House, and Williams was responsible for much of their success or failure. When a member sought to recall an approved bill providing for taxation, apparently on behalf of property owners who objected, Williams resisted. "The people who oppose this bill are those who do not want to pay their taxes," he argued. Using procedural tactics, he supported moving the previous question in order to prevent the switching of votes: "I object to debate." The attempt to undermine the measure went down to defeat.[332]

Williams did not neglect home state advocacy. He supported enlarging the customhouse in Detroit, noting that rental costs for additional space had risen to the point where expanding the federal building would be more economical for the taxpayer.[333]

Two Civil War–related projects gained his support. In April, he introduced a joint resolution to authorize the erection of a statue to George A. Custer. In May, he presented a request on behalf of Gettysburg comrades Doubleday, Hancock, Slocum "and more than sixty other officers in the late war" to support the secretary of war and the army chief of engineers in memorializing the battle. John B. Bachelder had engaged in research and correspondence with participants and had produced graphics portraying the conflict. Williams introduced a resolution praying "that Congress provide in some adequate manner for the publication of the data in question, as well as for additional copies of the maps."[334]

In June, his advocacy extended to the nation's natural resources. He offered an amendment to provide appropriations for Yellowstone National Park in the amount of $810,000. The proposal was immediately opposed, but Williams persisted:

> *Mr. Atkins. I raise the point of order upon that amendment that there is no law authorizing the appropriation.*
>
> *Mr. Williams, of Michigan. There is not only a law authorizing it, but there is also a law which compels the Secretary of the Interior, so far as the law can do so, to protect and preserve this park.*
>
> …
>
> *Mr. Williams, of Michigan. I ask the Clerk to read section 2475 of the Revised Statutes.*
>
> *The Clerk read as follows:…*
>
> *The Chairman. The Chair thinks the law confers authority upon the Secretary of the Interior to have these things done. The Chair has frequently ruled that where authority was conferred to do a thing it was in order to make an appropriation to enable that thing to be done.…The Chair, therefore, rules the amendment in order.*
>
> …
>
> *So the amendment was agreed to.*[335]

The 2nd Session of the 45th Congress adjourned on June 20, 1878. Williams could go home and enjoy the cooler breezes along the Detroit River, rather than continue to suffer the stultifying summer heat along the Potomac. When the 3rd Session opened on December 2, he was back and answered the roll. The occasion, though, was bittersweet.

Williams had been defeated at the polls again. He lost his second reelection attempt in November 1878 largely due to a third-party candidate, John Heffron of the Greenback Party, who pulled 23.78 percent of the vote with a raw total of 5,760. The winner, Republican John S. Newberry, received 9,894 votes, 40.85 percent, to Williams's 8,567 votes, 35.37 percent. Nationally, voters "were not kind to former Union officers." Only three senators had that qualification; seventeen in the upper house were Confederate generals.[336]

Although a lame duck, Williams sought to continue representing the interests of his district and the District of Columbia. He immediately introduced three measures: on water rates within the District, to fix the rate of interest on bonds issued by the commissioners of the District and to grant an invalid pension. On December 11, he presented a request by Captain A.F. Rockwell, assistant army quartermaster, "relating to the improvement of a roadway leading from the Aqueduct Bridge to the Arlington National Cemetery." The next day, he asked approval for printing of a public health report for the District.[337] It was among the final times his name while alive would be noted in the *Record*.

CHAPTER 16

THE FINAL ACT

The House of Representatives convened at noon on Monday, December 2, 1878, and Williams answered the roll. His living quarters were steps away from the Capitol at 106 3rd Street NW, corner of Pennsylvania Avenue. He cast a vote on every record roll call through the eleventh of the month. He introduced a measure on the twelfth but was recorded as not voting during the yeas and nays. On Friday the thirteenth and Saturday the fourteenth, no roll call votes occurred.[338]

The Committee on the District of Columbia met in a hearing room on the third floor of the Capitol, where the committee rooms were located. Williams's committee room was on the West Front, next to the West Grand Staircase. It was a busy spot: members, staff and visitors passed the room on their way to other hearings or to the visitor galleries. Committee rooms served as the office space for the clerks. A long table, chairs, a desk and storage for the committee papers occupied most of the room. Meetings that drew a crowd meant participants had tight quarters.[339]

On Monday, December 16, the committee had scheduled to meet. It was the day specified by House procedure for consideration of business relating to the District of Columbia at 2:00 p.m., and there were measures to be advanced. Just before the appropriate time, Congressman Stephen L. Mayham of New York entered the room and greeted Williams. Mayham later recalled how "it was my privilege to spend the last half-hour of his eventful official life with him in his committee-room in this House." Nothing seemed out of order: "In apparent good health and in excellent

WASHINGTON, D. C.—THE JUDICIARY COMMITTEE OF THE HOUSE OF REPRESENTATIVES RECEIVING A DEPUTATION OF FEMALE SUFFRAGISTS, JANUARY 11TH—A LADY DELEGATE READING HER ARGUMENT IN FAVOR OF WOMAN'S VOTING, ON THE BASIS OF THE FOURTEENTH AND FIFTEENTH CONSTITUTIONAL AMENDMENTS.—See Page 347

1870s illustration of House committee hearing, U.S. Capitol. From *Leslie's Illustrated Newspaper. Collection of the U.S. House of Representatives.*

spirits, he conversed cheerfully and hopefully of passing through this House some measures of legislation matured in the committee in which he felt a lively interest and which he believed would promote the best interest of this District and the country." As the committee convened and began to conduct its business, Williams "was stricken." Obviously suffering a major health crisis, he was carried from the Capitol to his nearby residence. When the House convened at noon, Congressmen Mayham and Eppa Hunton of Virginia spoke to the committee's agenda in his stead.[340]

Several days went by while Williams fought for life. In Detroit, the Saturday, December 21 *Free Press* inserted a small item that indicated "conflicting reports with reference to Gen. Williams were flying around town yesterday." A private telegram announcing his death had caused flags to be lowered to half-mast until a second message reported that he remained alive. The next day's paper, however, gave the accurate conclusion. Under the headline "Death of Representative Alpheus S. Williams," the special dispatch from Washington reported the sorrowful news of his passing at 4:30 a.m. on the twenty-first, expiring in his 3rd Street residence. It listed the funeral details, including a list of pallbearers that would include war colleagues Joseph Knipe and Ezra Carman. General of the Army William T. Sherman and staff would escort the coffin to the Baltimore & Potomac rail station for departure to Toledo. "A feeling of deep sorrow" pervaded the capital city.[341]

The December 22 *Chicago Tribune* published several details under the headline "Gen. Williams, Death of the Michigan Congressman in Washington Yesterday." It reported he had "clung to life with the most remarkable tenacity for a number of days." It also reprinted a Detroit item how "all flags are at half-mast. Personally without an enemy, his political opponents were among the first to express sorrow." His son Larned had come from Philadelphia to be with him. Only a small estate was expected "owing to his free, open-hearted liberality." The *New York Times* of that date filled in more detail on his last days: he "had been sick nearly a week. He became unconscious Thursday noon, since which time little hope has been entertained of recovery, and the long-continued stupor ended yesterday morning with a quiet, painless death, due to effusion of blood upon the brain."[342]

The *Free Press* covered the story on its front page for several days. In the Christmas Day issue, cascading headlines announced "Farewell to the Hero-Statesman, Alpheus S. Williams," "A Spontaneous Outpouring of the People to Do Him Reverence," "Impressive and Touching Farewell Ceremonies" and "A Magnificent Procession Escorts the Remains to the Grave." Services had begun at the Williams residence, 499 Woodward Avenue, led by the pastor of the First Presbyterian Church, followed by the funeral liturgy at St. Paul's Episcopal Church on Woodward between Congress and Larned. An eight-man police detail bore the casket; honorary pallbearers included members of the Congressional delegation, former senator Chandler, ex-governor Baldwin, Charles C. Trowbridge and other distinguished citizens, including James F. Joy. The Detroit Light Guard served as escort. Among the many mourners were Colonels Wilkins and Pittman. Throngs along the route to Elmwood Cemetery attested, despite the intense cold, to the veneration of Detroiters for their fellow citizen. A military delegation from Fort Wayne fired the major general's salute at graveside, a farewell to "the gallant, modest, beloved, and chivalrous" hero.[343]

The *New York Times* also published a Christmas Day story, terming the funeral "the largest and most impressive ever seen" in Detroit, having "the entire community" involved. The "pall was the Union flag." After the interment at Elmwood on the wintry day, the hundreds of citizens "hurried through the deep snow-drifts to their carriages."[344]

The entry book at Elmwood recorded the details: funeral service on Christmas Eve at 4:00 p.m.; the lot and section; cause of death, "apoplexy," likely a stroke; and the name of the deceased, entered as "Gen. A.S. Williams." A massive stone monument would be erected next to his grave.[345]

Of his siblings, only sister Irene remained. Eldest brother Frederic had died in 1849 and Ezra, the business tycoon and legislator, in 1876. Their remains lay in New England. The Elmwood plot that had once seemed so capacious now hosted headstones for its original purchaser, his long-departed wife, two of their children and a grandchild.[346]

On January 7, 1879, Michigan Republican congressman Jay A. Hubbell announced his colleague's death to the U.S. House of Representatives. Per custom, the House adjourned for the day out of respect to his memory (as well as that of a Virginia member). On February 20, the House assembled for an evening session dedicated to memorializing its departed colleague from Michigan. Nathaniel Banks gave one of the testimonials. In addition to remarks by members, a letter from Sherman to Major Farquhar was quoted in which he spoke of their "close and mutual friendship" and of "the love and veneration of his men." Sherman recounted how they often rode together on the march and "was often delighted with [Williams's] cheerful disposition and love of wit." After three hours of tributes, the House adjourned.[347]

A.S. Williams grave monument, Elmwood Cemetery, Detroit. *Author's collection.*

Williams family plot, Elmwood Cemetery, Detroit. *Author's collection.*

The Michigan legislature conducted its own remembrance. On January 9, 1879, the Speaker of the House of Representatives announced that the Senate had passed a concurrent resolution to create a joint committee "to report appropriate resolutions expressive of the sense of both Houses" on the death of Williams. The House acted to concur. On January 29, both met in a joint convention to receive the committee report and to hear tributes. Governor Charles Croswell presided, and the Supreme Court and state officers attended. Also present were members of the bar and those of the Williams Memorial Association. Among the speakers was future U.S. Senator Thomas W. Palmer, who relayed a story conveyed to him by an aide of George H. Thomas. Once, when his subordinate commanders were bickering, the other "Old Pap" said, "[T]here is at least one man I can rely upon as reliable under all contingencies, and that is that solid old fighter General Williams." Mayor George C. Langdon of Detroit spoke. Wounded in the war, veteran William W. Duffield emphasized that "Williams' brilliant record as a soldier has somewhat obscured his great reputation as a civilian."[348]

The Memorial Association came into existence formally on February 25, 1879. Its purpose was to erect in Detroit "a monument or statue, which shall serve as a reminder to those who survive him and those who succeed him, of the gratitude and love of his fellow-citizens." Langdon was chair; others on the executive committee included James W. Romeyn, future U.S. Senator James McMillan and Samuel E. Pittman—"Pitt," as Williams had fondly called him. The late January day in Lansing served as an auspicious commencement to their work. Yet only Pittman of this roster would live to see its fruition. An early indication of the project's difficulty developed later that year. Congress had before it a joint resolution, H.R. 50, to donate condemned cannon to the association for purposes of adorning the Detroit monument. The measure did not emerge from committee.[349]

CHAPTER 17

REMEMBRANCE

I n 1880, less than two years after Williams's death, the U.S. War Department began publishing *The War of the Rebellion: A Compilation of the Official Records of the Union and Confederate Armies*. Containing reports, correspondence, tables and illustrations, the many thousand pages of the *Official Records* told the story of the Civil War as recorded by its participants. The collection would take decades to complete; when finished, it contained numerous references to and writings by Williams. Truth be told, though, his record began to unfold as part of the greater story from the pen of eyewitnesses promptly after the last shot. Almost universally, the publications were substantively positive.

One of Sherman's aides published an account of the "Grand March" from Atlanta through the Carolinas under an 1865 copyright. The book included assessments of other generals, including Williams. His appearance came in for comment as off-putting: he was described as unimpressive, of medium height and "heavily built," having "a large beard and still larger mustache." But his mien would win observers over "when the genial, kindly eyes light up in conversation." Williams's "singular" war experience as a frequent but always temporary corps commander deserved better:

> *This shifting and changing is part of the fortunes of war, and not the fault of Williams, for it is universally conceded that he is one of the best officers of the service. He has been in many trying positions, and no charge of blunder or failure lies at his door. A favorite with officers and men, he*

is delightfully hospitable, possesses an unfailing fund of good humor, is thoroughly subordinate, unenvious, unselfish, and as cool and self-possessed in the battle-field as at his quarters.[350]

The accounts of Williams typically arose, however, from regimental retrospectives written by those of lower rank. The very first, perhaps, was the history of the 2nd Massachusetts Infantry, the regiment of Robert Gould Shaw before he transferred to the 54th Massachusetts (Colored) Infantry. The 2nd's regimental historian, a chaplain, made this assessment of its divisional leader:

For three years the Second was in his command, and he kept their respect. Brave, cool, genial, experienced in Mexico, he was a favorite. If not, he would never have got the pet title of "Papa,"—shortened by and by into "Pap." When the men, in after years, used to say "Here comes 'Pap,'" they felt that matters would go on right.

The chaplain wrote that Williams had exercised corps command both "bravely and wisely."[351]

Another veteran of that regiment echoed this assessment. Henry N. Comey rose from private to captain and served through the entire war. His copious writings were not published until 2004, but as a contemporary record of people and events they bear unaffected authenticity. Comey served under Williams from October 1861 until mustering out. In a letter home in August 1864, he wrote that "Williams is recommended for Major General, which is as it should be." He was "an excellent officer" who had become "a great military leader."[352]

In 1871, another regimental history spoke of Williams's popularity among the men in the ranks. His elevation to division command in June 1862 received approval from his soldiers: "He was familiarly known as 'Old Pap,' and in truth he was a fatherly old man;—one who never rose to great height or fame, but who filled his position well, and always retained the esteem and confidence of his men."[353]

Ten years after Gettysburg, battlefield historian John Bachelder published a guidebook for visitors to the hallowed ground. Unlike Meade's report or the Congressional resolution, Williams received mention and favorably. The guide recorded how Williams immediately sought to attack the Confederate left flank on July 1. It discussed how he had gone to the aid of the Union center on July 2. And it gave a full portrayal of the events early on July 3 in the recovery of Culp's Hill by the XII Corps, acknowledging that "General Williams commanded the corps."[354]

A different kind of remembrance was reflected in a Detroit news item in 1879. Angell's gallery was featuring an exhibition of a "bust portrait" of Williams completed by artist Samuel Conkey. Though missing the "familiar eye-glasses," the sculpture drew admiration from "all who knew and loved the grand old man."[355]

George H. Gordon published three volumes of his war reminiscences, beginning in 1882, that contributed colorful, and less than flattering, vignettes on Williams. Besides the incident when Williams had to be awakened in his night wear in the Winchester hotel, another came after Antietam while the 1st Division encamped at Maryland Heights. Gordon described special treatment of the commander: three log houses had been constructed at Williams's order: "one for an office, one for a mess-room and one for himself and his daughters who were visiting him."[356]

Williams's war service next received mention, not completely flattering, when *The Century* magazine published a compendium of articles in the mid-1880s. In Jacob Cox's article on Antietam, the IX Corps general noted how command had passed to Williams, who "had only time to take the most general directions from Hooker, when the latter also was wounded." Those familiar with the events on the right wing that frightful morning could have deduced that the corps, under Williams's emergency elevation, had performed ably. Such an inference was contradicted by a Cox comment that Williams fought "a losing battle at all points but one," that being where Greene's division reached the Dunker church.[357] In the same volume, the editors published, in smaller type, a letter by General Silas Colgrove on "The Finding of Lee's Lost Order." Containing several errors of recollection, the piece gave complete credit to Pittman and none to Williams for seeing the value in the document.

Accounts of Gettysburg in *Battles and Leaders* drew Williams into view next. An article by John Gibbon, previously appearing in the *Philadelphia Weekly Press*, recounted the council of war late on July 2. Gibbon wrote that he and Hancock "doubly represented" the II Corps, as did Slocum and Williams the XII, unaware (or forgetful) of the wing organization that Meade had ordered. Relying on the Butterfield minutes, however, the article quoted how Williams voted to "stay" rather than retreat and that the next two generals followed with votes "same as Williams."[358] The XII Corps commander also came in for notice in an item on the right flank engagements during July 2–3. Slocum, however, was given credit for discerning the danger of sending all of the corps to support the center.[359] A laudatory article about Meade's performance served as frame for "The Meade-Sickles Controversy," largely a republishing of opposing communiqués by the principals as to the second day's affair at the Peach Orchard. Sickles's defense cited how Meade invited disputes with other corps commanders; he noted how Slocum had "arraigned [Meade] for a series of inaccuracies, to use the mildest phrase," and how Williams had sought to correct "four serious misstatements" in Meade's official report.[360]

In 1886, the posthumous memoirs of George B. McClellan appeared. The discussion of Williams's actions at Antietam contained a hint of that heroic performance: McClellan wrote how the command of the XII Corps "fell upon Gen. Williams" and how he "took command of the corps." No order from headquarters was cited; implicit was that in the maelstrom of combat and at a crucial moment in the morning's action, a volunteer brigadier general with no West Point training had taken it on himself to assume and exercise leadership competently, aggressively and at personal risk. The memoirs did refer to the unit then as "Gen. Williams's corps," as it was.[361] It would have taken a shrewd reader, though, to discern the implicit commendation.

In 1889, Michigan veterans came to Gettysburg to dedicate several monuments to Michigan units funded and erected by the state. In a companion publication appeared the address of General Luther S. Trowbridge of Detroit. Trowbridge criticized the popular fascination with Pickett's Charge to the detriment of other notable events, and he singled out one that had not yet received the attention it so "justly deserved." The XII Corps had been weakened on July 2 by having to send aid to the Union center. The effect on the army's fortunes could have been disastrous:

> *The enemy had succeeded in forcing his way, against most heroic resistance, to the Baltimore Turnpike, and thus secured a position practically in rear of the Army of the Potomac, and full of threatening danger. It is impossible to over-estimate the possibilities of disaster had he been able to hold that position until Pickett made his charge. From that position he was driven by the returning troops of the Twelfth Corps, on the morning of the 3d, after a fight beginning about daylight and lasting several hours.*

Credit went to those troops, but also to a Michigander:

> *The Twelfth Corps was not composed of Michigan troops, but it was commanded by a Michigan man, one of the most worthy and distinguished*

soldiers produced by any State. It was through his skillful and brilliant generalship that that most important result was gained. A most accomplished soldier, a genial, courteous and courtly gentleman, a citizen whose patriotism was unmarred by the slightest appearance of self-seeking, he filled the full measure of our ideal as a patriotic soldier. All honor to the brave, genial, unselfish General Alpheus S. Williams.[362]

On the twenty-fifth anniversary of the Battle of Chancellorsville, Samuel Pittman delivered remarks on Williams's role to a service organization full of combat veterans who likely would brook no nonsense. Pittman complained that all accounts published in the previous quarter century overlooked the contributions of the Red Star Division. It had been in the vanguard in stealing a march on Lee, coming on in his rear and, but for Hooker's change of plans, part of a great victory. Then, after the debacle on the Union right, Williams had led his men in arresting Jackson's flank attack and saving the army.[363]

Regimental histories continued to be published over the years, and that of the 28th New York Infantry in 1896 contained two fond remembrances of Williams. In one incident from May 1862, during Williams's temporary absence, a commanding officer adjured, "Let us give three cheers for Old Alf Williams, one of the best men the world ever saw." The "enthusiastic response indicated that the men agreed most heartily with the colonel's opinion of the Brigadier-General." Williams had merited "the unlimited confidence and love" of both rank and file and officers. In remembering how he often assumed corps command, it was a "position he always filled with distinction and ability."[364]

The work also contained an extensive remembrance entitled *In Memory of Dear Old "Pap Williams."* William F. Goodhue of the 3rd Wisconsin Infantry waxed poetic on its "brave old" and "devoted leader…of blessed memory":

> *Although I haven't seen the old general for thirty-one years, yet with memory's eye I see him to-day as plainly as ever.…His was a Cromwellian figure, sitting his horse like a centaur, sturdy, strong and imperturbable under all the circumstances of bloody warfare; his strong, kindly face and grizzled beard indicated the stanch and rugged nature of the man, while beneath his black slouched hat gleamed in the southern sun the glasses he constantly wore, scintillating like the jeweled eyes of a war god when giving to the warriors of the nation the inspiration of battle and holding firmly in his teeth the never-lighted stub of a cigar.*

Old "Pap" was ever at the front, Goodhue recounted, "and there he stayed" until the field was won. There was "not a drum beat in the Red Star Division that he didn't hear and was the first to answer its call." Recalling the only other general to merit that "affectionate sobriquet," George Thomas, Goodhue attested that "both were beloved by the troops they led through the war." For Williams, the years had not diminished "the abiding faith, the deep and hearty love and respect we then had and now have."[365]

Just before the century ended, the history of the "Lost Order" regiment appeared. The author promised that Williams's name "will appear again and again in this narrative." The relationship of division commander and men had begun immediately and endured: "From the start we had reason to respect him for his evident abilities and personal worth. Before the end we learned to venerate and love him, both as a great soldier and a great-hearted gentleman." After their transfer to the Western Theater, the 27th Indiana endured scorn from the veterans of Shiloh and Vicksburg. Williams looked for the right moment to prove that the disdain was unmerited; Resaca became that opportunity:

> *Old "Pap" Williams…was a Western man himself, at least by adoption, and was in full sympathy with Western people and their ways. But he could not resist the temptation to even up with men when he had such a good opportunity. As the men of the line that had been broken came tumbling back, and officers appealed to him with much warmth to come to their assistance, he said, "Yes, yes, get your men out of the way. I have some soldiers here (barely a slight emphasis on the word soldiers) from the Army of the Potomac, who can take care of these rebels."*[366]

After the turn of the century, a lieutenant colonel in the 107th New York Volunteer Infantry published *A History of the Twelfth and Twentieth Army Corps.* The study was bundled by the New York State Monuments Commission into a memorial volume on Slocum for the dedication of his statue at Gettysburg in 1904. A reader would find an extensive commentary on how Sherman supplanted Williams with Mower on the eve of Johnston's surrender:

> *It is difficult to reconcile this treatment of General Williams with any sense of fairness, honesty, or justice. He was not a graduate of West Point, but he had served with honor in the Mexican war. He had commanded the Twentieth Corps during a portion of the Atlanta campaign, and subsequently from Atlanta to Goldsborough. He commanded the Twelfth*

Corps with signal ability at Antietam and Gettysburg. As a brigadier general he outranked every officer in that army, and his commission as brigadier bore even date with that of Sherman himself. He commanded the famous "Red Star" Division in the Shenandoah Valley, in the spring of 1862, and had been at its head throughout the entire war, except when in command of the corps. He had never missed a battle or been absent from the army on any campaign; and on every battlefield where his troops were engaged he had displayed marked ability and achieved a marked success. Through all his long and brilliant service not an error or mistake had ever been laid to his charge; and now when the war was drawing to its close he was deprived of his command, and his place given to a favorite.

As for Sherman's *Memoirs*, the author regarded its "explanation worse than none." At war's end, Williams was one of two officers in the Union army who deserved promotion to major general more than any others.[367]

One of the most colorful portrayals of Williams came in a 1902 retrospective by a New York soldier. Charles E. Benton wrote of how "the boys affectionately" called him "old Pop," a "most efficient officer" who deserved to be major general. He did not usually betray his emotions, but the men had broken the code on his plans: they only needed to watch "the cigar which was carried in his mouth most of the time":

Was it lighted and emitting a cheerful cloud of smoke? All would be quiet for the day. Had it been allowed to go out, while the end was being violently chewed? The plans were maturing and some new movement was on foot. But when it was frequently shifted from side to side in his mouth and kept rolling over and over between the lips, "like a log in the peeler," as the paper-pulp man said, then there would surely be a fight before dark.[368]

On Memorial Day 1902, the leadership and citizens of Detroit commemorated the four decades since the Civil War in a significant ceremony. Chief speaker was Samuel W. Burroughs, a veteran and lawyer who had served as prosecuting attorney for Wayne County. At the conclusion of his remarks, he singled out Williams, reviewed his career and called for "erecting to his memory an equestrian monument and statue equal to that of Gen. Logan at Chicago."[369] The Williams Memorial Association effort had so far failed to achieve its task.

On February 6, 1910, the *Detroit Free Press* called its readers' attention to a centenary that would arrive later in the year. A gallant Michigan soldier deserved a "suitable memorial," it editorialized, equally for his heroic service in two wars as for his many contributions to civic affairs in his hometown. To know him was to admire him, "than whom there was no more daring, resourceful and effective commander in the field during the civil war." The 100th anniversary of Alpheus Williams's birthday in September marked a call to action.[370]

On June 4 of that year, a large crowd helped unveil an equestrian monument to George A. Custer in his hometown of Monroe, Michigan. President William H. Taft and Custer's widow, Libbie, were on hand. The ceremony drew veterans of the Michigan Cavalry Brigade, one of whom wrote a letter to the *Free Press* soon after. Of the "others of Michigan's sons" who deserved similar commemoration, one name stood out: "that grand old commander, Gen. Alpheus S. Williams, than whom a better soldier, a more patriotic man, a more capable officer, a truer gentleman, was not sent to the Civil War field by any state." The writer had confidence that Detroit in 1910 possessed the resources and civic spirit sufficient to "erect a truly grand monument to the commander of its military forces before the Civil War and altogether its most distinguished military representative in that war." The *Free Press* echoed the call in an editorial.[371]

Early the next year, a series of biographical articles on Williams authored by Detroit journalist Joseph Greusel appeared in the *Free Press*. They were compiled into a twenty-nine-page sketch in support of the monument campaign. Aside from the legislative memorials of 1879–80, the slender volume was the first full, albeit brief, recounting of Williams's life and Civil War career to be published.[372]

Greusel wrote of how the reports by superiors in the *Official Records* "make it plain that Williams never failed them, whether in charge of a division or an army corps." He saved Banks at Cedar Mountain; he grasped the importance of the Lost Order and forwarded it "without delay" to McClellan; he held back Stonewall Jackson at Chancellorsville; and for three days at Gettysburg he held the right flank "against superhuman efforts to penetrate from front and rear, made by day and night." Williams had "forced his way steadily upward by his mere soldier-like qualities to the rank of division and of corps commander…neither given himself to talking, nor much talked about, but was sought for whenever work was to be done. He made himself respected and valued accordingly by the great generals under whom he served." The people of Michigan ought to preserve "the glorious memory of Williams."[373]

By May 1911, a renewed effort was underway to erect a monument. A new association had been formed, and word was that "the monument movement will be vigorously pushed." Pittman served as chairman and speaker at a Central High School event to give "substantial impetus" to the project. He expressed renewed hope that the effort would "go on to a glorious consummation."[374]

Insufficient finances underlay the lack of prior success. The state did not come through in the 1880s, and support in the 1900s was directed to the Custer statue. In 1906, the Michigan chapter of the National Society of Colonial Dames of America had provided some funds. Contributions came in from children as well; the Detroit Board of Education authorized a veterans group to take up a collection in the schools, endorsing the idea that "the nickel of the school boy is as valuable as the dollars of the millionaire." These activities provided the springboard for others to become generous. In 1915, it was reported that the Michigan Commandery of the Loyal Legion had raised $30,000 and the City of Detroit had appropriated $10,000. Sufficient funding finally enabled taking a real step forward.[375]

The American Federation of Arts announced during the winter of 1911–12 that sculptor Henry Merwin Shrady had been chosen for the Williams monument project. Shrady was something of a phenom, having become prominent for winning the national competitions in 1901 and 1902 to design and cast equestrian statues of Washington and Grant. The monument to the Father of the Country was a simple horse and rider, to be erected at the Brooklyn entrance to the Williamsburg Bridge for $50,000. It was unveiled to great acclaim in 1906. The Grant project was enormous. It had a Congressional appropriation of $250,000, to be known as the Appomattox Memorial Monument to General Ulysses S. Grant, and the site was Union Square at the foot of the west side of the Capitol. In 1917, Shrady would receive the commission for a statue of R.E. Lee in Charlottesville, Virginia.[376]

The choice of architect for the Williams equestrian statue owed much to Michigander Charles Moore. As secretary to Senator McMillan, Moore had participated in Congressional efforts to redesign the National Mall. He was appointed in 1910 to the Commission of Fine Arts, serving with Daniel Burnham, Frederick Law Olmsted and Daniel Chester French to improve design in the nation's capital. Moore became director of the Detroit Museum of Art in 1914; in that capacity, he would oversee financial and artistic administration for the statue. Three years earlier had been this encounter:

I first saw Henry Merwin Shrady one morning at the Century Club, where he came to meet me.

"Why did you send for me?" he asked apprehensively. "Do you want to blow me up for my delay on the Grant statue?" "No," I answered, "I

want to offer you a commission to design for Detroit an equestrian statue of General Alpheus S. Williams." Astounded, Shrady exclaimed: "Good! Who was Alpheus S. Williams?"[377]

In 1921, a year before completion of the Lincoln Memorial on the Mall in Washington, the Williams monument was unveiled before a large crowd on Belle Isle in the Detroit River. Shrady had composed the statue with the rider looking downward at a map, an atypically unheroic pose suggesting of a soldiers' officer rather than one aloof. He wears an overcoat; the weather must be inclement. He has let the reins loose, evincing confidence in his horse's steadiness. The horse, popularly thought to be "Plug Ugly," is nearly identical to the mount featured in Shrady's statue of Washington. An aged and infirm Samuel Pittman, in one of his last acts, observed the ceremony from a motor car. He no doubt felt immense gratification for the special honor finally paid his good friend. Equestrian statues are the exception in monumentation; Michigan has but the two for the Civil War, and "of the millions of men who served the Union cause during the Civil War, just thirty

Williams equestrian statue, Belle Isle. *Author's collection.*

Williams statue detail. *Author's collection.*

have had their service commemorated with such a memorial." The sculpture gained approval from the family.[378]

The monument gained attention for Williams in Detroit, for a time. None of the works or references from 1865 until the eve of the Civil War Centennial, however, gained much notice for Michigan's most prominent citizen-general. Popular histories by Bruce Catton and Allan Nevins told of other more storied figures. In 1959 appeared the first collection of Williams's writings in print when Wayne State University Press published a four-hundred-page hardback edition of his wartime letters. The book gained kudos for its readability: "Williams possessed an unconscious literary flair that gives simple style and force to his letters; he also possessed eyes and a mind of his own, which sometimes led him to dispute the official records." Tragically, Dr. Milo M. Quaife, editor of the volume and author of its short biography, died in an automobile accident that September, leaving the book without its principal spokesperson.[379]

A quarter century later, a PhD candidate at Michigan State University submitted his dissertation entitled "Neglected Honor." Jeffrey G. Charnley's three-hundred-page typescript comprised the first complete biography of Williams in the century since his death. Charnley lauded his subject's military talents: "In the field and in battle, few Union generals exceeded the scope of his service. As a division and corps chief, he developed a record of exemplary service and constant improvement as a fighting leader, a soldier's general." Williams's lack of promotion lay with superiors who "either failed to notice his efforts or did not act to get him promoted." Historians had overlooked his importance, for he had "contributed significantly to the Northern war effort." As "Michigan's foremost citizen soldier," Williams's "life was one of neglected honor." The dissertation became part of the same legacy—it remains unpublished.[380]

Charnley authored a shorter piece that appeared in print in 1986. In the lead article of the scholarly *Michigan Historical Review*, Charnley partially revised his thesis. The Williams story had not received appropriate treatment because of "bad luck, political partisanship, a repetition of errors in interpretation and fact, and a lack of thoroughness in research." Professor Charnley concluded that Williams "deserves to rank as one of the best volunteer generals in the Civil War."[381]

In 1992, *Civil War*, the magazine of the Civil War Society, published an article on Williams in its July/August issue. Written by freelancer Greg Forster, the article was entitled "'Old Pap' Takes Care of Business" in the table of contents and "Alpheus Williams—'Old Pap'" in the text. Beginning with his efforts at Chancellorsville, the article maintained that "it was not the first or last time that General Williams would save the day for the Union." At Antietam, his corps performed admirably; at Chancellorsville he fought Jackson's flank attack to a standstill and then "adroitly managed his troops" against Jeb Stuart; and at Gettysburg, his performance was "superb." In the Western Theater, his leadership in vicious battles, often spearheading Sherman's advance, was overlooked by superiors and reporters. A "tough, aggressive officer," his service went unrewarded as a "victim of the press, of politics and his own unyielding personality."[382]

Three decades after the initial publication of *From the Cannon's Mouth*, the University of Nebraska Press issued a reprint under the same title. Added to the paperback was a new introduction by noted Civil War historian Dr. Gary W. Gallagher. Describing its subject's Civil War record as "admirable" and the man as "unquestionably a hard fighter" and nonprofessional soldier "who demonstrated aptitude for command during the Civil War," Gallagher nonetheless adjudged Williams as one who "often seemed satisfied merely to avoid decisive defeats and habitually urged caution." This attitude changed, he wrote, when Williams transferred to the Western Theater; thereafter, "his letters betray little of the excessive caution" of those in 1862–63. The continuing conflict transformed him from an opponent into an advocate of hard war. Williams's assessments of fellow officers drew praise for including "biting criticism and a touch of humor." Lack of promotion suggested that Williams's "notions about West Point favoritism may have been well founded." Gallagher considered Williams to have become a "reluctant convert" who held a "lukewarm attitude toward emancipation." As for the 1959 book, Gallagher termed it "a classic title" justifiably quoted "innumerable times" since first appearing.[383] In a later article, he encouraged readers to savor the volume for more than the history: "[T]hey will also discover that Williams, who seemed incapable of dull writing, invariably holds their attention."[384]

Civil War scholar Albert Castel added his perspective to the Williams canon in 1998. His "'Old Pap': Michigan's Top Civil War General" compared Williams with Custer, opining that the infantry general was the greater of the two since Williams "held higher commands and contributed far more to Northern victory than did Custer and…was superior to Custer in every military talent except the ability to publicize himself and secure promotion." Castel extolled Williams's military talents regardless of formal training, for he "displayed in his first full-fledged battle [Winchester] good judgment and coolness under fire." At Cedar Mountain "Williams showed that his skill on the battlefield matched his courage." Castel gave him credit for his role with the Lost Order and wrote, "Williams believed, and rightly so, that he had earned a major general's commission at Antietam." At Chancellorsville and Gettysburg, he "performed superbly, preventing an even greater Union defeat in the first and clinching a Northern victory in the second." After the latter battle, "no general in the Army of the Potomac not already possessing that rank deserved a major general's commission more than Williams." He performed equally well in the West, which culminated in having "saved Sherman at Bentonville from an embarrassing defeat." Castel summarized: "Without doubt Williams was a superior division commander and excellent corps commander and was capable by 1863 of being a successful army commander." Williams's writings also had high merit: "[F]rom a literary and historical standpoint, they are among the finest, if not the finest, letters written by any Civil War general."[385]

Nearly a century after its deposit in the Library of Congress in 1912, Ezra Carman's exhaustive study of the Antietam campaign came out in print. The work contains numerous passages about Williams and a pithy summary of the XII Corps performance under his leadership on September 17, 1862:

The whole corps, excepting the five new regiments, had been in continuous daily marches, and there was neither time nor opportunity to restore the spirit and vigor of the command. And yet, under all these adverse circumstances, this corps—as we shall see—repulsed the Confederates who were exultantly driving Hooker from the field, drove them out of the East Woods, back over the open fields and beyond the Hagerstown Road, and held these fields all day without yielding an inch of ground gained (except the woods it had seized around the Dunkard church).[386]

The years of the Civil War Sesquicentennial included three works with more than passing references to Williams.

In 2013–15, Mercer University published a detailed two-volume study of the beginning of the Atlanta Campaign, the product of twenty years of research and analysis by author/attorney Robert D. Jenkins Sr. It had a lot to say about Williams: "Perhaps the most unheralded, but successful general in all of the entire Federal armies," began the description. Williams "was tenacious, competent, and proved quite adept at responding to unexpected challenges throughout the war." His first success came at Cedar Mountain when his troops battered, drove and caused the Stonewall Brigade to break. Next came Antietam, when Williams "led a corps and drove Hood's Texans out of the East Woods and Miller cornfield." At Chancellorsville, "Williams's efforts helped to save General Hooker and the Army of the Potomac from annihilation." He had performed a key role at Gettysburg. Early in Georgia, his men "had fought well at Resaca, New Hope, and Kolb's Farm." In the Battle of Peach Tree Creek, "the beginning of the end for the Confederacy," Williams "would be called upon again to help stave off disaster." Jenkins ascribed Williams's lack of promotion to being "neither a Republican nor a West Pointer."[387]

In 2016, Professor John H. Matsui, Virginia Military Institute, published *The First Republican Army* on John Pope and the Army of Virginia. His thesis was that Pope's army served as a primary force that "pushed the Lincoln administration to destroy the Confederacy's armies, punish its civilians, and free its slaves," serving as "vanguard of the pro-emancipation and punitive turn of the overall Union war effort." This culture became possible by a growing preponderance in the army of generals who had not graduated from West Point. These leaders did not hold conservative views such as respecting Southerners' property, scorning Lincoln administration policies or favoring return to the antebellum status quo. The book did not identify Williams as an antislavery general, but it did not list him as among those cautious leaders who sought a limited conflict focused only on restoration of the Union. Thus, Williams did not fit the Army of the Potomac mold. Instead, Williams came in for praise as one of the Army of Virginia's three (of eight) competent generals who "demonstrated inspired leadership." The book also cited Williams for his criticisms of uncoordinated strategy and of Southern society and industry. Though he was not a Republican, the behavior that Williams exhibited was not conservative or merely political. Unlike Sickles at Gettysburg, whose infamous conduct "jeopardized the entire army," Williams "battled to hold the right wing" there and helped save the war for the Union.[388]

In 2017, an eight-hundred-page study of the Army of the Potomac by Civil War historian Stephen W. Sears appeared in retail outlets nationwide. The book's references to Williams were numerous and positive. He was prescient as to Stonewall Jackson's 1862 Shenandoah Valley Campaign, and it was his "command promise" that helped Banks's force survive "the Valley debacle." At Cedar Mountain, his division made the greatest gains and almost won an unlikely victory. Replacing Mansfield at Antietam, Williams led the XII Corps "to the most battlefield gains of anyone that day." Despite his contributions there and at Gettysburg, Sears recounted, and "despite his solid fighting history, citizen-soldier Alpheus S. Williams would never hold more than temporary command of the Twelfth Corps." Without the West Point credential, he would always carry the stigma of merely an amateur warrior.[389]

In the fall of 2013, the State of Michigan and Detroit authorities entered into a thirty-year lease to convert Belle Isle into a state park. Earlier in the year, the city had declared bankruptcy, and the park had become the subject of reporting on its deteriorating condition. The Michigan Department of Natural Resources, as the implementing agency, set to work on remediation. "Rich with history and natural beauty" hails a Michigan.org website, and the island's cultural resources are listed in a 2018 draft management plan that sought to build a case for improvements. On the list of resources is the "General Williams Equestrian Memorial."

Works on the Civil War will continue to emerge (witness this one). Attempting to survey and report on any mention of Williams in the hundreds of thousands of such publications, no matter how brief, would be herculean. As to all encountered in this effort,[390] very few suggest that Williams received anything like the honor he deserved.

Nearly 140 years after Williams's death, he featured prominently in the Summer 2018 issue of *Military Images* magazine. Featuring a number of

Above: Williams statue, rider and mount. *Author's collection.*

Right: Brigadier General A.S. Williams wearing Red Star Division Officer's Hardee (Dress) hat. *Library of Congress.*

privately held *carte de visite* images of its subject, the complimentary article decried "the neglected legacy" of a general officer who missed promotion because of his modesty, age and lack of West Point background. Quoting its subject's observation that unwritten history will be set right someday, the piece concluded, "Perhaps the time has come to do just that."[391]

EPITAPH

T wo monuments mark remembrance of "Old Pap" Williams in the city he spent four decades earnestly serving.

One is found in Historic Elmwood Cemetery: a distinctive stone monolith, bearing his name, dwarfs simple gravestones nearby where he, his beloved Jane and his many other loved ones are buried. The pathos of the Williams story is palpable. Inscriptions tell of premature deaths, of separations, of heartbreak. The monolith bears simple elements of military service, as do other markers close by, reminding the visitor that here lies a family who made great sacrifices for the people they cherished. One may kneel here, touch fingers to the chiseled words and dates and then stand in hushed reverence.

The other is on Belle Isle, an equestrian statue that looms ever taller as one approaches. Inscriptions mark the stone base, briefing on Williams's civic and military careers and those responsible for finally erecting this memorial. "An untiring servant of the people," so it says, although some who raise their eyes to the man on horseback see fatigue in the form. An expressionless face studies an unfolded map held with the right gloved hand, while the left clasps the reins and rests gently on the horse's neck. The collar of the greatcoat is pulled up, and the brim of the hat is pulled down; it is a cold day, or perhaps hostile weather is imminent. Regardless, there is an imperturbability conveyed by the work—no bravado, only the strength of a veteran leader who knows what he must be about.

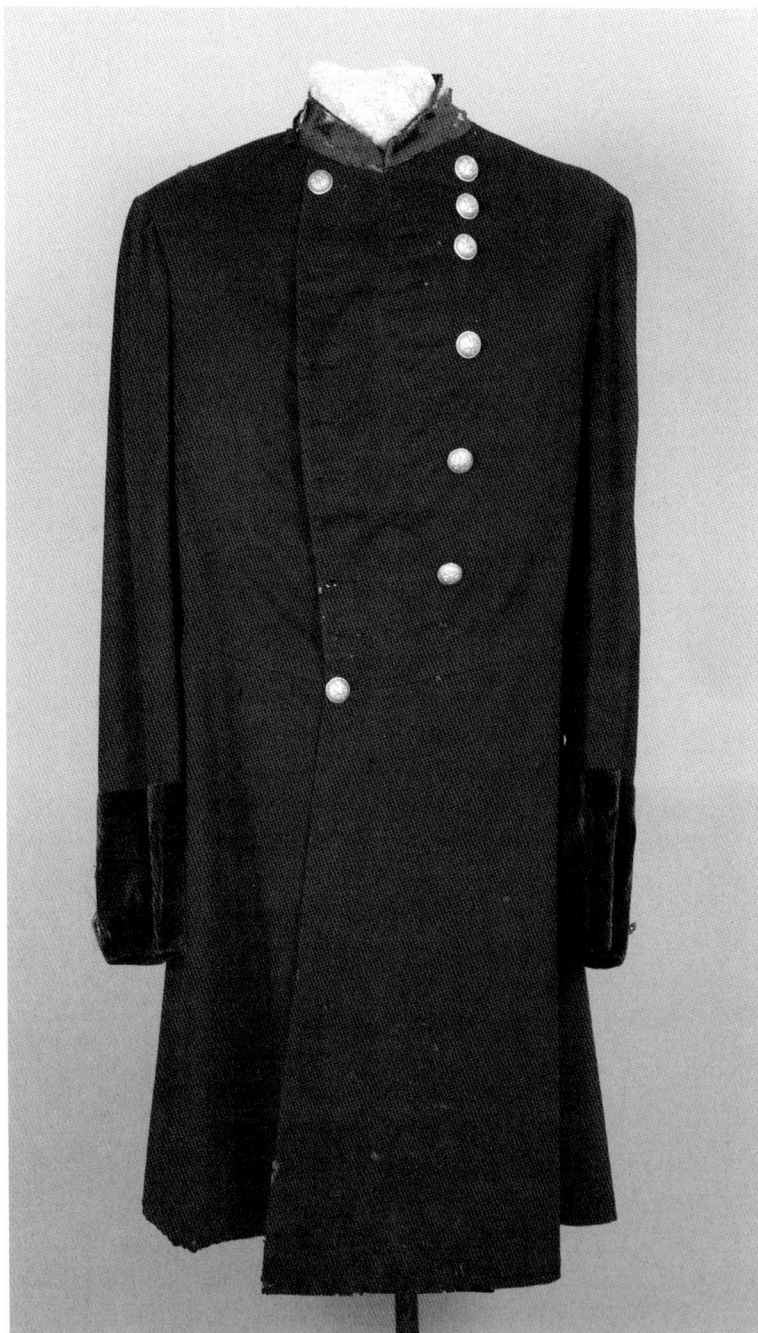

General "Pap" Williams's uniform coat, front view. *Detroit Historical Society.*

Uniform coat, rear view. *Detroit Historical Society.*

The visitor finds no trace of self-promotion at either site. This is, after all, the fatherly figure who eschewed "small fame at the expense of the great purpose we have in hand." At stake was "the freedom of mankind"; so, he carried on, despite dangers and affronts, because to do otherwise "would entail dishonor and disaster upon our posterity for many generations."

Those who read this volume are among those heirs, beneficiaries in that posterity. To them, these monuments invoke the same duty bequeathed to each succeeding generation, the same opportunity—to comprehend and to remember:

> *When this people forget or cease to recognize those grand achievements which determined the very existence of our free institutions, deathful apathy or fatal ingratitude will have so chilled the great heart of this Republic that freedom will find no champions, and national honor no brave defenders.*[392]

APPENDIX A

OFFICIAL REPORTS AND
RECORDS OF EVENTS[393]

March 5, 1862, Skirmish at Bunker Hill, Virginia—V, 517–18

March 7, 1862, Skirmish near Winchester, Virginia—V, 520–22

March 20, 1862 ff., "Abstract from 'Record of Events' in Williams' Division"—XII, pt. I, 378

May 27, 1862, Operations in Shenandoah Valley—XII, pt. I, 593–99

August 16, 1862, Cedar Mountain—XII, pt. II, 145–49

September 29, 1862, Antietam Campaign—XIX, pt. I, 474–81

May 15, 1863, Chancellorsville Campaign—XXV, pt. I, 676–84

August 22, 1863, Reports of Gettysburg Campaign—XXVII, pt. I, 770–72 [Division], 772–77 [Corps (three)]

January–March 1864, "Itineraries of 1st Division," XII and XX Corps—XXXII, pt. I, 26–29, 32

September 20, 1864, Reports of Atlanta Campaign—XXXVIII, pt. II, 17–19 [Corps], 26–37 [Division]

January 9, 1865, March to Sea (Part 1: Operations around Atlanta)—XXXIX, pt. I, 649–50

January 9, 1865, March to Sea (Part 2: Continuation of Savannah Campaign)—XLIV, 206–16

March 31 and May 27, 1865, Reports of Campaign of the Carolinas—XLVII, pt. I, 581–96 [Corps], 603–7 [Division]

January 20, 1865, "Memoirs upon the March" and "Report of Movement of Trains" from Atlanta to Savannah—Series 3, V, 398–402

CHART OF RELEVANT CORPS COMMANDS

Williams commanded first a brigade in 1861–62 and then a division for the balance of the war, with frequent stints as temporary commander of an army corps, shown here.

II Corps, *Army of Virginia*

Nathaniel P. Banks	June 26, 1862–Sept. 4, 1862	71 days
ASW	August 10, 1862	1 [394]
ASW	Sept. 4, 1862–Sept. 12, 1862	9

XII Corps, *Army of the Potomac*

ASW	Sept. 12, 1862–Sept. 15, 1862	4
Joseph K.F. Mansfield	Sept. 15, 1862–Sept 17, 1862	3
ASW	Sept. 17, 1862–Oct. 20, 1862	34
Henry W. Slocum	Oct. 20, 1862–Apr. 28, 1863	191
ASW	Apr. 28, 1863–Apr. 30, 1863	3
Slocum	Apr. 30, 1863–June 30, 1863	62
ASW	July 1, 1863–July 4, 1863	4
Slocum	July 4, 1863–Aug. 31, 1863	59
ASW	Aug. 31, 1863–Sept. 13, 1863	14
Slocum	Sept. 13, 1863–Sept. 24, 1863	12

Slocum	324 days
Williams	69
Mansfield	3

XII Corps, *assigned to Department of the Cumberland*

Joseph Hooker	Sept. 25, 1863–Oct. 6, 1863	12
Daniel A. Butterfield	Oct. 6, 1863–Oct. 9, 1863	4
Slocum	Oct. 9, 1863–Apr. 4, 1864	147

XX Corps, *Army of the Cumberland*

Hooker	Apr. 4, 1864–July 27, 1864	115
ASW	July 27, 1864–Aug. 27, 1864	32
Slocum	Aug. 27, 1864–Nov. 11, 1864	77

XX Corps, *Left Wing, Military Division of the Mississippi and Army of Georgia*

ASW	Nov. 11, 1864–Apr. 2, 1865	143
Joseph A. Mower	Apr. 2, 1865–June 9, 1865	69

TOTALS

Slocum	548 days
ASW	244
Hooker	127
Banks	71
Mower	69
Butterfield	4

Williams wrote that his assumption of command on April 28, 1863, was "for the sixth time." This chart lists it as the fifth; see chapter 8 for communications suggesting others.[395] All but Williams held the rank of major general.

FAREWELL ORDER TO TROOPS OF 1ST DIVISION, XX CORPS, NEAR WASHINGTON, D.C., JUNE 6, 1865

GENERAL ORDERS NO 8

The time having arrived when this Division is to be broken up and the Regiments are to be separated, some going to their homes and some to service for awhile in other Departments, the Brevet Major General Commanding embraces the occasion to thank officers and men for their long, gallant and faithful services to the Republic and for their uniformly respectful and dutiful deportment to himself personally and as their commander.

Some of you have been under his command for more than three and a half years; all of you for more than a year.

In this comparatively brief period, during a series of extraordinary and decisive campaigns, have been concentrated the severe labors, exposures, and great events that rarely fall within the experiences of any single human life.

To all of you—Comrades in these eventful years and scenes—your commanding General bears an affection kindred to that of a fond father to faithful and dutiful sons.

Most of you, commencing your military career in Virginia with the Army of the Potomac, kept pace in its marches and on its battlefields to the great crowning triumph at Gettysburg. Then, turning westward to the succor of our western armies beleaguered in Chattanooga, you opened communications with them through the vallies of Tennessee.

After Lookout Mountain and Mission Ridge, you became a part of the "Army of the Cumberland" of Sherman's Grand Army in that memorable campaign of "a hundred days under fire," ending in the capture of Atlanta. Then, breaking your communication with the North, you launched forth into that unheralded and mysterious "March to the Sea" and found your egress in the captured City of Savannah; then turning northward through the Carolinas and occupying in succession their submissive Capitals, you have, after a mid-winter campaign of incredible difficulties and hardships—scarcely delayed in your daily progress by numberless swamps and swollen rivers and seemingly impassable roads and the barriers and battles of hostile armies—at length completed the gigantic circuit of your toilsome marches in the proud Capital of the Nation, exultant in the peace you have helped to win and joyful in the near prospect of sitting down again in love and gratitude at home.

To recite your long and varied services were to write a history of the great campaigns in the East, in the West, and in the South. Your banners bear the names of the proudest battlefields of the War.

Comrades! Let the recollections of the fatigues the dangers and the exposures you have undergone—the memorable battles you have fought—the eventful and decisive campaigns you have taken part in, be not only enduring topics of a just pride, but active incentives to lives of future usefulness and of undying devotion to your Country's honor and welfare.

Your old commander bids you an affectionate farewell!

A.S. Williams
Bvt Major General Commanding[396]

REMARKS TO SOCIETY OF THE ARMY OF THE CUMBERLAND, OPERA HOUSE, DETROIT, NOVEMBER 15, 1871

GENERAL A.S. WILLIAMS, CHAIRMAN OF THE LOCAL EXECUTIVE COMMITTEE, IN BEHALF OF THE CITY OF DETROIT, WELCOMED THE SOCIETY IN THE FOLLOWING WORDS:

Comrades:

As the organ of your Local Executive Committee, and observing the pleasant custom of your former meetings, I congratulate you upon the return of another Reunion of this Society. As a citizen of Detroit, I cordially welcome you to our city.

I congratulate you, because in these reunions old friendships, formed amid the exposures and privations of camp-life, are revived and invigorated; loyal sentiments are nurtured and strengthened; generous purposes and high aims are formed and established.

I welcome you as you should be welcomed in every loyal city—the representatives of that grand army upon whose tattered banners are inscribed Perryville, Shiloh, Stone River, Chickamauga, Lookout Mountain, Mission Ridge, Resaca, Kenesaw, Peach Tree Creek, Atlanta, Jonesborough, Bentonville, Franklin, Nashville, and hundreds of other battles and combats which cluster like stars upon your army's escutcheon, and make up the brilliant constellation of your glorious record.

I welcome you, as should be welcomed the valiant soldiers who came to the succor of this great nation when its political life was imperiled—who threw their vigorous manhood into the gigantic struggle that was to decide the momentous issue between freedom and slavery—between Union and political disruption—between established order and endless anarchy.

With no less cordiality I greet the representatives of the other great armies, and those distinguished commanders who honor our Reunion with their presence to-day.

There are here those who fought at Donelson and Vicksburg, and were your brave comrades at Shiloh and in the battles for Atlanta and in the campaigns of Georgia and the Carolinas.

There are here, those who swept the enemy from Missouri and the central Mississippi, and came to join their arms with yours around Corinth; and those who so bravely defended Fort Saunders and the beleaguered city of Knoxville, and fought by your side afterward in those "one hundred days under fire" in the Atlanta campaign, and in the shining victories of Franklin and Nashville. They are here, too, those from the Eastern armies, who upheld the old flag with signal valor and fidelity on the Peninsula, at Cedar Mountain, at Antietam, at Chancellorsville, at Gettysburg, in the Wilderness, and around and beyond Petersburg, to the grand rebel finale at Appomattox. And those, too, are here who, in the beautiful valley of the Shenandoah, scattered the rebel columns with decisive victories, and joined in the final triumph in Central Virginia—and those covered with victorious laurels gathered at Fort Fisher, who, with their comrades of the Ninth Corps from their successful campaigns in Mississippi and East Tennessee, came to meet Sherman's columns at Goldsboro'. Some we claim as of the prolific family of the Cumberland—by birth or adoption—and all of that great brotherhood of loyal soldiers who, in a common cause, bore the "gorgeous ensign of the Republic" to a triumphant issue.

The suggestions of these occasions, Comrades, are not all, however, of a joyous character.

The memories of the fallen and of the departed come back to us with all the intensity of freshest sorrow as we greet and embrace the living comrade.

And foremost of all sinks into our saddened thoughts the recollection of our immeasurable loss in the death of that great hero and commander, whose official chair, draped in the emblems of mourning, stands, by your resolve, at all your Reunions as a perpetual memorial that his heroic spirit still lives in our hearts, and ever presides in our united as in our individual memories. How can we render a fitting tribute to the virtues of him in whom all the elements of goodness and greatness were so wonderfully and so beautifully blended? His pure, serene, and consistent life speaks his highest and best eulogy, and the hearts of his veteran soldiers respond with a spontaneous homage of love and devotion to the memory of their sainted commander,

"Take him for all in all,

We ne'er shall look upon his like again."

Comrades, we meet for no self-glorying purpose. In the language of our constitution, our Society is formed "to perpetuate the memory of the fortunes and achievements of the Army of the Cumberland, and to preserve an unanimity of loyal sentiment and a kind and cordial feeling, which have been an eminent characteristic of our army."

Noble and elevated purposes these, and worthy of the men whose names are written with those decisive battle-fields, where the priceless life of this great nation hung upon their valor, their constancy, and their fidelity.

Patriotic purposes, too! for they look to the future welfare and glory of the Republic.

When this people forget or cease to recognize those grand achievements which determined the very existence of our free institutions, deathful apathy or fatal ingratitude will have so chilled the great heart of this Republic that freedom will find no champions, and national honor no brave defenders. Far from the future fortunes of our beloved country, Comrades, may that day be when the remembrance of the past sacrifices and gallant services of her sons stir not the hearts of her people, when national pride makes no response to the recollections of national glory or individual heroism.

While we live, Comrades, our friendships will live; and yet your hearts can not be unconscious that, year after year, continued separation and the engrossments of active life corrode and weaken the links that bound our earlier sympathies and feelings. You can not have failed to observe that public recognition and the manifestations of national gratitude, year by year, weaken and lessen as great current events interpose to cloud and dim the popular remembrance of the momentous exploits of our late civil war.

It is in these Reunions that we must rekindle and keep alive these blessed friendships. It is on these occasions that we must collect and perpetuate those sacred memories, and preserve and transmit those faithful records, upon which the future historian may erect an enduring and truthful monument to the valor, the patriotism, and the fidelity of the Army of the Cumberland.

The address was received by the Society with enthusiasm.[397]

Notes

A complete bibliography can be located at jackdempseybooks.com.

Preface

1. Joseph Greusel, *General Alpheus S. Williams* (Detroit, MI: Seidel, 1911).
2. Milo M. Quaife, ed., *From the Cannon's Mouth: Civil War Letters of General Alpheus S. Williams* (Detroit, MI: Wayne State, 1959, reprinted, Lincoln: University of Nebraska, 1995).
3. Jack Dempsey and Brian James Egen, *Michigan at Antietam: The Wolverine State's Sacrifice on America's Bloodiest Day* (Charleston, SC: The History Press, 2015).
4. Union military units, smallest to largest: company, regiment, brigade, division, corps, army.
5. "Brigadier General Alpheus S. Williams…was paternal enough at fifty-four to be universally known as Pop." Lloyd Lewis, *Sherman: Fighting Prophet* (New York: Harcourt, Brace, 1932), 400.

Chapter 1

6. Ulysses S. Grant, *Personal Memoirs*, vol. 1 (New York: C.L. Webster, 1885–86), 1; National Society, Daughters of the American Republic, *American Monthly Magazine* 26 (January–June 1905): 294; Hepzibah: Isaiah 62:4 (KJV).

7. David D. Field, *Statistical Account of the County of Middlesex in Connecticut* (Middleton, CT: Clark & Lyman, 1819), 92, 99; Connecticut SHPO, *Historical and Architectural Resources Inventory for the Town of Deep River, Connecticut* (Norwalk, CT, 2011–12), 18, 24, 28; *History of Middlesex County Connecticut* (New York: J.B. Beers, 1884), 543, 549; Frank J. Mather, *"Old Deep River"* (Deep River, CT: New Era, 1914), 7, 14; *Connecticut: A Guide to Its Roads, Lore and People* (Boston: Houghton Mifflin, 1938), 76. Elder brother Ezra became a distinguished town leader and member of the Connecticut legislature.

8. Hepzibah and children were recorded on August 7, 1820, 4th U.S. Census, NARA roll M33_3, image 370, page 372; A.S. Williams to Irene Williams Chittenden, September 20, 1869, *Alpheus Starkey Williams Papers*, 1810–1922, Burton Historical Collection, Detroit Public Library (hereafter *ASWP*). Grandmother Irene died in 1839. Starkey and Williams family burials occurred in Fountain Hill and River View Cemeteries, Middlesex County, Connecticut, where gravestones provide dates. He would also outlive grandchild Laura, born on August 11, 1869, in Detroit to Mary Howard Williams and Francis Ulrich Farquhar. She died at Milwaukee on November 11, 1869; a stone inscribed "Our Little Laura" marks her Detroit grave. William L. Learned, *The Learned Family: Learned, Larned, Learnard, Larnard, and Lerned* (Albany, NY: Weed-Parsons, 1898), 339.

9. *Connecticut: A Guide*, 31–35, 44.

10. Yale University, *Catalogue*, 1827, 22, 23; 1828, 19; 1829, 16; 1830, 13, 24–26, 27, 28 (emphasis in original); Ebenezer Baldwin, *Annals of Yale College* (New Haven, CT: Hezekiah Howe, 1831), 234–35; John Farmer, *American Quarterly Register* 7, no. 2 (November 1834), 330; Quaife, *From the Cannon's Mouth*, 388. Appreciation to Jansen Hasbrouck, Kingston, New York.

11. Robert B. Ross, *Early Bench and Bar of Detroit from 1805 to the End of 1850* (Detroit, MI: R.P. Joy and C.M. Burton, 1907), 225; Quaife, *From the Cannon's Mouth*, 3; Jeffrey G. Charnley, "'Neglected Honor': The Life of General A.S. Williams of Michigan, 1810–1878," PhD diss., Michigan State, 1983, 9. It is likely that Williams's life story became garbled with Wikoff's, who had "escaped from the tiresome discipline of a protracted University career. Having come into the control of an ample fortune," he devoted "some years to a wide tour of Europe." Henry Wikoff, *My Courtship and Its Consequences* (New York: J.C. Derby, 1855), 27–28. His father's death in 1826 made him "heir to the greater part of his fortune." Henry Wikoff, *Reminiscences of an Idler* (New York: Fords, Howard & Hulbert, 1880), 11.

12. Distribution of Estate of Mr. Ezra Williams, deceased, Probate Court Records, vol. 7, 278–79, April 4, 1820, Chester, Connecticut. Kudos to Ms. Marian Staye and Deep River Historical Society for this research. Williams inherited $3,417.02 upon his mother's death, ibid.

13. Hall became attorney general in 1839, served in the New York legislature and in 1847 became New York City counsel. Yale University, *Catalogue*, 1833–34, 9.

14. Washington's Virginia militia experience may have inspired Williams.

15. Wikoff, *Reminiscences*, 44, 48; Yale University, *Catalogue*, 1833–34, 8; *Journal, ASWP.*

16. *Journal, ASWP.* The 1849 wreck of the *Sylvie* remains in the Columbia River.

17. Lawrence Barrett, *Edwin Forrest* (Boston: James R. Osgood, 1881), 1–2, 152; Wikoff, *Reminiscences*, 77, 133, 194–95.

18. To the suggestion that they visit exotic locales (Russia and Egypt), Williams refused. Wikoff, *Reminiscences*, 153, 191–92; *Journal, ASWP.* Years later, he fondly recalled Vallombrosa in Tuscany. Quaife, *From the Cannon's Mouth*, 109.

Chapter 2

19. *ASWP*; Kenneth E. Lewis, *West to Far Michigan* (East Lansing: Michigan State, 2002), 220–21; Willis F. Dunbar, *Michigan: A History of the Wolverine State* (Grand Rapids, MI: Eerdmans, 1970), 263; Clarence M. Burton, *When Detroit Was Young: Historical Studies*, ed. Milo M. Quaife (Detroit, MI: Burton Abstract & Title, 1951), 38–42; *Digest of Detroit Daily Advertiser* 1, no. 303, 278–79; Peter Gavrilovich and Bill McGraw, *Detroit Almanac: 300 Years of Life in the Motor City* (Detroit, MI: Free Press, 2001), 39.

20. Dunbar, *Michigan*, 245–46, 263; Paul Taylor, *"Old Slow Town": Detroit during the Civil War* (Detroit, MI: Wayne State, 2013), 9; Quaife, *From the Cannon's Mouth*, 276.

21. Ross, *Early Bench and Bar of Detroit*, 212.

22. Timothy D. Lusch, "Robert E. Lee and the Lake Erie Survey Expedition of 1835," *Michigan History* 101, no. 4 (July/August 2017): 53–54; John T. Blois, *Gazetteer of the State of Michigan, in Three Parts, Containing a General View of the State* (Detroit, MI: Sydney L. Rood & Company, 1839), 416.

23. Franklin B. Dexter, *Biographical Notices of Graduates of Yale College* (New Haven, CT, 1913), 232; *Obituary Record of Graduates of Yale University*

Deceased from June, 1880, to June, 1890 (New Haven, CT: Tuttle, Morehouse & Taylor, 1890), 367; *ASWP*. The William L. Clemens Library collections include bank correspondence with statesman Lucius Lyon.

24. For the Exchange, see the cover of *Michigan and the Civil War: A Great and Bloody Sacrifice* (Charleston, SC: The History Press, 2011); Fred Carlisle, *Chronology of Notable Events in the History of the Northwest Territory and Wayne County* (Detroit, MI: O.S. Gulley, Bornman, 1890), 327–291; *Journal, ASWP*.

25. Don Faber, *Boy Governor: Stevens T. Mason and the Birth of Michigan Politics* (Ann Arbor: University of Michigan, 2012), 102–7; *Journal, ASWP*.

26. *ASWP*; Julius P.B. MacCabe, *Directory of the City of Detroit, with its Environs, and Register of Michigan, for the Year 1837* (Detroit, MI: William Harsha: 1837), 79. Charles Larned died in 1834; his father served as aide-de-camp to George Washington. Ross, *Early Bench and Bar of Detroit*, 225.

27. *Michigan Historical Collections*, vol. 36 (Lansing, MI: Wyncoop Hallenbeck Crawford, 1908), 139; Steve Lehto, *Michigan's Columbus: Life of Douglass Houghton* (Royal Oak, MI: Momentum, 2009), 30; *Three Sermons Preached on Important Occasions* (Detroit, MI: Jabez Fox, 1850); *Presbyterian Reunion: A Memorial Volume, 1837–1871* (New York: De Witt C. Lent, 1870), 235; George I. Reed, *Bench and Bar of Michigan: A Volume of History and Biography* (Chicago: Century, 1897), 205; Amy Elliott Bragg, *Hidden History of Detroit* (Charleston, SC: The History Press, 2012), 114; *Detroit Illustrated: The Commercial Metropolis of Michigan* (Akron, OH: Harry Hook, 1891), 93.

28. *ASWP*. Also born in 1810 and an immigrant to Detroit in 1836, Romeyn became a prominent citizen. Williams previously practiced law with John G. Atterbury. Clarence M. Burton, William Stocking and Gordon K. Miller, *City of Detroit, Michigan, 1701–1922*, vol. 2 (Detroit, MI: S.J. Clarke, 1922), 1,146.

29. *ASWP*. The club dates to 1839—its Belle Isle facility stands. Burton, *When Detroit Was Young*, 51; Gavrilovich and McGraw, *Detroit Almanac*, 289; Charnley, "Neglected Honor," 43, 256.

30. *ASWP*; Silas Farmer, *History of Detroit and Michigan or The Metropolis Illustrated* (Detroit, MI: Silas Farmer, 1884), 190, 864.

31. Kenneth C. Martis, *Historical Atlas of Political Parties in the United States Congress, 1789–1989* (New York: MacMillan, 1989), 31; Jon Meacham, *American Lion: Andrew Jackson in the White House* (New York: Random House, 2008), 289; James Z. Schwartz, *Conflict on the Michigan Frontier: Yankee and Borderland Cultures, 1815–1840* (DeKalb: Northern Illinois, 2009), 8, 13, 22, 26–27.

32. *Journal, ASWP*. Charles died on November 8, 1919.

33. Burton, *When Detroit Was Young*, vol. 1, 326–28; Farmer, *History of Detroit*, 143. He was alderman again in 1858, Farmer, *History of Detroit*, 756. Irene died on April 7, 1907, and Mary on February 7, 1935. Elmwood inscriptions, records, *ASWP.*

34. William D. Wilkins, "Traditions and Reminiscences of the Public Schools of Detroit (Read Before the Teachers' Institute of Detroit, February 13th, 1871)," *Michigan Historical Collections*, vol. 1, 2nd ed. (Lansing, MI: Robert Smith Printing Company, 1907 reprint of 1877 edition), 448–56.

35. James H. Welling, *Directory of the City of Detroit and Register of Michigan for the Year 1845* (Detroit, MI: Harsha & Willcox, 1845), 85 (same author/title printed Detroit: A.S. Williams, Printer, 1846, 147); Farmer, *History of Detroit*, 190, 195, 682; Charnley, "Neglected Honor," 51; Tom S. Applegate, "A History of the Press of Michigan," *Michigan Historical Collections*, vol. 6 (Lansing, MI: Wynkoop Hallenbeck Crawford Company, 1907, reprint of 1884 edition), 62–63.

36. Farmer, *History of Detroit*, 190, 195, 682; Ross, *Early Bench and Bar of Detroit*, 225–26; K. Jack Bauer, *Mexican War, 1846–1848* (Lincoln: University of Nebraska, 1992), 223; Burton, Stocking and Miller, *City of Detroit*, vol. 1, 366; *Rode's United States Post Office Directory and Postal Guide* (New York: Charles R. Rode, 1853), 46; Michael F. Holt, *Rise and Fall of the American Whig Party: Jacksonian Politics and the Onset of the Civil War* (Oxford: Oxford University, 1999), 511; *Shove's Business Advertiser and Detroit Directory for 1852–1853* (Detroit, MI: Free Press, 1852), 230. He also served on Wednesdays in 1849 as city police watch captain. Farmer, *History of Detroit*, 203; Gavrilovich and McGraw, *Detroit Almanac*, 289. Appreciation to Mike Maurer, secretary, Zion Lodge No. 1, Detroit.

37. "Jeanie" may actually be "Janie." *Journal, ASWP*; Paul H. Scheidler, "Ever Truly Yours, E. Wright," *Michigan History* 97, no. 6 (2013): 5; Farmer, *History of Detroit*, 303–4; Le Roy Barnett and Roger Rosentreter, *Michigan's Early Military Forces* (Detroit, MI: Wayne State, 2003), 338–41, 344, 502–3; Russel H. Beatie, *Army of the Potomac: Birth of Command*, vol. 1 (Cambridge: Da Capo, 2002), 463.

38. Elmwood inscription. She left an estate of $1,400. Michigan Works Progress Administration, *Probate Records from Archives of Wayne County, Michigan*, vol. 3, entry 2072½ (1936). McIntosh died in 1892 and was buried in the Williams plot. Compare the similar experience of Thomas Jefferson.

39. Friend Palmer, *Early Days in Detroit* (Detroit, MI: Hunt & June, 1906), 235–36. This source also states that Williams served as volunteer fireman (page 357); *ASWP.* Julia's absence in the 1850 census is curious.

40. Don E. Fehrenbacher, *Prelude to Greatness: Lincoln in the 1850s* (Stanford, CT: Stanford University Press, 1991), 3, 29.

41. Charnley, "Neglected Honor," 54–55.

42. William Stocking, ed., *Under the Oaks: Commemorating the Fiftieth Anniversary of the Founding of the Republican Party, at Jackson, Michigan, July 6, 1854* (Detroit, MI: Detroit Tribune, 1904), 26; *Prominent Newspapermen in Michigan*, Michigan Historical Collections, vol. 36 (Lansing: Michigan Historical Commission, 1915), 159; Martin J. Hershock, *Paradox of Progress: Economic Change, Individual Enterprise, and Political Culture in Michigan, 1837–1878* (Athens: Ohio University, 2003), 131.

43. Martin J. Hershock, "'Agitation Is as Necessary as Tranquility Is Dangerous': Kinsley S. Bingham Becomes a Republican," *Congress and the Crisis of the 1850s*, ed. Paul Finkelman and Donald R. Kennon (Athens: Ohio University, 2012), 144, 151, 154. Williams was not a teetotaler. He took pleasure at imbibing "the most refreshing drink of cinchona [quinine] and whiskey that was swallowed by mortal throat" during one hot summer day. Quaife, *From the Cannon's Mouth*, 199. U.S. Grant also identified as a Whig.

44. Willard Klunder, *Lewis Cass and the Politics of Moderation* (Kent, OH: Kent State, 1996), 279, 301; *Johnston's Detroit City Directory and Advertising Gazetteer of Michigan for 1856–7* (Detroit, MI: Detroit Daily Tribune, 1856), 44; Charnley, "Neglected Honor," 77–79.

45. Ross, *Early Bench and Bar of Detroit*, 226; Steve Soper, *"Glorious 'Old Third'": A Brief History of the Third Michigan Infantry Regiment Veteran Volunteers, 1855 to 1865* (n.p.: Old Third Michigan, 2014; rev. edition), 42–44, 58–59, 63–64, 69, 73; Pioneer Society, *Michigan Historical Collections*, vol. 1, 2nd ed. (Lansing, MI: Robert Smith Printing Company, 1907, reprint of 1877 edition), 90–91; vol. 12, 2nd ed. (Lansing, MI: Robert Smith Printing Company, 1907, reprint of 1877 edition), 334–37, 340.

46. *Journal of the Proceedings of the Common Council of the City of Detroit, from May 31, 1859, to January 10, 1860, Inclusive* (Detroit, MI: W.F. Storey, 1860), 98–99; *ASWP*; *Umberhine's Detroit City Business Directory for 1860–61* (Detroit, MI: Daily Advertiser, 1860), 120. Bagley became governor in 1873.

47. A forty-year-old Massachusetts-born woman, J.A. Bloss, was also recorded. She was likely related to J.B. Bloss, a seed dealer who lived next door and was listed as such in the 1857 (Johnston's) Detroit city directory, 154, 259.

48. Gavrilovich and McGraw, *Detroit Almanac*, 289.

49. Charnley, "Neglected Honor," 82.

Chapter 3

50. *Detroit Free Press*, April 13, 1861, 1.

51. William H. Withington, *Michigan in the Opening of the War* (Detroit, MI: Ostler, 1889), 7.

52. John Robertson, *Michigan in the War* (Lansing, MI: W.S. George, 1882), 17, 22.

53. Withington, *Michigan in the Opening of the War*, 10; *Detroit Free Press*, April 18, 1861, 1; Frank B. Woodford, *Father Abraham's Children: Michigan Episodes in the Civil War* (Detroit, MI: Wayne State, 1961), 28–30.

54. Clayton R. Newell, *Regular Army Before the Civil War, 1845–1860* (Washington, D.C.: Center of Military History, 2014), 48, 52.

55. Soper, *"Glorious 'Old Third,'"* 140, 145, 154; Robertson, *Michigan in the War*, 165–67.

56. Camp Williams Michigan Historical Marker, S0679, Adrian College, west side of South Madison south of Williams Street; Martin N. Bertera and Kim Crawford, *4th Michigan Infantry in the Civil War* (East Lansing: Michigan State, 2010), 7–8, 13; Generals' Reports of Service, *War of the Rebellion*, vol. 3, Alpheus S. Williams, Report No. 17, March 20, 1864, U.S. Army Generals' Reports of Civil War Service, 1864–87, U.S. National Archives, Archives Unbound, Gale Document no. SC5004593381 (hereafter *AGI*), 2; Robert E. Mitchell, "The Organizational Performance of Michigan's Adjutant General and the Federal Provost Marshal General in Recruiting Michigan's Boys in Blue," *Michigan Historical Review* 28, no. 2 (Fall 2002): 115, 120. Special thanks to Kathy Petlewski, electronic resources librarian, Plymouth District Library, and Gale/Cengage Learning.

57. See Federal Judicial Center, "Wilkins, Ross," https://www.fjc.gov/history/judges/wilkins-ross; Ross, *Early Bench and Bar of Detroit*, 217.

58. Beatie, *Army of the Potomac*, 463–64 (emphasis in original).

59. Quaife, *From the Cannon's Mouth*, 16.

60. Ibid.; Adjutant General's Office, *Official Army Register, for September, 1861* (Washington, D.C.: Government Printing Office, 1861), 13; *Senate Executive Journal*, August 5, 1861, 544, 553, 557–58; Albert A. Nofi, *Civil War Treasury* (Boston: Da Capo, 1995), 381.

61. *War of the Rebellion: A Compilation of the Official Records of the Union and Confederate Armies* (Washington, D.C.: Government Printing Office, 1880–1901), series I, vol. 51, pt. I, 455 (hereafter, series I references are implicit).

62. Ibid., vol. 51, pt. I, 473.

63. Ibid., 481.

64. *AGI*, 2, 37; Russell Duncan, ed., *Blue-Eyed Child of Fortune: Civil War Letters of Robert Gould Shaw* (Athens: University of Georgia, 1992), 252. Larned joined him from September 1861 until after the Winchester defeat in May 1862. He then moved to Philadelphia, marrying there after the war. Quaife, *From the Cannon's Mouth*, vii, 16–17, 20, 79, 141.

Chapter 4

65. *Official Records*, vol. 51, pt. I, 493.

66. Quaife, *From the Cannon's Mouth*, 18–19; *AGI*, 2.

67. Banks's Division was constituted as of August 4, 1861. *Official Records*, vol. 5, 15–16. Vol. 2, operations near Harpers Ferry, June–July 1861, refers to a subordinate of General Robert Patterson as "Brigadier-General Williams." It indexes (1,099) this individual as "Williams, Alpheus S." The corrections (2–3, 6) are silent. Various studies repeat this mistake: Pennsylvanian Edward C. Williams commanded the brigade under Patterson during the campaign. Samuel P. Bates, *History of the Pennsylvania Volunteers, 1861–65*, vol. 1 (Harrisburg, PA: B. Singerly, 1869), 68 note *; *Commemorative Biographical Encyclopedia of Dauphin County, Pennsylvania* (Chambersburg, PA: J.M. Runk, 1896), 244–45. Confirmed with Gary Gimbel, president, Falling Waters Battlefield Association. The same error appears in *Official Records*, vol. 51, pt. I, 423.

68. Quaife, *From the Cannon's Mouth*, 8; *AGI*, 43.

69. *Official Military Atlas of the Civil War* (New York: Arno, 1978), Plate VII; *Official Records*, vol. 5, 32.

70. *Official Records*, vol. 51, pt. I, 498–500, 502; vol. 5, 34, 388.

71. Quaife, *From the Cannon's Mouth*, 24; *AGI*, 2.

72. Quaife, *From the Cannon's Mouth*, 25; *Official Records*, vol. 5, 34, 339; James A. Morgan III, *A Little Short of Boats: Civil War Battles of Ball's Bluff & Edwards Ferry* (New York: Savas Beatie, 2011), 172–76, 187–93.

73. George B. McClellan, *McClellan's Own Story: The War for the Union* (New York: Charles Webster, 1886), 188.

74. Quaife, *From the Cannon's Mouth*, 27–28, 59; Lyman R. Comey, *A Legacy of Valor: The Memoirs and Letters of Captain Henry Newton Comey, 2nd Massachusetts Infantry* (Knoxville: University of Tennessee, 2004), 25; David H. Strother, "Personal Recollections of the War," *Harper's New Monthly Magazine* 33, no. 196 (September 1866): 424–28; *Official Records*, vol. 5, 339.

75. Morgan, *Little Short of Boats*, 184, 191; Gary W. Gallagher, *Lee and His Generals in War and Memory* (Baton Rouge: Louisiana State, 1998), xi.

Chapter 5

76. Alonzo H. Quint, *Record of the Second Massachusetts Infantry, 1861–65* (Boston: J.P. Walker, 1867), 30; Duncan, *Blue-Eyed Child of Fortune*, 159, 162, 164; *AGI*, 2; Quaife, *From the Cannon's Mouth*, 43, 46. Williams spelled the name "Dollarson." Quaife, *From the Cannon's Mouth*, 18; a contemporaneous city directory lists a "Geo W Dolarson, colored, baker, 167 Russell" and "Dolarson Mrs, embroider, 165 Russell." *Johnston's Detroit City Directory and Advertising Gazetteer of Michigan* (Detroit, MI: H. Barns & Company, 1861), 149.

77. *AGI*, 2; Quaife, *From the Cannon's Mouth*, 36, 45, 52, 61; *Official Records*, vol. 51, pt. I, 521, 533, 539. Williams was in Washington on January 4 to visit Rene, rushed back, "overtook" the brigade and preceded it to Hancock. Quaife, *From the Cannon's Mouth*, 53–54, 60, 90.

78. *Official Records*, vol. 51, pt. I, 529, 531; Peter Cozzens, *Shenandoah 1862: Stonewall Jackson's Valley Campaign* (Chapel Hill: University of North Carolina, 2008), 1,191; George K. Johnson, "Battle of Kernstown," in *War Papers Read Before the Commandery of the State of Michigan*, vol. 1 (Detroit, MI: Winn & Hammond, 1890), 3; Quaife, *From the Cannon's Mouth*, 40.

79. *AGI*, 2–3; Quaife, *From the Cannon's Mouth*, 61–62; Cozzens, *Shenandoah 1862*, 126; *Official Records*, vol. 5, 517–18.

80. Quaife, *From the Cannon's Mouth*, 62, 63; Cozzens, *Shenandoah 1862*, 131, 134; *AGI*, 3; *Official Records*, vol. 5, 520–21; Richard R. Duncan, *Beleaguered Winchester: A Virginia Community at War, 1861–65* (Baton Rouge: Louisiana State, 2007), ix–x, 48–51; Steven S. Raas, ed., *With the 3rd Wisconsin Badgers: The Living Experience of the Civil War through the Journals of Van R. Willard* (Mechanicsburg, PA: Stackpole, 1999), 48–49.

81. Duncan, *Beleaguered Winchester*, 59; Quaife, *From the Cannon's Mouth*, 64.

82. George P. Sanger, ed., *Statutes at Large*, vol. 12 (Boston: Little, Brown, 1863), 319. A March 13 statute required promulgation as an article of war a prohibition on the U.S. military returning fugitives to their claimed owners on penalty of court-martial. Ibid., 354.

83. Courtesy of Virginia Historical Society. David F. Riggs, "Robert Young Conrad and the Ordeal of Secession," *Virginia Magazine of History and Biography* 86, no. 3 (July 1978): 259–74; Duncan, *Beleaguered Winchester*, 65–66.

84. *AGI*, 3, 44; *Official Records*, vol. 12, pt. I, 378. Schenck applied directly to new Secretary of War Edwin M. Stanton. *Official Records*, vol. 51, pt. I, 546–47; vol. 5, 21–22, 733, 757. Israel B. Richardson of Pontiac, West Point 1841, received promotion to division command on March 14, ibid., vol. 51, pt. I, 552; Jack C. Mason, *Until Antietam: The Life and Letters of Major General Israel B. Richardson, U.S. Army* (Carbondale: Southern Illinois, 2009), 125; *Official Records*, vol. 5, 732.

85. *Official Records*, vol. 51, pt. I, 547; vol. 5, 18, 755.

86. *Official Records*, vol. 51, pt. I, 549, 551–52.

87. *Official Records*, vol. 12, pt. I, 378; vol. 5, 56. The 2nd Brigade became part of another corps.

88. *Official Records*, vol. 12, pt. I, 426. He came in for implied criticism for not supporting a cavalry action on the twenty-seventh, ibid., 448; *AGI*, 4; Cozzens, *Shenandoah 1862*, 246, 276; Quaife, *From the Cannon's Mouth*, 72–73.

89. Cozzens, *Shenandoah 1862*, 288, 290, 307; *Official Records*, vol. 12, pt. I, 545–49.

90. Cozzens, *Shenandoah 1862*, 340–42; Quaife, *From the Cannon's Mouth*, 73–75.

91. Quaife, *From the Cannon's Mouth*, 78–79; *Official Records*, vol. 12, pt. I, 593–95. One history is critical of Williams's dispositions, credits Gordon's version and regards Banks as "misguided." James G. Hollandsworth Jr., *Pretense of Glory: The Life of General Nathaniel P. Banks* (Baton Rouge: Louisiana State, 1998), 64–65. Gordon wrote two decades later that Williams "was calmly sleeping" and that "loud calls" were required to bring him to his door "where, as his red face beamed above his long flannel night-shirt, he was a spectacle to behold." George H. Gordon, *From Brook Farm to Cedar Mountain in the War of the Great Rebellion, 1861–62* (Boston: Houghton, Mifflin, 1883), 226. One historian categorizes Gordon's recollections as unreliable. Cozzens, *Shenandoah 1862*, 556 n6. Instead, the officer in his hotel room was Gordon, ibid., 350.

92. Quaife, *From the Cannon's Mouth*, 79–80, 82; *AGI*, 5; *Official Records*, vol. 12, pt. I, 580, 595–96, 701–2; Cozzens, *Shenandoah 1862*, 361–69.

93. *Official Records*, vol. 12, pt. I, 597–98, 607; Quaife, *From the Cannon's Mouth*, 82–86; John M. Gould, *History of the First-Tenth-Twenty-ninth Maine Regiment* (Portland, ME: Stephen Berry, 1871), 127.

94. *Official Records*, vol. 12, pt. I, 553, 607, 611, 706; Quaife, *From the Cannon's Mouth*, 66, 88–90.

95. Cozzens, *Shenandoah 1862*, 381; *AGI*, 6; *Official Records*, vol. 12, pt. I, 540, 545, 638; pt. III, 434; Quaife, *From the Cannon's Mouth*, 97–99.

96. Quaife, *From the Cannon's Mouth*, 84, 87, 98–99.

Chapter 6

97. *Official Records*, vol. 11, pt. III, 264–65.

98. Ibid., vol. 12, pt. III, 435–38. Major General Frémont did not countenance being commanded by an inferior in rank.

99. Ibid., 439–40, 456–58, 467, 472–73; *AGI*, 6.

100. *Official Records*, vol. 12, pt. 3, 486, 491, 509, 516, 520; Edward J. Stackpole, *From Cedar Mountain to Antietam* (Harrisburg, PA: Stackpole, 1959), 31–35; Robert K. Krick, *Stonewall Jackson at Cedar Mountain* (Chapel Hill: University of North Carolina, 1990), 1.

101. *AGI*, 6–7; Quaife, *From the Cannon's Mouth*, 99; *Official Records*, vol. 12, pt. III, 524–27, 535–36, 547, 551; Stackpole, *From Cedar Mountain to Antietam*, 35–36. According to Pope, Banks's strength was "only about 8,000." *Official Records*, vol. 12, pt. II, 20, 25. Crawford was U.S. Army prewar.

102. *Official Records*, vol. 12, pt. III, 553; pt. II, 133–34; Janet B. Hewett, ed., *Supplement to the Official Records of the Union and Confederate Armies*, Series 2 (Wilmington, NC: Broadfoot Pub. Company, 1994–98), 520; Stackpole, *From Cedar Mountain to Antietam*, 38.

103. *AGI*, 7; *Official Records*, vol. 12, pt. II, 133–34, 145. Pope later contended that he wanted Banks to maintain the defensive; Banks cited a verbal order from Pope to attack. Krick, *Stonewall Jackson at Cedar Mountain*, 43.

104. *Official Records*, vol. 12, pt. II, 55; Quaife, *From the Cannon's Mouth*, 100; Stackpole, *From Cedar Mountain to Antietam*, 56–59; Darrell L. Collins, *Army of Northern Virginia: Organization, Strength, Casualties, 1861–1865* (Jefferson, NC: McFarland, 2016), 264; Darrell L. Collins, *Army of the Potomac: Order of Battle, 1861–1865, with Commanders, Strengths, Losses and More* (Jefferson, NC: McFarland, 2013), 45. Krick, *Stonewall Jackson at Cedar Mountain*, 45, concluded Jackson's superiority was fifteen thousand to nine thousand. Williams estimated the Rebel force "exceeded 20,000 men, though probably not all were brought into action." *AGI*, 8. Williams made sure the initially "bad" position of his division was corrected by "immediately" securing Banks's approval. Quaife, *From the Cannon's Mouth*, 100–101.

105. Quaife, *From the Cannon's Mouth*, 100; *AGI*, 7–8. Collins, *Army of the Potomac*, 45, gives 1st Division strength as 3,700.

106. Stackpole, *From Cedar Mountain to Antietam*, 64, 66–67; Krick, *Stonewall Jackson at Cedar Mountain*, 150–51, 156, 187; *Official Records*, vol. 12, pt. II, 183; Bruce Catton, *This Hallowed Ground: The Story of the Union Side of the Civil War* (Garden City, NJ: Doubleday, 1956), 156.

107. Stackpole, *From Cedar Mountain to Antietam*, 67–69, 79; Krick, *Stonewall Jackson at Cedar Mountain*, 205; Quaife, *From the Cannon's Mouth*, 101.

108. Stackpole, *From Cedar Mountain to Antietam*, 69–71, 73; *AGI*, 8; Hewett, *Supplement to Official Records*, 521.

109. Krick, *Stonewall Jackson at Cedar Mountain*, 299; *Official Records*, vol. 12, pt. II, 134, 184; Stackpole, *From Cedar Mountain to Antietam*, 76–77; James I. Robertson Jr., *The Stonewall Brigade* (Baton Rouge: Louisiana State University Press, 1963–91), 132–35; Gordon, *From Brook Farm to Cedar Mountain*, 351.

110. Gordon, *From Brook Farm to Cedar Mountain*, 320; *Official Records*, vol. 12, pt. II, 134; Quaife, *From the Cannon's Mouth*, 101.

111. *Official Records*, vol. 12, pt. II, 136–39; Quaife, *From the Cannon's Mouth*, 101–2.

112. Quaife, *From the Cannon's Mouth*, 100–103.

113. *Official Records*, vol. 12, pt. II, 134–35. Pope reported that the corps' conduct "was beyond all praise" but omitted Williams from the list of gallant generals in his official account, ibid., 28.

114. Quaife, *From the Cannon's Mouth*, 103–5; *AGI*, 9; *Official Records*, vol. 12, pt. II, 27; Hewett, *Supplement to Official Records*, 705.

115. Quaife, *From the Cannon's Mouth*, 103–13; *Official Records*, vol. 12, pt. II, 28–29. Fort Albany's location today is near the Pentagon and boundary of Arlington National Cemetery.

116. Quaife, *From the Cannon's Mouth*, 109–11.

117. Ibid., 111, 119–20.

Chapter 7

118. *Official Records*, vol. 19, pt. II, 590–94, 598–600.

119. Thomas M. O'Brien and Oliver Diefendorf, *General Orders of the War Department, Embracing the Years 1861, 1862, and 1863*, vol. 1 (New York: Derby & Miller, 1864), 389; *Official Records*, vol. 19, pt. I, 67; pt. II, 279; Quaife, *From the Cannon's Mouth*, 111; *AGI*, 10.

120. *Official Records*, vol. 19, pt. II, 202, 214, 297.

121. *Official Records*, vol. 51, pt. I, 814–17, 821, 823; vol. 19, pt. I, 39–40, 43, 479; Quaife, *From the Cannon's Mouth*, 119–21; Pittman letter to E.A. Carman, May 24, 1897, Pittman Papers, Williams College.

122. Stephen W. Sears, *Lincoln's Lieutenants: The High Command of the Army of the Potomac* (Boston: Houghton Mifflin Harcourt, 2017), 358.

123. Samuel E. Pittman, "Story of the 'Famous Lost Dispatch,'" *Ladies Evening*, Michigan Commandery, Military Order of the Loyal Legion of the United States, March 5, 1903, Samuel Pittman Papers, Williams College, 3–4; Silas Colgrove, "The Finding of Lee's Lost Order," *Battles & Leaders of the Civil War*, vol. 2, ed. Robert U. Johnson and Clarence C. Buel (New York: Century, 1887), 603; Wilbur D. Jones, *Giants in the Cornfield: The 27th Indiana Infantry* (Shippensburg, PA: White Mane, 1997), 229–31; Charles B. Dew, "How Samuel E. Pittman Validated Lee's 'Lost Orders' Prior to Antietam: A Historical Note," *Journal of Southern History* 70, no. 4 (November 2004): 865–70; Samuel E. Pittman Papers, Burton Historical Collection, Detroit Public Library. See *Michigan at Antietam*, chapter 2.

124. *Official Records*, vol. 19, pt. II, 281.

125. Quaife, *From the Cannon's Mouth*, 121.

126. *AGI*, 11; Bradley M. Gottfried, *Maps of Antietam* (New York: Savas Beatie, 2012), 129.

127. Quaife, *From the Cannon's Mouth*, 125.

128. *Official Records*, vol. 19, pt. I, 55.

129. *AGI*, 11; John M. Priest, *Antietam: The Soldiers' Battle* (Shippensburg, PA: White Mane, 1990), 74; Quaife, *From the Cannon's Mouth*, 125; *Official Records*, vol. 19, pt. I, 475. Mansfield approached a Maine regiment and ordered it to cease firing on "our own men," although the soldiers in the ranks knew better: "The General took out his glass, but immediately his horse was shot in the right hind leg and became unruly. Then the General was shot." Hewett, *Supplement to Official Records*, series 3, 562–63.

130. *Official Records*, vol. 19, pt. I, 475; Walter H. Hebert, *Fighting Joe Hooker* (Lincoln: University of Nebraska Press, 1999), 142; Quaife, *From the Cannon's Mouth*, 126; Stephen W. Sears, *Landscape Turned Red: The Battle of Antietam* (New Haven, CT: Ticknor & Fields, 1983), 300; John W. Schildt, *Twelfth Corps at Antietam* (Sharpsburg, PA, 2012), 99; Jim Murphy, *A Savage Thunder: Antietam and the Bloody Road to Freedom* (New York: Simon & Schuster, 2009), 45; *AGI*, 11.

131. Collins, *Army of Northern Virginia*, 275; *Official Records*, vol. 19, pt. I, 67; Sears, *Landscape Turned Red*, 364–65.

132. Comey, *Legacy of Valor*, 73, 77; *AGI*, 12–13.

133. Bruce Catton, "Crisis at the Antietam," *American Heritage* 9, no. 5 (August 1958); Phillip T. Tucker, *Miller Cornfield at Antietam: The Civil War's Bloodiest Combat* (Charleston, SC: The History Press, 2017), 44–46.

134. *AGI*, 13. Crawford claimed that a thigh wound forced him to leave the field. Others (Williams and Ezra Carman of the 13th New Jersey)

believed that he had skulked. Sears, *Lincoln's Lieutenants*, 387; Quaife, *From the Cannon's Mouth*, 255.

135. Gottfried, *Maps of Antietam*, 160; Quaife, *From the Cannon's Mouth*, 126–27.

136. Tucker, *Miller Cornfield at Antietam*, 189.

137. Stackpole, *From Cedar Mountain to Antietam*, 470 (D. Scott Hartwig commentary). Sumner, a Regular army officer since 1819, shared McClellan's disdain for volunteer officers. Marion V. Armstrong Jr., *Unfurl Those Colors: McClellan, Sumner, and the Second Army Corps* (Tuscaloosa: University of Alabama, 2008), 108–9.

138. Stackpole, *From Cedar Mountain to Antietam*, 470–71. Future Ohio governor Jacob Cox criticized Sumner and lauded Williams as "a cool and experienced officer" who performed capably on September 17. Jacob D. Cox, *Military Reminiscences of the Civil War*, vol. 1 (New York: Charles Scribner's, 1900), 319, 328–29; Quaife, *From the Cannon's Mouth*, 128.

139. Greene's battle description (343 words) bordered on terseness. *Official Records*, vol. 19, pt. I, 504–6. Armstrong, *Unfurl Those Colors*, 178; *AGI*, 14–15; Catton, *Crisis at the Antietam*; Bruce Catton, *Mr. Lincoln's Army* (Garden City, NJ: Doubleday, 1962), 280. Greene was West Point, class of 1823.

140. That night, Williams "for the first time in nearly twenty-four hours" found food. *AGI*, 17.

141. *Official Records*, vol. 19, pt. I, 24–25, 30–33. West Point seems the commonality. McClellan's tabulation listed VI Corps casualties at 439, ibid., 195–96, a fourth of those sustained by XII Corps and 40 percent of Williams's Division, ibid. 199.

142. *Official Records*, vol. 19, pt. I, 199, 474, 507, 510; Sears, *Lincoln's Lieutenants*, 417 (letter of April 18, 1863); Duncan, *Blue-Eyed Child*, 238 (August 29, 1862 letter).

143. Quaife, *From the Cannon's Mouth*, 127, 130–31.

144. *Official Records*, vol. 19, pt. I, 36. Adding to the oversight: Hooker made no report and Sumner's merely referenced Williams's, even though both had verbally complimented him, ibid., 275–77; Quaife, *From the Cannon's Mouth*, 136.

145. Ralph Waldo Emerson, "The President's Proclamation," *The Atlantic*, November 1862. Williams, "a very experienced brigadier," was after Antietam "deserving of higher rank." Perry D. Jamieson, *Death in September: The Antietam Campaign* (Abilene, TX: McWhiney, 1999), 60; Quaife, *From the Cannon's Mouth*, 131, 142, 378.

Chapter 8

146. McClellan assigned Slocum to command on October 5. *Official Records*, vol. 19, pt. II, 431; Quaife, *From the Cannon's Mouth*, 136, 141. Williams continued as temporary corps commander during Slocum's absences. *Official Records*, vol. 25, pt. II, 86, 102–7; *AGI*, 18–19; *Official Records*, vol. 21, 754–55; Charnley, "Neglected Honor," 280 n32 and 292 n72, ascribes the lack of promotion to Stanton, not Lincoln.

147. *Official Records*, vol. 25, pt. II, 3; Charles E. Slocum, *Life and Services of Major General Henry Slocum* (Toledo, OH: self-published, 1913), 67. The area of XII Corps' winter quarters east of Stafford Court House is today bisected by an Amtrak rail line.

148. Quaife, *From the Cannon's Mouth*, 159, 162–64.

149. *Official Records*, vol. 25, pt. II, 152; pt. I, 682.

150. *Official Records*, vol. 25, pt. II, 273–75; Quaife, *From the Cannon's Mouth*, 180–81.

151. *Official Records*, vol. 25, pt. I, 671, 677. Ruger was West Point, class of 1854.

152. Bruce Catton, *Never Call Retreat* (Garden City, NJ: Doubleday, 1965), 144; *Official Records*, vol. 25, pt. I, 676–77; Slocum, *Life and Services of Major General Henry Slocum*, 77; Samuel E. Pittman, *Operations of General Alpheus S. Williams and His Command in the Chancellorsville Campaign* (Detroit, MI: Wm. S. Ostler, 1888), 8; Quaife, *From the Cannon's Mouth*, 185. Fairview had been a Chancellor farmstead. The structure burned several weeks after the battle. Geary was a Mexican-American War veteran.

153. John Bigelow Jr., *Campaign of Chancellorsville: A Strategic and Tactical Study* (New Haven, CT: Yale, 1910), 237, 248; Quaife, *From the Cannon's Mouth*, 185–86; *Official Records*, vol. 25, pt. 1, 677. He was not alone in this opinion.

154. Quaife, *From the Cannon's Mouth*, 187; *AGI*, 21; *Official Records*, vol. 25, pt. I, 677; pt. II, 326, 328, 765.

155. Bigelow, *Campaign of Chancellorsville*, 259, 293; *Official Records*, vol. 25, pt. II, 363. Williams was clear that aid ought to go where Jackson was headed—to the Union right.

156. Quaife, *From the Cannon's Mouth*, 188; *AGI*, 21.

157. Bigelow, *Campaign of Chancellorsville*, 295–97, 301; *AGI*, 22; Collins, *Army of Northern Virginia*, 292, gives Jackson's strength at 36,135.

158. *Official Records*, vol. 25, pt. I, 678; Pittman, *Chancellorsville Campaign*, 10–17; Charles C. Coffin, *Boys of '61* (Boston: Estes & Lauriat, 1881), 196. Coffin was a *Boston Journal* reporter. Quaife, *From the Cannon's Mouth*, 190; Bigelow, *Campaign of Chancellorsville*, 302.

159. *Official Records*, vol. 25, pt. I, 669–70. The 1ˢᵗ Division went into the maelstrom "with a loud cheer," ibid., 678, and "a yell of defiance," *AGI*, 22.

160. Quaife, *From the Cannon's Mouth*, 193–95.

161. Ibid., 195–200. "Old Plug" proved "a regular old soldier." In late July, he and Williams suffered an "eight or ten feet" fall, not the first or last accident accompanying the horse's "five or six wounds." His rider felt "a great love" for him, ibid., 237.

162. National Park Service signage at Fairview; *Official Records*, vol. 25, pt. I, 671.

163. Quaife, *From the Cannon's Mouth*, 188–89.

164. Ibid., 178–203 (Erebus: mythic Greek underworld).

165. *Official Records*, vol. 25, pt. I, 183–84; Quaife, *From the Cannon's Mouth*, 202; Markenfield Addey, *"Old Jack" and His Foot-Cavalry* (New York: John Bradburn, 1864), 210–12.

166. Bigelow, *Campaign of Chancellorsville*, 223, 485; *Official Records*, vol. 25, pt. I, 171.

167. Bigelow, *Campaign of Chancellorsville*, 316–19; Robert K. Krick, "The Smoothbore Volley that Doomed the Confederacy," *Chancellorsville: The Battle and Its Aftermath*, ed. Gary W. Gallagher (Chapel Hill: University of North Carolina, 1996), 120–21 (see page 17 in the Krick essays published under the title by Louisiana University Press in 2002); Douglas S. Freeman, *R.E. Lee: A Biography*, vol. 2 (New York: Charles Scribner's, 1962), 560.

Chapter 9

168. "Fields of Fire," Virginia Historical Highway Marker T57, Hunter Mill Road (Route 674) south of Baron Cameron Avenue, Vienna; *Official Records*, vol. 17, pt. I, 143; Quaife, *From the Cannon's Mouth*, 214.

169. *Official Records*, vol. 27, pt. I, 143, 782, 798, 825; vol. 51, pt. I, 1,063; Quaife, *From the Cannon's Mouth*, 215, 220–21, 223–24.

170. *Official Records*, vol. 27, pt. III, 458.

171. Ibid., pt. I, 771, 816, 758; Quaife, *From the Cannon's Mouth*, 224; Edwin B. Coddington, *The Gettysburg Campaign: A Study in Command* (New York: Charles Scribner's, 1979), 314; *AGI*, 27.

172. *Official Records*, vol. 27, pt. I, 777, 810–11.

173. Quaife, *From the Cannon's Mouth*, 224–25; David L. Ladd and Audrey J. Ladd, eds., *The Bachelder Papers: Gettysburg in Their Own Words*, vol. 1 (Dayton, OH: Morningside, 1994), 213.

174. John B. Bachelder, *Gettysburg: What to See, and How to See It* (Boston: self-published, 1873), 36; *Official Records*, vol. 27, pt. I, 773.

175. Gary W. Gallagher, "Confederate Corps Leadership on the First Day at Gettysburg," *The First Day at Gettysburg* (Kent, OH: Kent State, 1992), 51–53; Chris Mackowski and Kristopher D. White, "Second-Guessing Dick Ewell: Why Didn't the Confederate General Take Cemetery Hill on July 1, 1863?," *Civil War Times* 49, no. 4 (August 2010): 34.

176. Douglas S. Freeman, *R.E. Lee: A Biography*, vol. 3 (New York: Charles Scribner's, 1963, originally published in 1935), 77–78. Freeman embellished this argument in a chapter entitled "Ewell Cannot Reach a Decision" in *Lee's Lieutenants: A Study in Command* (New York: Charles Scribner's, 1944), 90; Coddington, *Gettysburg Campaign*, 320. Note the identical subtitle.

177. *Official Records*, vol. 27, pt. I, 758–59, 825; Coddington, *Gettysburg Campaign*, 321.

178. Ibid., 760. Locations are on a map in Slocum's report.

179. The 1st Brigade of 2nd Division formed in rear. *Official Records*, vol. 27, pt. I, 773, 804, 825–26; Quaife, *From the Cannon's Mouth*, 226; A. Wilson Greene, "'A Step All-Important and Essential to Victory': Henry W. Slocum and the Twelfth Corps on July 1–2, 1863," *The Second Day at Gettysburg*, ed. Gary W. Gallagher (Kent, OH: Kent State, 1993), 105, 108, 117. Ruger was also a favorite of Williams. Quaife, *From the Cannon's Mouth*, 254.

180. *Official Records*, vol. 27, pt. I, 773, 826; *AGI*, 28; Quaife, *From the Cannon's Mouth*, 226.

181. *Official Records*, vol. 27, pt. I, 773; Quaife, *From the Cannon's Mouth*, 227.

182. *Official Records*, vol. 27, pt. I, 773–74; *AGI*, 29; Gary W. Gallagher, ed., *Fighting for the Confederacy: The Personal Recollections of General Edward Porter Alexander* (Chapel Hill: University of North Carolina Press, 1989), 232; Sears, *Lincoln's Lieutenants*, 565.

183. *Official Records*, vol. 27, pt. I, 116, 765–66, 774, 778, 783, 804, 806, 809, 812, 883; Coddington, *Gettysburg Campaign*, 418; Jeffrey C. Hall, *The Stand of the U.S. Army at Gettysburg* (Bloomington: Indiana University, 2003), 143; Harry W. Pfanz, *Gettysburg: The Second Day* (Chapel Hill: University of North Carolina, 1987), 409.

184. Daniel G. Crotty, *Four Years Campaigning in the Army of the Potomac* (Grand Rapids, MI: Dygert, 1874), 91.

185. *Official Records*, vol. 27, pt. I, 826; Quaife, *From the Cannon's Mouth*, 229.

186. Collins, *Army of Northern Virginia*, 308; Jesse H. Jones and George S. Greene, "The Breastworks at Culp's Hill," *Battles and Leaders of the Civil War*, vol. 3 (New York: Century, 1884–88), 316–17 (hereafter *B&L*); *Official Records*, vol. 27, pt. I, 774.

187. John Gibbon, "The Council of War on the Second Day," *B&L*, 313–14. See Bill Hyde, ed., *The Union Generals Speak: The Meade Hearings on the Battle of Gettysburg* (Baton Rouge: Louisiana State University Press, 2003), 258–59.

188. Quaife, *From the Cannon's Mouth*, 229–30.

189. *Official Records*, vol. 27, pt. I, 774–75; *AGI*, 30; Quaife, *From the Cannon's Mouth*, 230.

190. *Official Records*, vol. 27, pt. I, 761, 774–75; *AGI*, 30; Coddington, *Gettysburg Campaign*, 471; John D. Hoptak, *Confrontation at Gettysburg: A Nation Saved, a Cause Lost* (Charleston, SC: The History Press, 2012), 183–84, 190.

191. *Official Records*, vol. 27, pt. I, 775; *AGI*, 31.

192. Sears, *Lincoln's Lieutenants*, 593; William A. Blair and Bell I. Wiley, *A Politician Goes to War: The Civil War Letters of John White Geary* (University Park: Pennsylvania State University Press, 1995), xi.

193. Collins, *Army of Northern Virginia*, 314; Allen C. Guelzo, *Gettysburg: The Last Invasion* (New York: Alfred A. Knopf, 2013), 113–14; Isaac R. Trimble, "The Battle and Campaign of Gettysburg," *Southern Historical Society Papers*, vol. 26 (Richmond, VA, 1898), 128.

194. *Official Records*, vol. 27, pt. I, 763; Quaife, *From the Cannon's Mouth*, 239.

195. *Report of the Joint Committee on the Conduct of the War, at the Second Session Thirty-Eighth Congress*, Army of the Potomac: Battle of Petersburg (Washington, D.C.: Government Printing Office, 1865), 336; Bachelder, *Gettysburg*, 56.

196. *Official Records*, vol. 27, pt. I, 184–85; Collins, *Army of Northern Virginia*, 308.

197. Quaife, *From the Cannon's Mouth*, 245.

198. Meade's pursuit of Lee engendered immediate dissatisfaction, starting with the president. See July 14 Halleck letter to Meade, *Official Records*, vol. 27, pt. I, 92; George P. Sanger, ed., *Statutes at Large*, vol. 13 (Boston: Little, Brown, 1866), 401. Two other resolutions were adopted that day, honoring Banks for Port Hudson's surrender and Burnside without specific rationale. Sanger, ed., *Statutes at Large*.

199. Guelzo, *Gettysburg*, 352–56; Ron Chernow, *Grant* (New York: Penguin, 2017), 992.

200. Richard A Sauers, *Gettysburg: The Meade-Sickles Controversy* (Washington, D.C.: Potomac, 2003), 141–52.

201. Quaife, *From the Cannon's Mouth*, 284; *Official Records*, vol. 27, pt. I, 114 (Meade) and 139 (Williams).

202. *Official Records*, vol. 27, pt. I, 758–61. The report totaled 1,200 words for July 1–3.

203. Ibid., 770–72 (division) and 772–77 (corps).

204. Ibid., 776. Williams also sent Geary's report back for correction, ibid., 777.

205. *Official Records*, vol. 27, pt. I, 777 (Ruger) and 765 (Williams); Quaife, *From the Cannon's Mouth*, 279–84. Private letters reveal his feelings as "terribly disgusted," "chagrined," "astonished," "pretty mad," "vexed," "annoyed" and, on Meade's report, as "defective" and "unholy." Quaife, *From the Cannon's Mouth*, 271–72, 288. The William L. Clements Library in Ann Arbor possesses an undated photograph captioned "Corps commanders, Army of the Potomac, Battle of Gettysburg," exhibiting the usual suspects—and Williams.

206. *Official Records*, vol. 27, pt. I, 763 (Slocum) and 120 (Meade).

207. Ibid., 769–70. Meade here admitted that he had not read Williams's Corps report or to have questioned his attendance at the council of war, although "I of course sent for corps commanders." A letter from George Greene confirmed Meade's nonfeasance and regret. Quaife, *From the Cannon's Mouth*, 294. In 1865, Williams recorded that he asked Meade at the Leister House, in view of Slocum's presence, whether he should withdraw: "he directed me to stay." *Bachelder Papers*, 217.

208. Slocum had written to the president on Williams's behalf on June 5. Quaife, *From the Cannon's Mouth*, 204–5. There does not appear to be a reply. U.S. Senator Jacob M. Howard had written Stanton and received a "wish a washy" reply, ibid., 206.

Chapter 10

209. *Official Records*, vol. 30, pt. I, 197–98; pt. III, 792 (September 23, received 10:00 p.m.); pt. I, 168 (received 10:35 p.m.); Walter Stahl, *Stanton: Lincoln's War Secretary* (New York: Simon & Schuster, 2017), 311.

210. Stahl, *Stanton*, 311–13; Tyler Dennett, *Lincoln and the Civil War in the Diaries and Letters of John Hay* (New York: Dodd, Mead, 1939), 93. Lincoln issued peremptory orders to Burnside to hasten from Knoxville to Chattanooga; he never made it. Similarly, Sherman's relief expedition stretched from Corinth, Mississippi, to Memphis; he never made it either. Daniel, *Days of Glory*, 345.

211. *Official Records*, vol. 29, pt. I, 147–48; *AGI*, 33; Quaife, *From the Cannon's Mouth*, 258. He would miss assistance from Wilkins, who had returned to Detroit after a prisoner exchange. Quaife, *From the Cannon's Mouth*, 255; *Official Records*, vol. 51, pt. I, 1092.

212. *Official Records*, vol. 29, pt. I, 151–52, 159, 162, 164, 166, 175. The War Department had extensive communications with railroad lines on the transit. See Roger Pickenpaugh, *Rescue by Rail: Troop Transfer and the Civil War in the West* (Lincoln: University of Nebraska, 1998). The historic depot exists at 10877 Willow Drive in Bealeton.

213. The Relay House is six miles southwest of Baltimore in Arbutus, junction of Railroad and Viaduct Avenues. Pickenpaugh, *Rescue by Rail*, 3–6, 77, 82–83, 87–89, 95, 98, 102, 110, 114, 117, 120, 127, 131; *Official Records*, vol. 29, pt. I, 180, 184.

214. Chernow, *Grant*, 311; *Official Records*, vol. 29, pt. I, 185, 194; Allan Nevins, *War for the Union*, vol. 3 (New York: Charles Scribner's, 1971), 202; James M. McPherson, *Battle Cry of Freedom: The Civil War Era* (New York: Oxford, 1988), 675; *AGI*, 34; Quaife, *From the Cannon's Mouth*, 265.

215. *Official Records*, vol. 29, pt. I, 156, 184; vol. 30, pt. II, 713–14; pt. IV, 137, 163–64, 397–98.

216. Ibid., vol. 30, pt. IV, 446–47; Quaife, *From the Cannon's Mouth*, 266, 276–78, 288.

217. Michael R. Bradley, *With Blood & Fire: Life Behind Union Lines in Middle Tennessee, 1863–65* (Shippensburg, PA: Burd, 2003), xv–xvi, 2, 39–40; Quaife, *From the Cannon's Mouth*, 266, 276, 278, 291 (an 1863 four-hundred-page study). He likely had read *Little Dorritt* years earlier (see "circumlocution"). Quaife, *From the Cannon's Mouth*, 23.

218. Pickenpaugh, *Rescue by Rail*, 152.

219. Edmund R. Brown, *Twenty-Seventh Indiana Volunteer Infantry in the War of the Rebellion, 1861 to 1865, First Division 12th and 20th Corps* (Monticello, IN: 1899), 448. Williams did not mention encountering Grant.

220. It would have been his singular chance to perform under Grant's eyes.

221. Pickenpaugh, *Rescue by Rail*, 159–60, 204; *AGI*, 34; Sears, *Lincoln's Lieutenants*, 598.

Chapter 11

222. Earl J. Hess, *Battle of Ezra Church and the Struggle for Atlanta* (Chapel Hill: University of North Carolina, 2015), xi. Williams's "battles": Resaca,

May 14–15; Peach Tree Creek, July 20; "combats": New Hope Church, May 25; Kolb's Farm; June 22; *Official Records*, vol. 38, pt. I, 52–54; *AGI*, 35; Quaife, *From the Cannon's Mouth*, 304.

223. *Official Records*, vol. 38, pt. I, 62–63; pt. II, 27; vol. 32, pt. II, 32; Quaife, *From the Cannon's Mouth*, 296–97; Generals' Reports of Service, *War of the Rebellion*, vol. 9, Alpheus S. Williams, Report 30, March 20, 1864, U.S. Army Generals' Reports of Civil War Service, 1864–87, U.S. National Archives, Archives Unbound, Gale Document no. SC5004595051 (hereafter *AGII*), 2. Again, special thanks to Ms. Petlewski and Gale. Craig L. Symonds, *Joseph E. Johnston: A Civil War Biography* (New York: W.W. Norton, 1994), 3, 267, 284.

224. Symonds, *Joseph E. Johnston*, 270.

225. *AGII*, 2–3; *Official Records*, vol. 38, pt. IV, 17.

226. *Official Records*, vol. 38, pt. I, 64; pt. II, 27–28; *AGII*, 3.

227. *Official Records*, vol. 38, pt. I, 64; pt. II, 28; *AGII*, 3. Williams "was much complimented," and General Howard gave him personal thanks. Newspaper accounts ignored him. Quaife, *From the Cannon's Mouth*, 308, 317, 319. Stanley was West Point, class of 1852.

228. *Official Records*, vol. 38, pt. II, 22, 28–29; *AGII*, 4–5.

229. *Official Records*, vol. 38, pt. II, 28–29; Robert P. Broadwater, *General George H. Thomas: A Biography of the Union's "Rock of Chickamauga"* (Jefferson, NC: McFarland & Company, 2009), 171; Quaife, *From the Cannon's Mouth*, 219, 309; *AGII*, 6.

230. *Official Records*, vol. 38, pt. I, 64–65; *AGII*, 7.

231. *Official Records*, vol. 38, pt. II, 29–30; Quaife, *From the Cannon's Mouth*, 312; *AGII*, 8–9; Broadwater, *General George H. Thomas*, 172. He again received congratulations. Quaife, *From the Cannon's Mouth*, 313. His leadership style continued to place him in harm's way. Williams's horse was hit. The next day, Williams felt "a sharp sting on my elbow joint." A spent Minié ball struck him near the "funny bone," leaving a lump and temporary loss of feeling. He put himself within sharpshooter range, and officers "quite near him" were shot. Once, at great risk, he "stood on the slender rail piles in the front rank." Quaife, *From the Cannon's Mouth*, 313–14, 316, 320, 331.

232. Earl J. Hess, *Kennesaw Mountain: Sherman, Johnston, and the Atlanta Campaign* (Chapel Hill: University of North Carolina, 2013), 6–27, 32; *Official Records*, vol. 38, pt. I, 66–68; *AGII*, 11–14.

233. *Official Records*, vol. 38, pt. IV, 627; Hess, *Kennesaw Mountain*, 29.

234. *Official Records*, vol. 38, pt. I, 68; *AGII*, 14–17; Daniel, *Days of Glory*, 407.

235. Symonds, *Joseph E. Johnston*, 309. It is too much to afford Williams the credit for Hood's elevation, one of the most fateful changes in Rebel army commands. Fate proved its fickleness with Kolb's Farm.

236. The structure today is the McAdoo Historic Event Center, 1706 Powder Springs Road Southwest near its intersection with Macland Road, Marietta. Jim Miles, *Fields of Glory: A History and Tour Guide of the War in the West, The Atlanta Campaign, 1864* (Nashville, TN: Cumberland, 2002), 137; Georgia Historical Commission Marker 033-10 (1952); National Park Service, *The Powder Springs Road Community and the Battle of Kennesaw Mountain*, brochure; *AGII*, 18–20.

237. Earl J. Hess, *The Battle of Peach Tree Creek: Hood's First Effort to Save Atlanta* (Chapel Hill: University of North Carolina, 2017), 67, 104; *AGII*, 21–23.

238. Hess, *Peach Tree Creek*, 152, 154–55, 160–63, 166; Albert Castel, *Decision in the West: Atlanta Campaign of 1864* (Lawrence, KS: University Press, 1992), 377–78, 380; William F. Fox, "Slocum and His Men: A History of the Twelfth and Twentieth Army Corps," *New York State Monuments Commission: In Memoriam: Henry Warner Slocum 1826–1894* (Albany, NY: J.B. Lyon, 1904), 261–63; *Official Records*, vol. 38, pt. II, 35; Hewett, *Supplement to Official Records*, series 5, 24; *AGII*, 21–26 (losses: 580); Daniel, *Days of Glory*, 414.

239. Hess, *Peach Tree Creek*, 265–68.

240. *Official Records*, vol. 38, pt. V, 272–74, 292, 302, 637, 670; Geary, Butterfield and Brigadier General William T. Ward, 3rd Division, were passed over. Knipe temporarily commanded the 1st Division. *AGII*, 27–29. Four months earlier, Williams had heard from Senator Howard that the president had him marked for "the next promotion." Quaife, *From the Cannon's Mouth*, 297; Hess, *Ezra Church*, 8. Hooker professed friendship for Williams, but according to George H. Thomas, in April 1864 Hooker was suggesting replacing him as division commander. Thomas passed the information on without comment to Sherman, who did not reply or concur in the suggestion. Hooker's two other disfavorites, Carl Schurz and Adolph von Steinwehr, were replaced. *Official Records*, vol. 32, pt. III, 271–72, 292, 341; Larry J. Daniel, *Days of Glory: The Army of the Cumberland, 1861–1865* (Baton Rouge: Louisiana State University Press, 2004), 385. Williams was not on the guest list for "a special dinnery-party" at Hooker's Wauhatchie headquarters, which included Thomas, Howard and other general officers. Daniel, *Days of Glory*, 390.

241. Hess, *Peach Tree Creek*, 270–71; Quaife, *From the Cannon's Mouth*, 341; *Official Records*, vol. 38, pt. II, 35; pt. V, 768, 777, 781; Hewett, *Supplement*

to Official Records, series 5, 31. A telegram from Slocum to Halleck arrived an hour before Sherman's. *Official Records*, vol. 38, pt. II, 778; *AGII*, 30.

242. Catton, *This Hallowed Ground*, 349.

243. Carl Sandburg, *Abraham Lincoln: The War Years*, vol. 3 (New York: Harcourt, Brace, 1939), 229.

244. James I. Robertson Jr., ed., *A Rebel War Clerk's Diary: At the Confederate States Capital*, vol. 2, *August 1863–April 1865* (Lawrence, KS: University Press, 2015), 250–52.

245. On Election Day, he voted for Lincoln at the polls of the 1st Michigan Engineers; Quaife, *From the Cannon's Mouth*, 348, 351; *Official Records*, vol. 38, pt. I, 86.

246. *Official Records*, vol. 38, pt. II, 37; *AGII*, 30; Quaife, *From the Cannon's Mouth*, 306, 309, 334–35, 338.

Chapter 12

247. *Official Records*, vol. 39, pt. III, 627, 701, 713; Quaife, *From the Cannon's Mouth*, 351.

248. *AGII*, 31; Quaife, *From the Cannon's Mouth*, 343–49.

249. *Official Records*, vol. 39, pt. III, 743–44. One letter revealed that he thought to quit "when I can do so honorably." That time never arrived, and Pittman's departure left Williams homesick and "pretty blue." He also lost Knipe to transfer. Quaife, *From the Cannon's Mouth*, 297, 311, 332, 342–44; *Official Records*, vol. 44, 206, 213; Coffin, *Boys of '61*, 392–93; March to the Sea Heritage Trail marker (hereafter *MTSHM*), Philadelphia United Methodist Church, 2194 West Hightower Trail, Conyers, Georgia.

250. *MTSHM*, "Centreville: Federal Encampments," adjacent to Jersey Community Building, 123 Main Street. The nearby Dallys Chapel Baptist Church on H D Atha Road recalls this history. Appreciation to Dewayne Powers for invaluable assistance.

251. Coffin, *Boys of '61*, 392–93; *Official Records*, vol. 44, 867; Quaife, *From the Cannon's Mouth*, 151.

252. *MTSHM*, "Social Circle: Lightning Strikes Twice," W. Hightower Trail west of North Cherokee Road; *MTSHM*, "Rutledge Station: A Tranquil Community Touched by War," Morgan County, Georgia, features a classic Williams photograph; *Official Records*, vol. 44, 206–7.

253. *MTSHM*, "Madison Station: As Near a Paradise as Anything I Ever Saw," 287 West Jefferson Street; Jeff Prugh, "The Town Sherman Refused to

Burn," *Washington Post*, October 14, 1979; Anna S. Rubin, *Through the Heart of Dixie: Sherman's March and American Memory* (Chapel Hill: University of North Carolina Press, 2014), 15. Eatonton is the birthplace of Joel Chandler Harris.

254. Rubin, *Through the Heart of Dixie*, 17; James C. Bonner, "Sherman at Milledgeville in 1864," *Journal of Southern History* 22, no. 3 (August 1956): 273, 275, 280, 282, 284–85; *MTSHM*, "The Old Governor's Mansion: Utmost Disorder and Confusion," and "State House Square: '…pretty well ransacked and things torn up generally,'" center of Milledgeville; *Official Records*, vol. 44, 207.

255. *MTSHM*, "Brown House: A Bed and a Meal for General Sherman," and "Washington County Courthouse: 'We had fought for the town and it was our plunder,'" 268 North Harris Street and 132 West Haynes Street, Sandersville; *MTSHM*, "Tennille Station: Sherman's 'Wings' Converge," Smith and West North Central Avenue; *Official Records*, vol. 44, 207.

256. *MTSHM*, "Crossing the Ogeechee River: A Classic Military Maneuver," west side of T E Buchanan Road in picnic area 0.3 miles north of U.S. 221, west of Louisville, and "The Sacking of Louisville: 'thoroughly and completely ransacked,'" East Broad Street west of Green Street, Louisville.

257. *Official Records*, vol. 44, 207.

258. *MTSHM*, "Battle of Buck Head Creek; 'fire one volley and fall back,'" Big Buckhead Church Road west of US-25, northeast of Old Louisville Road, near Perkins, Jenkins County.

259. *Official Records*, vol. 44, 207–8.

260. "Monteith Road" is crossed by I-95 south of exit 109. H. David Stone Jr., *Vital Rails: The Charleston & Savannah Railroad and the Civil War in Coastal South Carolina* (Columbia: University of South Carolina, 2008), 237.

261. *Official Records*, vol. 44, 208.

262. Ibid.

263. Alexander A. Lawrence, *A Present for Mr. Lincoln: The Story of Savannah from Secession to Sherman* (Macon, GA: Ardivan, 1961), 195–96.

264. Ibid., 208–9; *Autobiography of Oliver Otis Howard*, vol. 2 (New York: Baker & Taylor, 1907), 93; *Official Records*, vol. 44, 974 (Hardee dispatch to Davis, December 21, from Hardeeville); Noah A. Trudeau, *Southern Storm: Sherman's March to the Sea* (New York: Harper Collins, 2008), 453; *AGII*, 39–40.

265. *Official Records*, vol. 44, 7, 12, 209. Howard wrote that a friendly debate ensued over which unit first entered Savannah, but Geary, Williams's Corps, had the honor; *Autobiography of Oliver Otis Howard*, 94.

266. *Official Records*, vol. 44, 783, 809–10.

267. Ibid., 44, 966, 970, 974.

268. Ibid., 210–12. Williams claimed the figures for fodder were likely understated by 1.5 million pounds.

269. The column ranged for up to fifteen miles in length. *Official Records*, vol. 44, 212. Coleraine plantation was on the west bank of the Savannah River across from Onslow Island, south of (St.) Augustine Creek, near where present Georgia Route 25 (North Coastal Highway) crosses, Port Wentworth. Frank T. Wheeler, *Savannah River Plantations: Photographs from the Collections of the Georgia Historical Society* (Charleston, SC: Arcadia Publishing, 1998), 40.

270. *Memoirs of General William T. Sherman: By Himself* (New York: D. Appleton, 1875), vol. 2, 244–45; *Official Records*, vol. 44, 502. Rubin, *Through the Heart of Dixie*, 23, submits that Davis pre-planned ridding himself of the refugees. Another history states that Davis was responsible for three such incidents, including an earlier one at Buckhead Creek and a third at Lockner Creek. J.D. Dickey, *Rising in Flames: Sherman's March and the Fight for a New Nation* (New York: Pegasus Books, 2018), 201–2, 228–30. A third, while admitting that Davis abandoned human beings "to their fate," regards Williams as "a civilian at heart" and "old," though "a proven soldier and a leader." Nathaniel C. Hughes Jr. and Gordon D. Whitney, *Jefferson Davis in Blue: The Life of Sherman's Relentless Warrior* (Baton Rouge: Louisiana State University Press, 2002), 300, 309.

271. Quaife, *From the Cannon's Mouth*, 18, 46 n8. Living at 195 Russell Street one year later and eventually on Croghan Street in Detroit, he died in May 1889. *Charles F. Clark's Annual of the City of Detroit, 1866–7* (Detroit, MI: Charles F. Clark, 866), 134; *Detroit Free Press*, May 10, 1889, 3.

272. Dr. Martin Luther King Jr., *Emancipation Proclamation Centennial Address*, New York Civil War Centennial Commission Emancipation Proclamation Observance, New York City, September 12, 1962.

273. Lawrence, *Present for Mr. Lincoln*, 229, 309; Quaife, *From the Cannon's Mouth*, 355, 385; William Waud's sketch names Sherman, Williams and other officers. Frederic E. Ray, *Alfred A. Waud: Civil War Artist* (New York: Viking, 1974), 174.

Chapter 13

274. *AGII*, 41; Quaife, *From the Cannon's Mouth*, 379. On a list of "Appointments Confirmed by the Senate" "To be Major-Generals of Volunteers by Brevet" were "Brigadier-Generals A.S. Williams, Judson Kilpatrick, and

Absalom Baird, U.S. Vols., January 12, 1865." *United States Service Magazine*, vol. 3 (New York: Charles P. Richardson, 1865), 289; *Senate Executive Journal*, January 30, 1865, 105–6; February 14, 1865, 161, 166–67.

275. Coffin, *Boys of '61*, 437; *AGII*, 42–43; *Official Records*, vol. 47, pt. I, 581–83, 591–93; Clement Eaton, ed., "Diary of an Officer in Sherman's Army Marching through the Carolinas," *Journal of Southern History* 9, no. 2 (May 1943): 243 (emphasis in original); Dexter Horton, Groveland Township, served as captain and commissary of subsistence. Robertson, *Michigan in the War*, 980.

276. Quaife, *From the Cannon's Mouth*, 373–74; Mark Hoffman, *"My Brave Mechanics": First Michigan Engineers and Their Civil War* (Detroit, MI: Wayne State, 2007), 245, 269.

277. *Official Records*, vol. 47, pt. I, 583–84; pt. II, 719; Eaton, "Diary of an Officer in Sherman's Army," 247.

278. Quaife, *From the Cannon's Mouth*, 373–74; *Official Records*, vol. 47, pt. I, 584–85, 594–96; Sherman, *Memoirs*, 295; *Official Records*, vol. 47, pt. II, 807; *Sherman's March through North Carolina: A Chronology*, ed. Wilson Angley, Jerry L. Cross and Michael Hill (North Carolina Division of Archives and History, 1995), 23–24.

279. John G. Barrett, *Civil War in North Carolina* (Chapel Hill: University of North Carolina, 1963), 319–22; *Official Records*, vol. 47, pt. I, 585–86; *AGII*, 55–56.

280. *Official Records*, vol. 47, pt. I, 65, 586; Mark L. Bradley, *Last Stand in the Carolinas: The Battle of Bentonville* (Campbell, CA: Savas Woodbury, 1996), 132.

281. *Civil War in North Carolina*, 331; *Official Records*, vol. 47, pt. I, 587; Bradley, *Last Stand*, 194.

282. Bradley, *Last Stand*, 194–95, 200–203; *Civil War in North Carolina*, 335, 587–88.

283. *Official Records*, vol. 47, pt. I, 588; *Sherman's March through North Carolina*, 39; *Official Records*, vol. 47, pt. II, 919; Bradley, *Last Stand*, 307. Excellent graphics are contained in Mark A. Moore, *Old North State at War: The North Carolina Civil War Atlas* (North Carolina Department of Cultural Resources, 2015), 151–56.

284. Quaife, *From the Cannon's Mouth*, 376–77; *Official Records*, vol. 47, pt. I, 596, 603.

285. *Official Records*, vol. 47, pt. I, 588; *AGII*, 66.

286. *Official Records*, vol. 47, pt. III, 73–75; Quaife, *From the Cannon's Mouth*, 375–80; *Civil War in North Carolina*, 339; Joseph T. Glatthaar, *March to the Sea and Beyond* (New York: New York University, 1985), 23. One historian

attributed Williams's demotion to his "gentlemanly" demeanor. John G. Barrett, *Sherman's March through the Carolinas* (Chapel Hill: University of North Carolina, 1956), 33; *Civil War in North Carolina*, 348. Another evaluated him as merely "competent and timely" and the demotion because "Williams, apparently unambitious militarily and politically, seemed content with doing his job. He reminds one of George Thomas." Nathaniel C. Hughes Jr., *Bentonville: The Final Battle of Sherman and Johnston* (Chapel Hill: University of North Carolina, 1996), 228–29. In Brady's valedictory May 1865 photograph "Sherman and His Generals," Mower represented XX Corps. Several histories attribute the move as fulfilling a long-standing promise to Mower.

287. The Army of Georgia received formal designation on March 28. *Official Records*, vol. 47, pt. III, 43, 185, 214, 268–69; pt. I, 603–4; Hoffman, *"My Brave Mechanics,"* 286–87; Quaife, *From the Cannon's Mouth*, 161, 381; Mark L. Bradley, *This Astounding Close: The Road to Bennett Place* (Chapel Hill: University of North Carolina, 2000), xiii–xiv.

288. *Official Records*, vol. 47, pt. I, 604–5.

289. Ibid., 605.

290. Quaife, *From the Cannon's Mouth*, 380, 388.

291. *ASWP.* Swift, an ex-prisoner of war, received a brevet brigadier generalship for gallant and meritorious service at the Battle of Spotsylvania.

292. Fox, "Slocum and His Men," 315; Quaife, *From the Cannon's Mouth*, 390.

293. *Official Records*, vol. 47, pt. I, 605–6; Quaife, *From the Cannon's Mouth*, 367–68.

294. *Official Records*, vol. 42, pt. III, 584; *AGII*, 72.

295. *AGII*, 73. On May 26, the last Rebel army surrendered.

296. Rachel S. Thorndike, ed., *Sherman Letters: Correspondence Between General and Senator Sherman from 1837 to 1891* (New York: Charles Scribner's, 1894), 260; *Report of the Proceedings of the Society of the Army of the Tennessee* (Cincinnati, OH: F.W. Freeman, 1885), 115–16 (Jacob D. Cox remarks, April 1881); Mark A. Smith and Wade Sokolosky, *"No Such Army Since the Days of Julius Caesar": Sherman's Carolinas Campaign from Fayettville to Averasboro, March 1865* (California: Savas Beatie, 2017), 92.

Chapter 14

297. *Official Records*, vol. 46, pt. III, 1,247; Quaife, *From the Cannon's Mouth*, 356, 381, 389–91.

298. *AGII*, 73; *Official Records*, vol. 47, pt. III, 620, 679–81; vol. 48, pt. II, 1,049–50, 1,111; *United States Service Magazine*, vol. 4 (New York: Charles B. Richardson, 1865), 70. George H. Thomas also supported his retention. Quaife, *From the Cannon's Mouth*, 390–91. On July 18, Grant wrote Stanton seeking appointment of John W. Geary, once Williams's subordinate, to a full major generalship. *Official Records*, vol. 47, pt. III, 678. Reynolds was West Point class of 1843.

299. *New York Times*, July 19, 1865, 4.

300. *Detroit Free Press*, August 13, 1865, 1; *AGII*, 73–74, 83.

301. Charnley, "Neglected Honor," 237; Ezra J. Warner, *Generals in Blue* (Baton Rouge: Louisiana State, 2006), 452.

302. Quaife, *From the Cannon's Mouth*, 384; *AGII*, 74; Ed Bearss and Arrell M. Gibson, *Fort Smith: Little Gibraltar on the Arkansas* (Norman: University of Oklahoma, 1969), 303–9; *Report of the Joint Committee on Reconstruction at the First Session Thirty-Ninth Congress* (Washington, D.C.: Government Printing Office, 1866), 48–59, 69–77, 79–99, 119–20, 124–29, 153–55, 168–70; Eric Foner, *Reconstruction: America's Unfinished Revolution* (New York: Harper Collins, 2002), 45.

303. *AGII*, 74–75; *United States Service Magazine*, vol. 5 (New York: Charles B. Richardson, 1866), 181 (General Orders No. 168, "Brevet Major-General E.D. Townsend, Assistant Adjutant-General").

304. *ASWP*; *Statutes at Large*, Act of April 17, 1866, 39th Congress, 1st Session, Chap. 46, 38–39; *Journal of the Missouri State Senate at the Regular Session of the Twenty-Sixth General Assembly* (Jefferson City, NC: Horace Wilcox, 1871), 275–76.

Chapter 15

305. Hershock, *Paradox*, 185–91.

306. David M. Jordan, *Winfield Scott Hancock: A Soldier's Life* (Bloomington: Indiana University, 1996), 5–6, 30–31, 165, 204, 307; Harriette M. Dilla, *Politics of Michigan 1865–1878* (New York: Columbia, 1912), 62, 64.

307. Hershock, *Paradox*, 191; Charnley, "Neglected Honor," 239–40. Crapo's vote exceeded 1864's. Stocking, *Under the Oaks*, 65; Michael J. Dubin, *United States Gubernatorial Elections, 1861–1911: The Official Results by State and County* (Jefferson, NC: McFarland, 2010), 270–71.

308. Stocking, *Under the Oaks*, 85; Hershock, *Paradox*, 192; Elizabeth R. Varon, *Andrew Johnson: Campaigns and Elections*, available at https://millercenter. org/president/johnson/campaigns-and-elections.

309. Quaife, *From the Cannon's Mouth*, 9–10; Susan S. Robeson, Caroline F. Stroud and Kate H. Osborn, *An Historical and Genealogical Account of Andrew Robeson* (Philadelphia, PA: J.B. Lippincott (1916), 382; *ASWP*. Still, he concluded with: "Love to the Major, and believe me, as ever, your affectionate Father."

310. *Senate Executive Journal*, December 14, 1866, 4; David N. Camp, ed., *American Year-Book and National Register for 1869* (Hartford, CT: O.D. Case, 1869), 81–82; Paul H. Bergeron, ed., *Papers of Andrew Johnson*, vol. 2 (Knoxville: University of Tennessee, 1994), 546, gives the date as December 10; *Senate Executive Journal*, February 27, 1867, 276, Committee Chair Charles Sumner; *Senate Executive Journal*, March 2, 1867, 327–28.

311. Jay C. Martin, *General Henry Baxter, 7th Michigan Volunteer Infantry* (Jefferson, NC: McFarland, 2016), 147; Charnley, "Neglected Honor," 242.

312. Farmer, *History of Detroit*, 948. Its remnant exists west of I-96 between MLK Boulevard and Michigan Avenue. *Journal of the Missouri State Senate*, 275–76; *Society of the Army of the Cumberland Fourth Reunion* (Cincinnati, OH: Robert Clarke, 1870), 33, 265. See Appendix D. He also joined the Army of the Potomac veterans organization. Dilla, *Politics of Michigan*, 111, 119.

313. He was then boarding at 68 West Fort Street. *Hubbell & Weeks' Annual City Directory for 1872–3* (Detroit, MI: Tribune Book and Job Office, 1872), 507; Dilla, *Politics of Michigan*, 145; *Society of the Army of the Cumberland Sixth Reunion* (Cincinnati, OH: Robert Clarke, 1872), 118; *Society of the Army of the Cumberland Seventh Reunion* (Cincinnati, OH: Robert Clarke, 1873), 127, available at http://www.presidency.ucsb.edu/ws/index.php?pid=29579 and http://www.presidency.ucsb.edu/ws/?pid=29580.

314. *Record of Service of Michigan Volunteers in the Civil War, 1861–1865*, vol. 45 (Kalamazoo, MI: Ihling Bros. & Everhard), 186; Palmer, *Early Days*, 904; *Chicago Tribune*, December 22, 1878, 2. She died in Arlington Heights, Massachusetts, November 1903. *Detroit Free Press*, November 17, 1903, 5. Her burial in Elmwood was not in the Williams plot. The painting of the first election in Michigan, now exhibited in the Detroit Institute of Arts, was "for many years in the possession of Mrs. A.S. Williams." Farmer, *History of Detroit*, 112.

315. *AGII*, 41.

316. Dubin, *United States Gubernatorial Elections*, 231. Prohibition Party candidate Charles P. Russell received forty-eight votes. Stocking, *Under the Oaks*, 91.

317. Sherman, *Memoirs*, vol. 1, 3.

318. *Sherman's Historical Raid: The Memoirs in the Light of the Record, A Review Based upon Compilations from the Files of the War Office* (Cincinnati, OH: Wilstach,

Baldwin, 1875). Brother-in-law Charles W. Moulton came to Sherman's defense with *Review of General Sherman's Memoirs Examined, Chiefly in Light of Its Own Evidence* (Cincinnati, OH: Robert Clarke, 1875).

319. See note 220; the salutation is "My dear General," suggesting another recipient. Letter Commenting on Sherman's Memoirs, mssHM 3730, Huntington Library, San Marino, California, 2, 9, 32–33. Sherman's passage is at vol. 2, 333, and his eulogy is in *Journal of the House of Representatives of the State of Michigan*, vol. 1 (Lansing, MI: W.S. George, 1879), 278.

320. *Congressional Record*, 44th Congress, 1st Session, Vol. 4 (Washington, D.C.: Government Printing Office, 1876), 166. The Constitution provided for Congress to meet annually "and such Meeting shall be on the first Monday in December." Article One, Section 4, Clause 2 (revised by the Twentieth Amendment). The 43rd Congress held its 2nd Session from December 7, 1874, until March 3, 1875.

321. *Congressional Record*, 44th Congress, 1st Session, vol. 4, 167, 171, 183; Ben P. Poole, *Congressional Directory, Compiled for the Use of Congress*, 44th Congress, 1st Session, 1st ed. (Washington, D.C.: Government Printing Office, 1875), 144–45, 152. It was not an undesirable back row location. Ben P. Poole, *Congressional Directory*, 44th Congress, 2nd ed. (Washington, D.C.: Government Printing Office, 1877), 167. In the *Directory*'s biography, Williams's command of XII Corps at South Mountain was listed. *Chicago Tribune*, December 22, 1878, 2.

322. *Centennial of the United States Military Academy at West Point, New York, 1802–1902*, vol. 2 (Washington, D.C.: Government Printing Office, 904), 388. The Board of Visitors continues today. *Congressional Record*, 44th Congress, 1st Session, Vol. 4, 183, 250–51, 330, 2,082; Poole, *Congressional Directory* (1875), 78. The House voted unanimously to impeach former secretary of war William W. Belknap in March 1876. The Williamses lived at 499 Woodward Avenue, with his office at "14 Telegraph Block" during his service in Congress. *J.W. Weeks & Company's Annual Directory of Detroit, for 1875–76* (Detroit, MI: Tribune Printing Company, 1875), 611; *…for 1876–77* (Detroit, MI: Wm. A. Scripps, 1876), 660; *…for 1877* (Detroit, MI: J.W. Weeks & Company, 1877), 705; *…for 1878* (Detroit, MI: J.W. Weeks & Company, 1877), 760.

323. *Reports of Committees of the House of Representatives for the First Session of the Forty-Fourth Congress, 1875–76* (Washington, D.C.: Government Printing Office, 1876), 1–4, 75, XV (Report Nos. 53, 75, 191); *Congressional Record*, 44th Congress, 1st Session, vol. 4, 2,565, 3,018.

324. Charles K. Hyde, "'Detroit the Dynamic': The Industrial History of Detroit from Cigars to Cars," *Michigan Historical Review* 27, no. 1 (Mt. Pleasant: Central Michigan University, 2000), 57; *Congressional Record*, 44th Congress, 1st Session, Vol. 4 (Washington, D.C.: Government Printing Office, 1876), Appendix, 323–24.

325. *Congressional Record*, 44th Congress, 2nd Session, Vol. 5 (Washington, D.C.: Government Printing Office, 1877), 3, 1,050.

326. Ibid., Appendix, 176–77.

327. William H. Rehnquist, *Centennial Crisis: The Disputed Election of 1876* (New York: Alfred A. Knopf, 2004), 248.

328. Dubin, *United States Gubernatorial Elections*, 238; Stocking, *Under the Oaks*, 94. William Wilkins was credited with helping Williams get elected to Congress twice. *Detroit Post and Tribune*, "Col. Wilkins Dead," April 1, 1882; *Michigan Historical Collections*, vol. 4 (Lansing, MI: Wynkoop Hallenbeck Crawford Company, 1906, reprint of 1883 edition), 439. Wilkins died in 1882.

329. The American Presidency Project, "1876 Democratic Party Platform," https://www.presidency.ucsb.edu/documents/1876-democratic-party-platform.

330. Ben P. Poole, *Congressional Directory*, 45th Congress, 1st Session, 1st ed. (Washington, D.C.: Government Printing Office, 1877), 81, 84, 152–53, 159.

331. *Congressional Record*, 45th Congress, 2nd Session, Vol. 7 (Washington, D.C.: Government Printing Office, 1878), 223–26.

332. Ibid., 1,840, 4,831–33.

333. Ibid., 4,498.

334. Ibid., 2,926, 3,207.

335. Ibid., 4,557. His support may have been to establish a precedent for funding of Mackinac National Park.

336. Dubin, *United States Gubernatorial Elections*, 245. The Prohibition Party candidate received fifty-four votes. Hollandsworth, *Pretense of Glory*, 246 n34.

337. *Congressional Record*, 45th Congress, 3rd Session, Vol. 8 (Washington, D.C.: Government Printing Office, 1879), 8, 58, 59, 82, 127.

Chapter 16

338. *Congressional Record*, 45th Congress, 3rd Session, Vol. 8 (Washington, D.C.: Government Printing Office, 1879), 8, 127, 129; Ben P. Poole, *Congressional*

Directory for 45th Congress, Second Session, Second Edition, Corrected to June 10, 1878 (Washington, D.C.: Government Printing Office, 1878), 159.

339. Key details provided by Dr. Matthew Wasniewski and Ms. Farar Elliott, U.S. House of Representatives.

340. *Memorial Addresses on the Life and Character of Alpheus S. Williams* (Washington, D.C.: Government Printing Office, 1880), 6, 21; *Congressional Record*, 45th Congress, 3rd Session, vol. 8, 212, 219. George W. Hendee of Vermont, absent, was stated to be the committee chair.

341. *Detroit Free Press*, December 21, 1878, 1; December 22, 1878, 2. Knipe long held Williams in esteem. He delivered "a very flattering speech" in a sword presentation and named a son after Williams. Quaife, *From the Cannon's Mouth*, 162, 254.

342. *Chicago Tribune*, December 22, 1878, 2; *New York Times*, December 22, 1878.

343. *Detroit Free Press*, December 25, 1878, 1.

344. *New York Times*, December 25, 1878, 1; *Chicago Daily Tribune*, December 25, 1878, 2, reprinted the *Times* item.

345. *Record Book*, Elmwood Historic Cemetery.

346. Yet it held space enough for all the family.

347. *Congressional Record*, 45th Congress, 3rd Session, Vol. 8 (Washington, D.C.: Government Printing Office, 1879), 365–66, 1,683–97.

348. *Journal of the House of Representatives of the State of Michigan*, 1879, vol. 1 (Lansing, MI: W.S. George, 1879), 68, 274–75, 280, 282, 288.

349. Ibid., 36; *Congressional Record*, 45th Congress, 3rd Session, Vol. 8 (Washington, D.C.: Government Printing Office, 1879), 2,340, 2,346.

Chapter 17

350. George W. Nichols, *Story of the Great March from the Diary of a Staff Officer* (New York: Harper & Brothers, 1865), 287–88. Nichols's fame rocketed when he wrote about "Wild Bill" Hickock.

351. Quint, *Record of the Second Massachusetts Infantry*, 47–48, 276.

352. Comey, *Legacy of Valor*, 24, 188, 235.

353. Gould, *History of the First-Tenth-Twenty-ninth*, 147.

354. Bachelder, *Gettysburg*, 36, 52, 96–97.

355. *Detroit Free Press*, June 8, 1879, 6.

356. George H. Gordon, *A War Diary of Events in the War of the Great Rebellion* (Boston: James R. Osgood, 1882), 30. See n78 on Gordon's reliability.

357. Jacob D. Cox, "The Battle of Antietam," *B&L*, vol. 2, 630, 635; also 603.

358. *B&L*, vol. 3, 313–14.

359. Jones and Greene, "Breastworks at Culp's Hill," *B&L*, 316–17.

360. Though absent from Gettysburg due to wounds, Francis A. Walker wrote "Meade at Gettysburg," *B&L*, vol. 3, 406; ibid., 414–15.

361. McClellan, *McClellan's Own Story*, 591, 592, 601, 624. The book later referred to "Mansfield's corps," ibid., 601.

362. *Michigan at Gettysburg, July 1st, 2nd and 3rd, 1863: Proceedings Incident to the Dedication of the Michigan Monuments upon the Battlefield of Gettysburg, June 12th, 1889* (Detroit, MI: Winn & Hammond, 1889), 38–39.

363. Pittman, *Chancellorsville Campaign*, 17.

364. Charles W. Boyce, *A Brief History of the Twenty-Eighth Regiment New York State Volunteers* (Buffalo, NY, 1896), 24, 28.

365. Ibid., 61–62.

366. Brown, *Twenty-Seventh Indiana*, 104, 351, 469.

367. Fox, "Slocum and His Men," 295, 311–12.

368. *As Seen from the Ranks: A Boy in the Civil War* (New York: G.P. Putnam's, 1902), 138, 159–60.

369. *Detroit Free Press*, May 31, 1902, 2. The Logan monument was dedicated in 1897 after his 1886 death.

370. *Detroit Free Press*, February 6, 1910, 53.

371. David Ingalls and Karen Risko, *Michigan Civil War Landmarks* (Charleston, SC: The History Press, 2015), 96; *Detroit Free Press*, June 12, 1910, 38, 69. Correspondent William D. Mann had funded the printing of a history of the 7th Michigan Cavalry in 1893.

372. *Detroit Free Press*, March 5, 1911, 53.

373. Greusel, *General Alpheus S. Williams*, 5, 8–9, 15–24, 29. He made some small changes when including Goodhue's "centaur" quote in his biography. *Michigan Historical Collections*, vol. 39 (Lansing, MI: Wynkoop Hallenback Crawford, 1915), 378–86.

374. *Detroit Free Press*, May 27, 1911, 11.

375. *Journal Proceedings of the Board of Education of the City of Detroit for the Year 1910–11* (Detroit, MI: Griswold, 1912), 238, 256; *Prominent Newspapermen in Michigan*, Michigan Historical Collections, vol. 39 (Lansing: Michigan Historical Commission, 1915), 159 n1. MOLLUS funds came from both men and women.

376. American Federation of Arts, *Art and Progress*, vol. 3, November 1911–October 1912, 630. The Washington statue is in "Continental Army

Plaza" at the west East River approach to the Williamsburg Bridge on Roebling Street, south of South 4th Street. The Lee statue was the subject of early twenty-first-century controversy.

377. The Hall of American Artists, New York University, *Homage to Henry Merwin Shrady, Sculptor 1871–1922* (1942), 26. He also wrote *History of Michigan*, published in 1915 by Lewis Publishing of Chicago. Shrady's father ministered to U.S. Grant in his final illness.

378. Appreciation to Brian James Egen for these insights; for another, see Dennis A. Nawrocki, *Art in Detroit Public Places* (Detroit, MI: Wayne State, 2008), 118; John J. Hennessey, "Conservatism's Dying Ember: Fitz John Porter and the Union War, 1862," *Corps Commanders in Blue: Union Major Generals in the Civil War*, ed. Ethan S. Rafuse (Baton Rouge: Louisiana State, 2014), 14. The horse could represent "Yorkshire," the Detroit mount he had with him all four years; "Billy"; or "Major." Quaife, *From the Cannon's Mouth*, 19, 166, 293, 369, 371–72; Charles Moore Papers, 1905–17, Detroit Institute of Arts.

379. Review of Books, *New York Times*, November 29, 1959, 46.

380. Charnley, "Neglected Honor," "Abstract," i, 245–46. The dissertation held Williams partly at fault for the lack of promotion, maintaining that he should have been more assertive in seeking elevation.

381. Jeffrey G. Charnley, "Michigan's General A.S. Williams and Civil War Historians: A Century of Neglect," *Michigan Historical Review* 12, no. 1 (Spring 1986): 1–28.

382. Greg Forster, "'Old Pap' Takes Care of Business," *Civil War: The Magazine of the Civil War Society* 10, no. 4, issue no. 36 (July–August 1992): 18–22, 52–53.

383. Quaife, *From the Cannon's Mouth*, vii–xii. A currently popular historian would disagree with any equivocation about the West Point influence, decrying in a recent biography "the whole dismal parade of career hacks and self-promoting political generals on the Union side." Chernow, *Grant*, 431. George C. Marshall had scorn for officers who employed political pressure in aid of their advancement: "I may make a thousand mistakes in this war but none will be the result of political meddling....I don't like people who are seeking promotion." Speech of Dwight D. Eisenhower, May 23, 1964, George C. Marshall Research Library, Lexington, Virginia.

384. Gary W. Gallagher, "Seeing the War through Soldier's Letters: Military Memoirs Come Packed with Surprises," *Civil War Times* 50, no. 6 (December 2011): 22.

385. Albert Castel, "'Old Pap': Michigan's Top Civil War General," *Michigan History* 82, no. 4 (July/August 1998): 18ff.

386. Joseph Pierro, *The Maryland Campaign of September 1862: Ezra A. Carman's Definitive Study of the Union and Confederate Armies at Antietam* (New York: Routledge Taylor & Francis, 2008), 235.

387. Robert D. Jenkins Sr., *Battle of Peach Tree Creek: Hood's First Sortie, 20 July 1864* (Macon, GA: Mercer University, 2013), 302–4.

388. John H. Matsui, *First Republican Army: The Army of Virginia and the Radicalization of the Civil War* (Charlottesville: University of Virginia, 2016), 1–6, 52–53, 140, 156, 162 n8, 163 n33.

389. Sears, *Lincoln's Lieutenants*, 214, 293, 298, 417, 438. This judgment on Williams is not new. See Stephen W. Sears, *Chancellorsville* (Boston: Houghton Mifflin Company, 1996), 432; Stephen W. Sears, *Gettysburg* (Boston: Houghton Mifflin Company, 2003), 38.

390. Pickenpaugh, *Rescue by Rail*, 74 (Williams was "one of the least pretentious general officers in the Union army"); Hess, *Peach Tree Creek*, 152 ("one of the most thoroughly experienced division commanders in Sherman's army group during the Atlanta campaign," "an excellent division and corps commander" and "Michigan's most capable general of the war"); Richard Bak, *A Distant Thunder: Michigan in the Civil War* (Ann Arbor, MI: Huron River, 2004), 77, 176. See Thomas J. Goss, *The War within the Union High Command* (Lawrence, KS: University Press, 2003), 88, 148; "Slocum and Williams Steal the Initiative" in Matt Spruill, *Decisions at Gettysburg: The Nineteen Critical Decisions that Defined the Campaign* (Knoxville: University of Tennessee, 2011), 80. But see also Gerald Linderman, *Embattled Courage: The Experience of Combat in the American Civil War* (New York: Free Press, 1987), 164–66.

391. Ben Myers, "Old Pap: The Neglected Legacy of One of the Union's Most Loyal Brigadiers," *Military Images* 36, no. 3 (2018): 52–58.

Epitaph

392. John H. Franklin, *The Emancipation Proclamation* (Garden City, NJ: Doubleday/Anchor, 1965), 131; Quaife, *From the Cannon's Mouth*, 64, 348, 392. See Appendix D.

Appendix A

393. All but the last are in *Official Records*, series I.

Appendix B

394. *Official Records*, vol. 12, pt. II, 27 (an inaccurate figure). On September 12, Williams wrote, "Banks has been in command of the corps but a few days since the battle of Cedar Mountain"; Quaife, *From the Cannon's Mouth*, 120. It appears he was in official temporary command from the ninth to at least the eighteenth, ibid., 105. In 1864, he wrote that Banks resumed Corps command "on the march" from Culpeper to Alexandria; *AGI*, 9–10.

395. John H. Eicher and David J. Eicher, *Civil War High Commands* (Palo Alto, CA: Stanford University Press, 2001), 858, 861, 862; Quaife, *From the Cannon's Mouth*, 181. See Hewett, *Supplement to Official Records*, Series 3, 423.

Appendix C

396. *AGII*, 109–12 (original form).

Appendix D

397. *Society of the Army of the Cumberland, Fourth Reunion*, 12–15 (typos omitted).

INDEX

ACKNOWLEDGEMENTS

Besides those cited, sincere appreciation goes to Plymouth District Library, Michigan eLibrary, Library of Michigan, Bentley Historical Library, Burton Historical Library, William L. Clemens Library, Huntington Library, University of Pennsylvania Libraries, Library of Virginia, New York Public Library, U.S. Army Carlisle Barracks, Western Michigan University Library and Detroit Institute of Arts. For special research and analysis, I thank Don Conners of Deep River, Connecticut; Eric Minotti; Brian James Egen; Dr. Scott Stabler; Jerry and Jeanette Lee; Matt VanAcker; Keith Harrison; Rhonda Forristall; Betty Vaughn; Alonzo Lacey; Nan Card; Jim McConnell; Garry Adelman and American Battlefields Trust; Kirsten Neal; Civil War Talk Radio; Pam O'Connor; and Carol Bedford. For proficient manuscript assistance, I thank Jacqueline Tinney. For substantive counsel, I must thank Dave Dempsey and Dr. Martin J. Hershock, as well as Tom Dempsey for his constancy and fidelity.

For irreplaceable support and indulgence, I cherish Suzzanne, Anna and Daniel.

All errors herein are mine alone, any glory to him who "has His own purposes."

ABOUT THE AUTHOR

Jack Dempsey is author of the award-winning *Michigan and the Civil War: A Great and Bloody Sacrifice* and Civil War articles and coauthor (with Brian James Egen) of *Michigan at Antietam: The Wolverine State's Sacrifice on America's Bloodiest Day*. His fascination with the period dates to age eight. While counsel in the Ann Arbor office of Dickinson Wright PLLC, he served on the Michigan Historical Commission from 2007 to 2018, as its president from 2012 to 2017 and as chair of its Civil War Sesquicentennial Committee. Born in Detroit, he lives in Plymouth Township with his wife of forty-four years, Suzzanne.

http://jackdempseybooks.com

Proceeds from sales of this book benefit the Michigan Civil War Association.

Coat of arms of Michigan, encircled by a Civil War remembrance. *Author's collection.*